"Insightful and engaging—here's a mas[...]
sial issue by my friend Clay Jones. Rea[...]
analysis of a topic that has troubled ma[...]
in hand to underline the nuggets of wi[...]

Lee Strobel, Professor of Christian Thought,
Houston Baptist University

"I have read a number of books on the problem of evil, but this is one of the very best yet produced. Professor Clay Jones fearlessly and deftly addresses all the hard questions head-on with rational responses to them. There is no ducking of issues. Moreover, Jones skillfully weaves theology, biblical studies, and philosophy into a coherent, well-integrated book that is suited for both the scholar and the layperson. I highly recommend it."

J.P. Moreland, Distinguished Professor of Philosophy,
Talbot School of Theology, Biola University;
author of *The Soul: How We Know It's Real and Why It Matters*

"Dr. Clay Jones doesn't shy away from tough subjects. Instead, he tackles them with honesty, diligence, and resolve. In *Why Does God Allow Evil?* he engages one of the most difficult questions facing believers and skeptics alike. His treatment is God-honoring, straightforward, and accessible. If you're looking for a resource that acknowledges the severity of evil and the gravity of sin while taking the justice and grace of God seriously, *get this book!*"

J. Warner Wallace, senior fellow at the Colson Center for Christian Worldview,
Adjunct Professor of Apologetics at Biola, author of *Cold-Case Christianity*

"If you are looking for one book to make sense of the problem of evil, this book is for you. Clay Jones brings a lifetime of reflection to this difficult issue. He speaks with honesty and realism, and yet offers genuine hope. Both believers and skeptics will benefit from *Why Does God Allow Evil?*"

Sean McDowell, PhD, Biola University professor, speaker, author

"In this book, Clay Jones actually answers the question, 'Why does God allow evil?' So many books on the topic don't give an answer. Hence, this is a breath of fresh air. There is a bonus too. In his answer, Jones gives a full-arc presentation of the gospel. I've seen even seasoned Christians awaken to the depths of the gospel for the first time in response to Jones's material. I cannot recommend it more highly. Read it for yourself, then read with a church group. Don't be surprised if you detect palpable spiritual growth in everyone involved in studying this important book."

Craig J. Hazen, PhD, founder and director MA in Christian Apologetics,
Biola University; editor of *Philosophia Christi*, author of *Five Sacred Crossings*

"It's hard to imagine there could be a new much-needed book on the problem of evil when so much has already been written, but that's what this is. Clay strikes a rare balance of theological depth and accessibility on this difficult subject, making it an ideal resource for anyone seeking to better understand how evil and suffering can co-exist with a perfectly good and loving God. He answers questions you've always had, questions you're embarrassed to ask, and questions you didn't think to ask but should have…all in an engaging style that makes you not want to put it down."

Natasha Crain, author of *Keeping Your Kids on God's Side*

"Clay Jones has a novel and compelling approach to the problem of evil. In the search for answers, people frequently wonder if God is to blame. You'll find Clay's perspective on this matter eye-opening and even shocking."

William Lane Craig, Research Professor of Philosophy at Talbot School of Theology, Professor of Philosophy at Houston Baptist University

"Clay Jones offers a robust and comprehensive resource for addressing the problem of evil. Like the lectures he gives at Biola and around the world, *Why Does God Allow Evil?* is well-organized, engaging, and accessible. It's an important addition to the growing body of resources for twenty-first-century Christian apologetics."

Barry H. Corey, president of Biola University, author of *Love Kindness: Discover the Power of a Forgotten Christian Virtue*

"This book unashamedly provides biblical and theological answers to a significant challenge to the Christian worldview. My suspicion is that most readers will find things in this book that they immediately recognize are right—and that they are grateful to Jones for stating so forthrightly. I also suspect that most readers will find ideas they disagree with, and still others that they will need to consider at greater length. Truly important books are always this way. This is an insightful and courageous work—I cannot recommend it too highly."

Robert B. Stewart, Professor of Philosophy and Theology, Greer-Heard Professor of Faith and Culture, New Orleans Baptist Theological Seminary

WHY DOES
GOD
ALLOW
EVIL?

CLAY JONES

WHY DOES
GOD
ALLOW
EVIL?

HARVEST HOUSE PUBLISHERS
EUGENE, OREGON

Cover by Bryce Williamson, Eugene, OR

Cover Image © Sabphoto / Shutterstock

WHY DOES GOD ALLOW EVIL?
Copyright © 2017 Clay Jones
Published by Harvest House Publishers
Eugene, Oregon 97402
www.harvesthousepublishers.com

ISBN 978-0-7369-7044-0 (pbk.)
ISBN 978-0-7369-7045-7 (eBook)

Library of Congress Cataloging-in-Publication Data
Names: Jones, Clay, 1956- author.
Title: Why does God allow evil? / Clay Jones.
Description: Eugene, Oregon : Harvest House Publishers, [2017] | Includes
  index. |
Identifiers: LCCN 2017004436 (print) | LCCN 2017022940 (ebook) | ISBN
  9780736970457 (ebook) | ISBN 9780736970440 (pbk.)
Subjects: LCSH: Theodicy. | Future life.
Classification: LCC BT160 (ebook) | LCC BT160 .J653 2017 (print) | DDC
  231/.8—dc23
LC record available at https://lccn.loc.gov/2017004436

Printed in the United States of America

17 18 19 20 21 22 23 24 25 / VP-GL / 10 9 8 7 6 5 4 3 2 1

To the Lord God
Who is all-good and all-powerful.
Thank You that You so loved the world!

To Jean E.
My best friend, my lover, my faithful critic,
my constant encourager, my skilled helper,
my precious companion.
I look forward to enjoying eternity with you.
I thank God for you!

Contents

Preface

In 1994 I started writing a book on the problem of evil, and now, *only* 23 years later, that book has come to fruition. Although I had hoped to publish this book many years earlier, the Lord—who is all-good, all-knowing, and all-powerful—knew that I still had much to learn from theologians and philosophers, from students, from suffering, and, of course, from the Lord Himself.

Audience

This book is written primarily to explain to reflective Christians some of the most difficult theological concepts regarding evil and to encourage them in God's grand plan for their eternities. I spend too much time on the wonders of heaven for this to be directed to the skeptic. This is not to say that the principles aren't applicable to skeptics—they certainly are. It's just that I present them with the Christian in mind. I will say, however, that I have found information contained herein very helpful in my witness to non-Christians and my interactions with skeptics.

Related to the above, it's important to note that when presenting theodicy—that is, the justification of the ways of God to men—we are attempting to explain God's true reasons for allowing evil. We are trying to explain why God is good in spite of the evil in the world. That the skeptic might reply "I wouldn't worship a God like that" matters not. Our goal is to present a theodicy that is biblically based and coherent. If we succeed in that, the fact the skeptic doesn't like our answer is irrelevant. We are not trying to defend a god that the skeptic would worship. After all, a god that the skeptic would worship doesn't exist. We are explaining what the Bible says about the Lord's reasons for allowing evil.

Style

I have returned to the tradition of capitalizing the personal pronouns when they refer to God. I want to give Him all the honor I can possibly muster in a world that slanders Him.

Structure

I begin this book with an introduction that defines key terms, explains why many Christians think theodicy impossible, and examines false attempts to explain why God allows evil. In the first chapter I explain why Adam sinned, why we suffer for Adam's sin, and how natural evil entered our world. The second and third chapters examine the depth of human evil and whether there are any good humans. These two chapters may *temporarily* depress you, but I encourage you to keep reading and I conclude them with twelve reasons why such a study results in a positive transformation.

The fourth and fifth chapters examine two of the hardest questions for Christians—what is the destiny of the unevangelized, and, the most difficult question in theodicy, how can eternal punishment be fair?

The sixth, seventh, and eighth chapters examine the nature and value of free will, answer whether God could have allowed less evil, and look at how we could have free will in heaven but not sin.

The ninth and tenth chapters answer Christian misconceptions that make eternity appear boring, answer skeptical arguments that eternity will *necessarily* be boring, and explain how eternity will dwarf our sufferings to insignificance.

The eleventh chapter explains how our suffering here prepares us to be fit inheritors of the kingdom of God and qualifies us to reign over it forever with Jesus.

In the appendix I present a coherent but somewhat speculative explanation of Satan's rebellion and God's response to that rebellion. I present it in the appendix precisely because, as I said, it is somewhat speculative.

Acknowledgments

I thank the Lord who has forgiven me, who is using suffering in my life to transform me into His likeness, who has blessed me with the opportunity to write this book, and who has written our names in the Book of Life! I also thank my dear wife, Jean E., who helped me through all my degrees; has taught me many, many things; and gave me great help in writing this book. I shudder at what my dismal state might have been without God giving me such an intelligent, godly, knowledgeable, and caring wife to love and encourage me.

I'm thankful for my friend Craig Hazen for his many years of encouragement, for giving me the opportunity to teach in our department at Biola University, and specifically for giving me the opportunity to teach the course "Why God Allows Evil." I'm thankful for the help of my friend Joseph E. Gorra, who has encouraged me in this endeavor for many years, read the manuscript for this book, and has helped refine many of my ideas. I'm thankful for Mirhetu Gupta for his thoughtful comments on some of my chapters. I'm thankful for my many students who through the years have sharpened and encouraged me. Thank you also, Bill Farrel, for being the first one to encourage me to write a book. Thank you Terry Glaspey, Steve Miller, and Harvest House for your many suggestions and for giving me the opportunity to share my teaching on a larger scale.

Introduction

In Search of Answers About God and Evil

think I may have come to the problem of evil exactly backward. It seems to me that most Christians see evil, either in others' lives or their own, and then they ask why God would allow that evil. If these askers are in a position to do so, they then write a book or books on the topic. But that's not what happened to me.

My childhood was hard. I was sick *a lot*, had rheumatic fever, had what my parents thought was a life-threatening heart condition (it turned out to be a pronounced case of mitral-valve prolapse but they didn't know that back then), missed most of second grade, and wasn't allowed to play while in third grade. My parents worried that I was going to die. I was an insecure, sometimes bullied, abysmal student with a GPA under 2.0.

Thankfully I became a sincere Christian in junior high school, but at the beginning of my sophomore year in high school I thought I'd committed the unpardonable sin, which for months gravely depressed me.[1] I realize many people had much worse childhoods than I (my wife, Jean E., certainly did), but while I was growing up, I was often depressed. Yet something strange started happening: I began to see God work all my difficulties out for my good! My fear of dying gave me a *healthy* sense of my own mortality (valuable for anyone, whether Christian or not). And my fear of being damned resulted in my having a disciplined mind because the only way I could keep depression at bay was to force my mind to meditate on encouraging scriptures. All of this resulted in my having a sense that God loves me, and us, through suffering and uses it for our good.

I went to a university and then to seminary, and in 1981 I became a young associate pastor at a large church. It was then that I began to glimpse the glory of what it means to be a Christian now, and the glory that awaits Christians forever. To say this changed my life is an understatement. For the next few years I made the glory of what it means to be a Christian—now and forever—the major study of my life and the major topic of my teaching. Not only was I thrilled to understand our glorious eternal future, but along the way worldly lusts were diminished, I became a much more joyous Christian, and I realized that eternity would dwarf our suffering to insignificance. I was transformed.

Then as I began to think and pray these things through and to teach the greatness of our salvation, something else happened: I became curious as to where we came from. I wondered what the Bible taught about the nature of humankind without Christ, about our lost condition prior to our salvation. So I examined the depraved nature into which we were all born and contrasted that with what God is doing in the Christian now and what He will do for the Christian forever. Seeing God work good in my life *through* suffering, understanding the horror of human sin, and reveling in the greatness of our salvation had a strange effect on me when it came to hearing people talk about the problem of evil—I just didn't see the problem.

I realize that to some—maybe many—this will appear an outlandish, even outrageous claim. Some will think I'm terribly naïve, or stupid, or naïvely stupid. But that's what happened. When theologians would talk about this giant problem—the problem of evil—I just didn't see it as much of a problem.

I'm not alone in seeing human sinfulness and the glory that awaits us in heaven as central to understanding God's grand plan. The renowned

Bible expositor D. Martyn Lloyd-Jones wrote, "Most of our troubles are due to the fact that we are guilty of a double failure; we fail on the one hand to realize the depth of sin, and on the other hand we fail to realize the greatness and the height and the glory of our salvation."[2] I couldn't agree more. Similarly, C.S. Lewis emphasized the depth of human sinfulness in his writings, especially in *Till We Have Faces*, which was his favorite of his own works. In *Till We Have Faces*, the Queen's "complaint against the gods" is eventually answered (spoiler alert) by a revelation of her own sinfulness. And when it comes to eternity, C.S. Lewis wrote, "Scripture and tradition habitually put the joys of heaven into the scale against the sufferings of earth, and no solution of the problem of pain that does not do so can be called a Christian one."[3] The evil we now experience can only be understood from the perspective of where we, as Christians, have come and where we are going for all eternity.

Then in 1994 when it was suggested that I write a book, I thought, *I'd love to*. Little did I know it would take years for this to come to fruition, but God knew I still had much to learn.

After all, I'm not saying that in the years to follow there weren't questions that needed resolution—there were! I'm just saying that the basic problem of evil never seemed like much of one. Now, of course, some won't agree with the theodicy I present. That's okay—I look forward to dialoging with them! Also, I've lived long enough to realize that sometimes it has turned out that I've been mistaken on some things I previously was convinced were true. I know that in what follows I could be mistaken on any number of points. But if my underlying assumptions are correct (e.g., we have libertarian freedom), then I think the reader will find that what I'm presenting is a consistent and even compelling theodicy.[4]

For years now I've taught the course "Why God Allows Evil" every semester in Biola University's master of arts in Christian apologetics program, and I believe most of my students would agree that it's a coherent and, as they revolve the ideas in their minds, compelling theodicy. The reason I say "revolve the ideas in their minds" is because many students initially find some of the concepts counterintuitive.

Comprehending human evil is hard, and comprehending the other end of the spectrum—the glory that awaits us in heaven forever—is much harder.

My perspective on why God allows evil isn't unique. It's within the great tradition from Augustine to Thomas Aquinas that was well articulated by C.S. Lewis. Mostly what I'm doing differently is trying to illustrate and emphasize some teachings that are often not given the attention they deserve.

We need to know God's plan so that we can make sense of tsunamis, fires, cancers, strokes, rapes, tortures, and the fact that, except for the Lord's return, the only thing that will prevent us from watching everyone we know die will be our own death. If we don't understand that our good God can have a good purpose in allowing evil, we'll live confused Christian lives. We cannot, after all, love the Lord with all our minds and secretly suspect that Christianity can't answer the hard questions. We may repress doubts, but in time, they will wedge us from real confidence in Christ. Joy, peace, and boldness to witness, on the other hand, spring from a sense that God loves us through evil, suffering, and death, and that He will exalt us to inherit His kingdom and to reign over it with Jesus forever and ever.

What I seek to do, then, is much more than lay out tenets in a cerebral manner to create intellectual assent. Hopefully I do that! But I also seek to illustrate, as much as my limited skills allow, the horrors of evil, the glories of heaven, and the glory of Him who reigns over all things. I also pray for you, dear reader, along with all the saints, that we will somehow revel in the hope to which He has called us, the riches of His glorious inheritance, and the great power at work, right now, for us who believe (Ephesians 1:17-19).

When Adam and Eve ate from the Tree of the Knowledge of Good and Evil, they plunged us, their descendants, into a lifelong education of good and evil. This isn't a Bible sidebar topic. I'm always interested to hear a pastor, as a part of his teaching on a particular subject, tell his congregation how many times a word or concept—like *money*, or *love*, or *disciple*—appears in Scripture. They do it to tell us the relative importance of that topic. Well, if that is true, consider how often the Bible talks about good and evil.

The various forms of the words *good* and *evil* appear in the Bible almost 1100 times. Then when we add in the synonyms like *sin, wicked, holy, right, wrong, righteous, unrighteous, love, hate, obey*, and *disobey*, that brings the number to more than 5000 times. And this does not include other variations of words for evil like *bad, iniquity, corrupt, immoral, depraved*, or *profane*.

Nor does this include words for particular evils like *covet, adultery, idolatry, pride, lying, lust*, and so on. Nor words of particular types of goodness like *honor, truthfulness, faithfulness*, and *humility*. Nor words describing the inclination to do evil like *temptation* or *seduction*. Nor words about one's getting in good standing again with God after one has done evil, such as *atonement, sacrifice* (and the entire sacrificial system), *repentance*, and *forgiveness*. Nor words about the effects of evil, such as *sorrow, sadness, sickness, pain*, and *death*. Nor lengthy accounts of people sinning, like David and Bathsheba; of people suffering for their sin, like Judas; or of Jesus' atonement for sin like the crucifixion accounts. Nor does it include words describing the final destinations of the evil and the good, such as *judgment, hell*, and *heaven*. Nor words describing the goodness of God.

In other words, the Bible is largely about the knowledge of good and evil. We learn from it that God is good, that evil is horrific, and how to overcome evil with good. There is a problem of evil, all right. But it's not God's problem: It's ours.

Definition of Terms

If we are to understand the relevant literature on the problem of evil and suffering we need clarity on some core terms of the discussion.

Evil. As I wrote in *The Encyclopedia of Christian Civilization*, "Just as dark is defined in regards to the absence of light, so Christian thought has often defined evil as the absence of good; or to use Augustine's (AD 354–430) words, the privation of good (*privatio boni*)."[5] In short, "Evil then is what ought not to be, for evil is at the least unpleasant (as in a rotten peach) if not harmful or deadly (as in cancer or murder)."[6] I'm often asked where evil came from, or why God created evil, but evil is not a thing. There is no blob somewhere in the universe named evil. If there were such a blob, it would be difficult to explain why God would create such a blob. But evil is a corruption of the good, and evil arises from the misuse of the will. The will is misused for evil whenever we will things that are in contradiction to God's will (chapter 3 and chapters 6–8 will examine this more fully).

Christians have traditionally broken evil into two major categories. There is *moral evil*, which encompasses such things as lust, lying, child molesting, drunk driving, and murder. And there is *natural evil*, which encompasses such things as mold, tsunamis, earthquakes, measles, cancer, and, of course, death by natural causes. I will argue in the next chapter that what we call natural evils either result from us, the sins of others, or especially the sin of Adam.[7]

Related to these categories of evil there is what is called *gratuitous* or *pointless evil. Gratuitous evil* is evil that's considered to serve no greater good. Skeptics argue that gratuitous evil is that which a good God would have no reason to allow (this is discussed in the chapter "Wasn't There Another Way?").

Logical problem of evil. The *logical problem of evil* was famously formulated by Epicurus.[8] As eighteenth-century philosopher David Hume put it about God, "Epicurus' old questions are unanswered. Is he willing to prevent evil, but not able? then is he impotent. Is he able, but not willing? then is he malevolent. Is he both able and willing? whence then is evil?"[9] Note that the logical problem of evil attempts to show that there is an *internal* logical contradiction in Christianity. After all, Christians don't believe that logically contradictory things can be true, so *if* the logical problem of evil were to succeed, then Christianity would be logically contradictory and therefore false. Although theists answer this problem differently, most theists answer the logical problem by showing that a good God might have a *very good reason* for allowing evil—such as giving creatures free will. Because of this, the logical problem of evil has been discredited—even to atheists—and is now rarely employed, if ever.

As Paul Draper put it in the *The Oxford Handbook of Philosophical Theology*: "Although logical arguments from evil seemed promising to a number of philosophers in the 1950s and 1960s...they are rejected by the vast majority of contemporary philosophers of religion..."[10] Draper said this is because "some serious attempts" have demonstrated that evil is "logically compatible with God's existence." Draper gives the example of Alvin Plantinga's 1974 free will defense, which "persuaded many" that "God's existence is logically compatible with the existence of evil."[11] Draper says that "for a logical argument from evil to succeed, it is necessary to show that, for some known fact about evil, it is logically *impossible* for God to have a good moral reason to permit that fact to obtain. This, however, is precisely what most philosophers nowadays believe cannot be shown."[12] Thus, as atheist William L. Rowe put it, "The logical form of the problem is not much of a problem for theistic belief" because "efforts to establish the inconsistency between" God's omnipotence, omniscience, being all good, and the existence of evil "have been notoriously unsuccessful."[13] But skeptics now appeal to another argument from evil—the evidential problem.

Evidential problem of evil. William Rowe writes that the *evidential problem of evil* "is the view that the variety and profusion of evil in our world, although perhaps not logically inconsistent with the evidence of the theistic God, provides, nonetheless, *rational support* for atheism, for the belief that the theistic God does not exist."[14] In other words, even though there is no logical inconsistency in God allowing evil, does all the evil that we find in the universe make sense if there is an all-good, all-powerful God? Obviously because I'm writing a book on the subject, I believe that it does make sense, and that's the point of this book. Explaining God's good reasons for allowing the evil He allows is what is called *theodicy*.

Theodicy. Theodicy comes from the Greek *theos*, "God," and *dikê*, "justice." It is a justification of God. A theodicy attempts to explain God's true reasons for allowing evil. John Milton's *Paradise Lost* is a theodicy in which Milton set out to "justify the ways of God to men."[15] Theodicy is what I'm presenting here. I'm doing my best to present God's true reasons for allowing evil.

Anthropodicy. Anthropodicy is the justification of man. Those who engage in anthropodicy attempt to argue that humans are good and thus not deserving of what they suffer. Although you'll seldom hear the word *anthropodicy* written or spoken, skeptics regularly appeal to the goodness of individual humans and from that argue that God isn't good in allowing them to suffer.

The Problem (As Understood by Intelligentsia)

But is theodicy achievable? Can the Christian coherently explain why God allows evil? Sadly, for many Christians, most skeptics—and probably all atheists—the answer is no.

Christian Daniel Howard-Snyder writes that "no authoritative Christian source holds forth that we should expect to be able to understand why God would permit so much evil rather than a lot less." In fact, Howard-Snyder thinks "we do others a grievous disservice" to give them "any expectation to understand why God would permit so much evil." Otherwise these expectations "when left unfulfilled can become nearly irresistible grounds for rejecting the faith."[16]

Skeptic Bart D. Ehrman, in his book *God's Problem: How the Bible Fails to Answer Our Most Important Question—Why We Suffer*, agrees. Ehrman says that he was once a Christian, but "I realized that I could no longer reconcile the claims of faith with the facts of life." Ehrman wrote that "I could no longer explain how there can be a good and all-powerful God actively involved with this world, given the state of things." As a result, Ehrman wrote, "I have now lost my faith altogether. I no longer go to church, no longer believe, no longer consider myself a Christian."[17]

Atheist Sam Harris, in his book *Letter to a Christian Nation*, writes, "Somewhere in the world a man has abducted a little girl. Soon he will rape, torture and kill her. If an atrocity of this kind is not occurring at precisely this moment, it will happen in a few hours, or days at most."[18] Harris says that statistically, "this girl's parents believe—as you believe— that an all-powerful and all-loving God is watching over them and their family. Are they right to believe this? Is it *good* that they believe this? No. The entirety of Atheism is contained in this response."[19]

Although some will think me arrogant, or ignorant, or ignorantly arrogant to even suggest we can answer the question as to why God allows evil, that is, nonetheless, my contention. Over the years of teaching this subject every semester to our master's students (I have more than 70 students this semester alone), I've been reassured that these tough questions can be compellingly answered. I've also learned why people think the question is impossible to answer.

Why Some Think There Is No Answer

I've observed nine reasons people say that we do not know why God allows evil.

First, many are spiritually unreflective. By that I mean that they simply do not spend much time meditating on Scripture. If one isn't imbued with a gripping picture of what God is doing in the universe, then not only the problem of evil but much of what God is doing in every other aspect of creation will be obscure.

Second, most people, and even most Christians, fail to understand the depths of human depravity. This is true even for many of the students entering our master's program in Christian apologetics at Biola. This is the second major deficiency in attempts to present a compelling theodicy. After all, theodicy—the justification of God—is hardly even necessary, unless anthropodicy—the justification of man—succeeds. I examine this in detail in chapter 2, "Why Do Bad Things Happen to Good People?"

Third, some people are arrogant. When these individuals encounter doctrines that seem counterintuitive, they proudly opine that the doctrine must be mistaken rather than their intuition.[20] We need to come to Scripture in humility and wrap our minds around it, not the other way around. Our interpretive framework is indicted here: Do we simply read the Bible, or is the Bible permitted to ultimately and totally read us? Arrogance is also the problem when people think that if they haven't figured it out, then no one has. Of course, that's false on the face of it.

Fourth, many are ignorant of much Christian doctrine. The problem of evil, in one way or another, encompasses almost all Christian doctrine. Consider that the problem of evil encompasses, but is not limited to, the rebellion of Satan and his minions; the rebellion of Adam and Eve; the degradation of humankind; God's judgment of humankind in the flood; God's holiness and justice demonstrated through His choosing Israel and teaching them His ways; God's commanding them then to destroy the perverse Canaanites; Israel's committing the evil of the Canaanites and their subsequent exile;[21] Christ's ministry, death, and resurrection to save sinners; our preaching the good news; Christ's return to judge the world; hell; and Christians reigning with Christ forever and ever.

Fifth, many misunderstand Job. What I mean is that they read the last five chapters of Job, where the Lord asked Job, "Where were you when I laid the foundation of the earth?" (Job 38:4), and conclude that the major and maybe only takeaway from Job is that we should just be humble. Yes, we absolutely should be humble! But there's much more in Job than that. In the first two chapters we see a cosmic drama where Satan questions Job's loyalty and tells the Lord that the only reason Job serves Him is because the Lord doesn't let bad things happen to him. In other words, Satan contends that Job wouldn't serve God in the face of evil and suffering. But Satan is wrong (we'll talk more about that in the last chapter on reigning with Christ).

Sixth, some don't *want* the problem of evil answered. This is certainly true for atheists, as they appeal to this as a major reason for rejecting belief in God (I'll talk more about this shortly). But I've found that even some who call themselves Christians hold a grudge against God and they like that. They like the idea that "God's got this problem—this dirty open-secret—that the universe is a mess and somehow He's at fault." Just as people don't want to hear good things about humans whom they have a grudge against, they don't want to hear that God might be doing nothing wrong. Further, I've even heard people say that some Christians need to forgive God! One Christian magazine featured an article entitled, "Will You Forgive God?"[22] Let me be clear: God. Does. Not. Need. Your. Forgiveness. You need His.

Seventh, some hold to determinism. Let me say at the outset that the theodicy I present is compatible with Calvinist election and Arminian prevenient grace, but it is not compatible with determinism. If determinism is true—that God has determined every creature's every thought and deed so that they could never do otherwise—then the man who fantasized about how he would rape and torture to death the little girl next door, and then actually carried out his wicked scheme, was not able to do otherwise. This means that every exquisite torture, every penetration, burn, cut, crush, *ad infinitum, ad nauseam*, was indeed efficaciously arranged by God so that this torturer could not have done other than he did nor desired to do other than he desired.

Thus determinists not only struggle to explain why God allows evil, but most find it impossible.[23] For example, determinist R.C. Sproul concludes, "I do not know the solution to the problem of evil. Nor do I know of anyone who does."[24] As I said, my theodicy is compatible for those who hold to Calvinist election but not determinism. I discuss election and determinism further in the chapter "Wasn't There Another Way?"

Eighth, most people fail to understand the nature and value of free will. I spend three chapters dealing with free will, so I won't belabor that subject now.

Ninth, most fail to understand the glory that awaits Christians forever in heaven. This is the biggest deficiency among those who ponder the problem of evil. Not only does a failure to understand the glory of eternal life render answering the problem of evil almost impossible (if not impossible), a lack of comprehension of eternal life hinders the entire Christian experience. There is no bigger problem for Christians living in Western society than a shortsighted, this-world-focused Christianity. But those with a robust view of eternal life don't find the questions of life—even questions regarding why God allows evil—that difficult to consider.

False Starts

Before I present what I believe to be a scripturally faithful account of why God allows evil, it would be helpful to examine some attempts that may succeed, but do so at the expense of either logic or Scripture.

God Less Powerful

One way some people attempt to solve the problem of evil is by making God less than all-powerful—to say that God *can't* fix all the problems. Rabbi Harold Kushner takes this tack in his book *When Bad Things Happen to Good People*. For Kushner, God "cannot prevent" all the bad things that happen.[25] Kushner writes, "I recognize His limitations. He is limited in what He can do by laws of nature and by the evolution of human nature and human moral freedom."[26] Thus we need to "accept the idea that some things happen for no reason."[27] You need "to learn to love and forgive Him despite His limitations," just as you "once learned to forgive and love your parents even though they were not as wise, as strong, or as perfect as you needed them to be."[28] For Kushner, God cannot control it all. He couldn't make everything right even if He wanted to. That evil occurs in Kushner's world can be summed up as "Stuff happens!"

Another way people try to solve the problem of evil—and make God less powerful as a result—is offered by Gregory A. Boyd in his book *Satan and the Problem of Evil: Constructing a Trinitarian Warfare Theodicy*. Boyd is an open theist, and open theists hold that God doesn't know the future decisions of free beings. Thus Boyd concludes that "we must accept that at least sometimes God is *unable* to prevent them [certain occurrences of evil]."[29] This follows from Boyd's open theism— because God is a God of love and wanted other beings to enter into that love, when He created them He took the "risk" that they would rebel against Him.[30] Frankly, I really like Boyd's work, except that I don't believe open theism is accurate. Scripture reveals that God does, in fact, know the future decisions of free beings.[31]

God Less Good

Another way to make a theodicy work is to make God less good, or to at least change the definition of *good*. This was the tack taken by the late philosopher and theologian Gordon H. Clark, who wrote, "At this point it must be particularly pointed out that God's causing a man to sin is not sin. There is no law, superior to God, which forbids him to decree sinful acts."[32] Indeed, "God is not responsible for the sin he causes" because God "cannot be responsible for the plain reason that there is no power superior to him; no greater being can hold him accountable; no one can punish him; there is no one to whom God is responsible; there are no laws which he could disobey."[33]

But what, then, does it mean for us to call God *good*? After all, Jesus said in Matthew 5:48, "You are to be perfect, as your heavenly Father is perfect." But what does God's being perfect mean if He can cause sinful acts? As determinist Paul Helm comments, "The goodness of God must bear some positive relation to the sorts of human actions we regard as good. Otherwise, why ascribe goodness to God?"[34] Thus Helm is correct to say that this type of argument is "characteristic of philosophy but one which is extraordinary under any other circumstances."[35] This is sort of a worldly wisdom attempt to bail out a theology.[36]

Not Biblical

If one isn't going to diminish God's power or goodness to form a theodicy, there's another false start available: Ignore Scripture that contradicts what you want to believe. Perhaps the most famous exemplar of this approach is theologian John Hick. I like Hick's emphasis on soul-building (I think that's part of what God is doing here). But there's a major problem: To craft his theodicy, he ignores Scripture and embraces universalism—the belief that eventually, everyone goes to heaven. Hick writes that "only" if salvation "includes the entire human race can it justify the sins and suffering of the entire human race throughout all history."[37]

Well, as I said, if you're just going to discard the parts of Scripture that you don't like, then theodicy isn't hard to achieve. Ignoring parts of Scripture to form a theodicy is like assembling a picture puzzle without caring whether the finished puzzle resembles the picture on the box.

An Eternal Perspective

I hold that the Scripture is inerrant in the autographs and everything I present will be within the confines of historic Christian doctrine.[38] Also, as has been the majority position of historic Christianity,

I hold that God's omnipotence only extends to His doing what is logically possible as even God cannot create a square-circle, a married-bachelor, or a two-sided triangle. Similarly, God cannot give beings free will and not allow them to use it wrongly (that's as logical as it gets). Further, it was a greater good for God to create beings with free will than to not create them.[39] In the next chapter we will see how Adam got us into this mess and in the last three chapters we will see how eternity will ultimately dwarf our sufferings to insignificance.

Chapter 1

Why Do We Suffer for Adam's Sin?

When it comes to the matter of evil, one of the biggest issues is this: Why must *we* suffer for Adam's sin?[1] Indeed, how could it possibly be fair that we would *all* suffer for the sin that some distant couple committed a long time ago? To find the answer, we must go to the book of beginnings, the book of Genesis, and take it seriously.

The Setting

In Genesis 2:16-17, we read that "the LORD God commanded the man, 'You are free to eat from any tree in the garden; but you must not eat from the tree of the knowledge of good and evil, for when you eat from it you will certainly die.'" Then verse 25 says, "Adam and his wife were both naked, and they felt no shame."[2] God gave them only one prohibition: Do not eat from the Tree of the Knowledge of Good and Evil. I think they had it pretty good. All Adam and Eve had to do all day long was to garden and play with creation's *only* physically perfect and completely naked member of the opposite sex. Life wasn't so bad!

It's important to emphasize this because God is pro-pleasure—in fact, He created *all* the pleasures. C.S. Lewis, in his satirical book *The Screwtape Letters*, in which a senior tempter instructs a junior tempter on how to tempt Christians, wrote, "Never forget that when we are dealing with any pleasure in its healthy and normal and satisfying form, we are, in a sense, on the Enemy's ground." This, writes senior tempter Screwtape, is because pleasure is "His invention, not ours. He made all the pleasures: all our research so far has not enabled us to produce one."[3]

That's right—God created all the pleasures, including the enjoyment of food, drink, and sex. David praised the Lord in the Psalms that "at your right hand are pleasures forevermore" (Psalm 16:11 NKJV). So, again, Adam and Eve had it good—very good.

But this doesn't last.

Soon we learn in Genesis 3:4-5 that there was a serpent in the garden which said to the woman, "You will not surely die. For God knows that in the day you eat of it your eyes will be opened, and you will be like God, knowing good and evil" (NKJV). There it is. God says, "Don't eat this, or you will die." But this satanically inspired serpent tells the woman that, not only will she not die, but their lives will be better.[4] In other words, the serpent tells Eve that God is not acting in their best interest. Satan tells them that God is holding back something that would otherwise benefit them.

Isn't that the way teenagers often think? They will complain to their parents, "You're mean. Other parents let their kids do this!" Such teens are saying that their parents are not acting in their best interest, and are holding back something that would otherwise benefit them. I remember thinking that as well when I was a teen!

I'm convinced that God arranged the family, first and foremost, such that it is a microcosm of what is going on in the larger universe. Parents and teenagers have the opportunity to see, in their own interactions, much of what is going on when it comes to God acting in our best interest. It is important for parents, then, to make sure that they don't tell their kids *no* only because they just don't want to be bothered, but when it truly is the case that something isn't in their best interest. In so doing, parents model how God treats humankind. God's prohibitions are for our good, not because He is lazy or selfish.

Apparently Eve decided that God wasn't acting in her best interest. Thus, we read in Genesis 3:6, "So when the woman saw that the tree was good for food, and that it was a delight to the eyes, and that the tree was to be desired to make one wise, she took of its fruit and ate, and she also gave some to her husband who was with her, and he ate." And, of course, it turns out that Satan lied to them. In verses 7-8 we read about what happened next: "Then the eyes of both were opened, and they knew that they were naked. And they sewed fig leaves together and made themselves loincloths." And then they "hid themselves from the presence of the LORD." In other words, instead of feeling like gods, their nakedness embarrassed them. They were incapable of the intimate communion with God that they had once enjoyed.

Then God pronounced their punishment for disobedience, and it explains much about why we suffer. In Genesis 3:16 He said to the woman, "I will surely *multiply* your pain in childbearing; in pain you shall bring forth children.[5] Your desire shall be for your husband, and he shall rule over you." So there are two punishments: The first is that childbearing will now be very painful (that probably also includes everything related to childbearing, such as female reproductive problems). The second punishment is that the woman's desire will be for her husband, but he will now *rule* over her. A husband *ruling* over his wife wasn't a part of the original plan, and the world since then has witnessed many men treat women harshly and unjustly.[6]

The Origin of Natural Evil

Although increased pain in childbearing is a natural evil, there is more to come. In Genesis 3:17-19 the Lord told Adam, "Cursed is the ground because of you; in pain you shall eat of it all the days of your life; thorns and thistles it shall bring forth for you; and you shall eat the plants of the field. By the sweat of your face you shall eat bread, till you return to the ground, for out of it you were taken; for you are dust, and to dust you shall return."[7] So in response to Adam's sin, the Lord cursed the ground. Old Testament professor Robert R. Gonzalez points out that "just as 'childbearing' is a synecdoche for the woman's larger role of mother and wife, so 'the soil' does not limit God's curse merely to the sphere of agriculture...God is withdrawing his unqualified blessing and imposing a curse upon *the filling and the subduing* of the earth..."[8]

Thus later in Genesis 5:29 we read about "the ground that the LORD has cursed." Natural evil entered the world because God cursed the earth in response to Adam's sin. In fact, what pestilence—mold, decay, cancer, and so on—can't have ensued from God looking at planet Earth and saying, "I curse you"?

That creation is under a curse is further explained in Romans 8:19-23:

> For the creation waits with eager longing for the revealing of the sons of God. For the creation was subjected to futility, not willingly, but because of him who subjected it, in hope that the creation itself will be set free from its bondage to corruption and obtain the freedom of the glory of the children of God. For we know that the whole creation has been groaning together in the pains of childbirth until now. And not only the creation, but we ourselves...

Notice several things. First, creation's subjection to futility and corruption clearly occurred because of the Fall.[9] Otherwise one would have to argue that although in Genesis 1 the Lord called each day of His creation "good" (Genesis 1:4,10,12,18,25), and then summed up His overall creative work as "very good" (verse 31), what He meant by "very good" was that it was subject to "futility" and "corruption," and it was "groaning" and that animals were dying of cancer, etc. Nothing in the creation narrative suggests that.

In addition, the apostle Paul related creation's futility and corruption to man. As New Testament professor James D.G. Dunn explains:

> The point Paul is presumably making, through somewhat obscure language, is that God followed the logic of his purposed subjecting of creation to man by subjecting it yet further in consequence of man's fall, so that it might serve as an appropriate context for fallen man: a futile world to engage the futile mind of man...There is an out-of-sortedness, a disjointedness about the created order which makes it a suitable habitation for man at odds with his creator.[10]

This indeed is our experience with planet Earth. There is something desperately wrong with creation, and the hope for its renewal is linked to the revelation of the sons of God. Creation is groaning, and man groans while interacting with creation.

Consider also that Paul's comments about creation being corrupted are in the context of Romans 5:12: "Just as sin came into the world through one man, and death through sin, and so death spread to all men because all sinned." As Jesus' work on the cross will ultimately free humans from physical death, so will creation also be freed from its bondage at that time. For these and other reasons, a large majority of New Testament scholars relate Romans 8 to Genesis 3.[11]

Second, "creation" refers to *absolutely everything* but sentient beings. Commentator John Murray observed,

> *Angels* are not included because they were not subjected to vanity and to bondage to corruption. *Satan* and the *demons* are not included because they cannot be regarded as longing for the manifestation of the sons of God and they will not share in the liberty of the glory of the children of God. The *children of God* themselves are not included because they are distinguished from "the creation..."[12]

New Testament professor Douglas J. Moo says that the use of "'we ourselves'—plainly excludes believers from the scope of creation," so "[w]ith the majority of modern commentators, then, I think that creation here denotes the 'subhuman' creation."[13] Creation then is, again, everything else. New Testament professor Robert H. Mounce writes, "Currently, however, the entire universe is in travail as if it were giving birth."[14]

The phenomenon of creation being freed from corruption, as stated in Romans 8, is elucidated in Colossians 1. There, Jesus is identified as "the image of the invisible God," and we are told that "by him all things were created, in heaven and on earth, visible and invisible, whether thrones or dominions or rulers or authorities—all things were created through him and for him" (verses 15-16). Verses 19-20 go on to say, "In him all the fullness of God was pleased to dwell, and through him to *reconcile* to himself all things, whether on earth or in heaven, making peace by the blood of his cross."

Clearly, something must have happened to Jesus' relationship to creation—otherwise, why would "all things...in heaven and on earth" need to be reconciled to Jesus unless they were previously not reconciled? "All things" must include *everything* in subhuman creation, but if God originally created everything futile and corrupted, but called it "very good," then what is there for Jesus to reconcile to Himself? No one needs to be reconciled to anything unless previously they were at odds with each other. Thus, the separation of "all things," of creation, from Jesus, could only have occurred because of the fall of Adam.

Third, God subjected creation to corruption. As Murray points out, "Neither Satan nor man could have subjected it *in hope*; only God could have subjected it with such a design."[15] Likewise, Moo writes that "Paul must be referring to God, who alone had the right and the power to condemn all of creation to frustration because of human sin."[16]

But human woes don't stop with the Lord cursing the ground. Then the Lord did one final thing that sealed humankind's fate. In Genesis 3:22-23 we read, "The Lord God said, 'The man has now become like one of us, knowing good and evil. He must not be allowed to reach out his hand and take also from the tree of life and eat, and live forever.' So the Lord God banished him from the Garden of Eden to work the ground from which he had been taken."[17] So the Lord cursed the ground, presumably enabling all kinds of pestilence, and then He kicked Adam and Eve out of the Garden, removing them from the rejuvenating power of the Tree of Life.

And we've been attending funerals ever since.[18]

When it comes to natural evil, many people wrongly assume that when God said, "On the day that you eat of it you will surely die," He added, "in your sleep at a ripe old age of natural causes." But He didn't. He only said "you will surely die." And whether one dies at eight months old, or eighteen years old, or eighty-eight years old, we are all going to die. Here's some hard news: Only one thing is going to prevent you from watching absolutely every person you know die from murder, accident, or disease, and that will be your own death from murder, accident, or disease.[19] Have a nice day! But, seriously, that's a hard truth.

Of course, that observation isn't uniquely Christian! It's the same for all other religions and philosophies. You could become an atheist and add, "then worms will eat your body." Or you could become a Hindu or a Buddhist and then you could die again, and again, and again, and again.

Adam, because of his sin, passed on to us the only things he could pass on: flesh that was like his own, broken fellowship with God, and a world of hardship leading to death. Because Adam passed on *only* flesh, humans are prey to Satan and his demons.[20] Adam gave us his all, but all he could give was flesh like his—flesh that was weak, corrupt, and dying.

This is the bad news.

Why Did Adam Sin?

One question people frequently ask is, How could it be possible for Adam and Eve to sin if they were created without sin? Theologian John Hick opines, "It is impossible to conceive of wholly good beings in a wholly good world becoming sinful. To say that they do is to postulate the self-creation of evil *ex nihilo*! There must have been some moral flaw in the creature or in his situation to set up the tension of temptation..."[21] But there's nothing mysterious here. As C.S. Lewis explains: "The moment you have a self at all, there is the possibility of putting yourself first—wanting to be the centre—wanting to be God, in fact. That was the sin of Satan and that was the sin he taught to the human race."[22] Philosopher and theologian William A. Dembski further explains:

> Precisely because a created will belongs to a creature, that creature, if sufficiently reflective, can reflect on its creaturehood and realize that it is not God. Creaturehood implies constraints to which the Creator is not subject...The question then naturally arises, Has God the Creator denied to the creature some freedom that might benefit it? Adam and Eve thought the answer to this was yes (God, it seemed, had denied them the freedom to know good and evil). As soon as the creature answers yes to this question, its will

turns against God. Once that happens the will becomes evil. Whereas previously evil was merely a possibility, now it has become a reality. In short, the problem of evil starts with thinking that God is evil for "cramping their style." The impulse of our modern secular culture to cast off restraint wherever possible finds its roots here.[23]

I agree with Dembski, with one small caveat: I disagree that the will turns against God once it answers "yes to this question." Rather, the will turns against God when it answers yes, and then takes steps to try to remedy the situation. In other words, it happens when a being decides that God is withholding something that would benefit him and then decides to get what he wants against God's will. Otherwise, by Dembski's definition, Adam and Eve would have sinned *before* they ate of the fruit. Eating from the fruit would then be a subsequent sin, and that's not what the Bible teaches.

Why Do We Suffer for Adam's Sin?

So we've seen that when Adam sinned, God cursed the ground, thus enabling all kinds of pestilence. Then God kicked Adam and Eve out of the Garden, thus removing them from the rejuvenating power of the Tree of Life. But that still doesn't answer the question as to why we all suffer for the sin this couple committed thousands of years ago. How could that be fair?

In fact, many argue that the teaching of original sin is not only unfair, it is psychologically damaging. As self-esteem guru Nathaniel Brandon put it, "The idea of Original Sin…is anti-self-esteem by its very nature. The very notion of guilt without volition or responsibility is an assault on reason as well as on morality."[24] Philosopher Ian McFarland sums it up this way: "The idea that we are all guilty because of an ancestor's misdeed is viewed as morally outrageous and historically incredible, summing up for many everything that is wrong with Christianity."[25] Similarly, theologian John Hick asserts, "The policy of punishing the whole succeeding human race for the sin of the first pair is, by the best human moral standards, unjust and does not provide anything that can be recognized by these standards as a theodicy."[26] But Adam and Eve stand in a unique relationship to every one of us, and original sin makes sense if we think deeply about it.

Federal or Representative Headship

Several explanations about how we relate to Adam have merit. First, Adam is our federal, or representative, head.[27] Often, throughout history, a head has been chosen to represent a country. Once this head has been chosen, he may declare war without getting the country's individual citizens to vote on it. Similarly, Adam was the federal head of the human race, and he chose to rebel against God, thus making rebels of his race. That we didn't individually vote to make Adam the head of our race doesn't matter because God knows who can best represent us. Also, if God knew that *all of us* would have acted similarly, He does no wrong in choosing one person to represent us.[28]

Also, as systematic theologian William G.T. Shedd put it, "The sin of Adam...is imputed to posterity in the very same way that the righteousness of Christ is imputed to the believer—namely, undeservedly and gratuitously."[29] Indeed, Christians who still might think that suffering for Adam's sin is unfair should remember that it wasn't *fair* that Christ should die for them. Now, even though federal headship is a partial explanation for why we suffer for Adam's sin, I wouldn't bother arguing this point with an atheist. More persuasive reasons lie ahead.

Realistic or Seminal Union

Second, we all have a realistic, or seminal, union with Adam, so we really were "present in Adam when Adam sinned. All of humankind was in 'Adam's loins' when he rebelled, and since we were actually present at his sin, we also are therefore guilty of his sin."[30] Being ontologically present rendered Adam's sin as chargeable to us in the same way, as Shedd analogized, that "the hand or eye acts and sins in the murderous or lustful act of the individual soul."[31]

Hebrews 7:9-10 tells us that "one might even say that Levi himself, who receives tithes, paid tithes through Abraham, for he was still in the loins of his ancestor when Melchizedek met him." If Levi wasn't in any sense present in Abraham, then how could he have been said to have tithed to Melchizedek? First Corinthians 15:22 tell us that "in Adam all die" and we are all the offspring, the race of Adam. As Shedd wrote, "To die in Adam both spiritually and physically supposes existence in Adam both as to soul and body."[32] Similarly, theologian Millard J. Erickson said,

> So we were present in germinal or seminal form in our ancestors; in a very real sense, we were there in Adam. His action was not merely that of one isolated individual, but of the entire human race. Although we were not there individually, we were nonetheless there. The human race sinned as a whole. Thus, there is nothing unfair or improper about our receiving a corrupted nature and guilt from Adam, for we are receiving the just results of our sin. This is the view of Augustine.[33]

It takes time to wrap one's mind around this concept, but it is worth spending the time doing so.

Shedd said that one cannot hold to federal or representative headship *and* seminal identity because if we were actually present, then we didn't need a representative.[34] But I think both can be true because although we really were present when Adam sinned, we did not have individuated consciousnesses at the moment of Adam's sin; therefore, Adam can also serve as our representative.

Traducianism

Third, and related to the realistic (or seminal) union perspective mentioned above, there is a more compelling answer to why we suffer for Adam's and Eve's sin: They are our first parents, our original parents, and we are them. To understand why we suffer for their sin, on this we must be clear. Probably everyone reading this has studied sexual reproduction. Many of us have put it into practice, and others are hoping to. Adam and Eve sexually reproduced. We are the sexual *reproduction* of Adam and Eve. As Jesus said in John 3:6, "That which is born of the flesh is flesh, and that which is born of the Spirit is spirit." In other words, once Adam and Eve sinned, and then had a fallen nature, they could only reproduce their own fallenness. They couldn't reproduce something better than themselves.

We got our souls from Adam and Eve. In fact, we got our consciousnesses from Adam and Eve. After all, where did our consciousness come from? Obviously if there is no God, then we got our consciousness from our parents. There is something about the union of the sperm and the egg that can produce a being that is conscious. But if you do believe that there is a God, that doesn't change where you got your consciousness from—you still got it from your parents, who got it from their parents, and so on, all the way back to Adam and Eve. This concept that you received your soul from Adam and Eve—in fact, that in a very real sense you *are* Adam and Eve—is called *traducianism*.

The term *traducianism* comes from the Latin word *tradux*, which is translated *vine*. In the same way that a vine transfers its inherent nature, from its very root to every subsequent stem and leaf, so do we transmit our souls to our offspring when we reproduce. Augustine said it well:

> For we all were in that one man...The seminal nature was there from which we were to be propagated; and this being vitiated by sin, and bound by the chain of death, and justly condemned, man could not be born in any other state. And thus, from the bad use of free will, there originated the whole train of evil, which, with its concatenation of miseries, convoys the human race from its depraved origin, as from a corrupt root, on to the destruction of the second death, which has no end, those only being excepted who are freed by the grace of God.[35]

Millard Erickson put it similarly: "The entirety of our human nature, both physical and spiritual, material and immaterial, has been received from our parents and more distant ancestors by way of descent from the first pair of humans."[36] This doesn't mean that each sperm has a soul and each egg has a soul. J.P. Moreland explains how traducianism works:

> Traducianism is patterned after the ancient Aristotelian doctrine of substantial change in which two things come together, have the potential to form an entirely new substance in conjunction with each other, and they cease to exist as the new substance comes into existence. So each sperm and each egg has soulish potentialities to form a new ensouled body when they come together. So it isn't the soul of the father and mother that's relevant but the potentialities of egg and sperm.[37]

So it isn't that each sperm and each egg has a soul, but that the two of them combine to form a soul.

Shedd rightly said about traducianism that "the preponderance of the biblical representation favors it."[38] Eve was "taken out of Man" (Genesis 2:22-23), and there is no hint that God sent a soul into her. As Shedd put it, "the total female was supernaturally produced from the male."[39] After that, Genesis refers to Eve as "the mother of all living" (3:20), and says of Adam that "he fathered a son in his own likeness, after his image" (5:3). In other words, their children, or even a substantial part of their children, are from then on *not* created *ex nihilo* (out of nothing), but come from their sexual reproduction.

As we saw earlier, Jesus said in John 3:6, "That which is born of the flesh is flesh, and that which is born of the Spirit is spirit." Until we are born again, we are only Adamic flesh that needs to be born from above (John 3:3,7; 1 Peter 1:23). Jesus said in John 8:23, "You are from below; I am from above. You are of this world; I am not of this world." In other words, human souls are not specially created by God and do not come "from above." These and other passages support that we inherited our souls from Adam and Eve.[40] There are many other arguments for traducianism, but they are outside the scope of this endeavor.[41]

Now, there are some who argue against traducianism and for special creationism (the view that God specially creates a soul at the moment of conception and sends that soul into the conceptus). But Ephesians

2:3 says we are all "by nature children of wrath." If our souls were specially created by God, then the special creationist is in the awkward position of explaining why God would create a perfect soul and then send it into Adamic flesh, which immediately corrupts it and makes it worthy of God's wrath.[42]

Even though I've argued that we receive our souls from Adam and Eve, the rest of the theodicy that I will present doesn't depend on one holding to traducianism. Indeed, one can be a special creationist and hold to everything that follows. It's just that, as I said, the special creationist has to explain something that the traducian doesn't: Why would God create a perfectly good soul—the foundation of who you really are as a being—only to send it into Adamic flesh to be immediately corrupted and thus deserving of the wrath of God? Either way, the soul is corrupt at conception. Traducianism, however, removes an extra step from theodicy.

That we received our souls from Adam and Eve is particularly troublesome to those who have a strong sense of Western individualism. Many of us like to think that we are all individual units *not* all that connected to everyone else. But there is an organic union between all of us. In my interactions with students from Asia, by the way, I've found that they don't struggle to accept this sense of corporate identity as much as Westerners do.

I used to wonder why the Bible doesn't mention Adam more often when he is so significant to our existence. Then I learned that the word *adam* occurs regularly in the Old Testament, and the reason we don't realize this is that English Bibles translate the Hebrew word *adam* as "man" or "human." In other words, those who read the Hebrew text would see the word/name *adam/Adam* throughout the Old Testament. For example, the phrase "son of man" is used about 250 times in the Old Testament, and the Hebrew word translated "man" in all those occasions is *adam*. For instance, the Lord said in Ezekiel 14:12-14,

> Son of man [*adam*], when a land sins against me by acting
> faithlessly, and I stretch out my hand against it and break its
> supply of bread and send famine upon it, and cut off from it

man [*adam*] and beast, even if these three men, Noah, Daniel, and Job, were in it, they would deliver but their own
lives by their righteousness, declares the Lord GOD.

Thus, the reader of the Hebrew Old Testament wouldn't be confused
about our identity with Adam.[43]

What this all means, then, is that we were all born with natures
inclined to sin. Indeed, David confessed in Psalm 51:5, "Surely I was
sinful at birth, sinful from the time my mother conceived me" (NIV). In
class I show my students a black-and-white album cover of Lady Gaga
with color only on her metallic blood-red lips. Her disheveled platinum
mane, her mouth open in a growl, her black eye shadow with a thick
stripe of black underscoring intense eyes gives her a wild, ravenous look,
and the album's title is *Born This Way*. And to that I say, "Oh, yes, you
were!" We were all born that way.

However one gets to the doctrine of original sin, it has great explanatory power. As philosopher Alvin Plantinga put it, "The doctrine of
original sin has been verified in the wars, cruelty, and general hateful-
ness that have characterized human history from its very inception to
the present."[44] Even atheist Michael Ruse agrees: "I think Christianity is
spot on about original sin—how could one think otherwise, when the
world's most civilized and advanced people (the people of Beethoven,
Goethe, Kant) embraced that slime-ball Hitler and participated in the
Holocaust?"[45]

Sometimes people ask how, if traducianism is true, Jesus could have
been born without a sinful nature, as He would have inherited a sinful nature from Mary. Frankly, I don't see the problem. God is certainly
capable of working that out, especially because with Jesus' conception,
the man's sperm was absent. Also, Genesis tells us that the serpent-
crusher will come from the seed/offspring of the woman (Genesis 3:15).
The Lord could easily have said that the serpent-crusher would come
through the seed/offspring of both the man *and* the woman, but He
didn't. It's entirely possible that the sinful nature is passed through the
man's sperm and not the woman's ovum.

Now, of course, God could have done it another way, but we don't need to know the exact mechanism God used any more than I need to understand aerodynamics to fly on a plane. All that's important for our present purposes is the fact that Adam's seed was corrupted. In the next chapter, we will examine the ruinous evil that Adam's family perpetrates.

I've had the parents of infants complain that there's no possible way that their little bundles of joy could be born corrupted—they're so cute. But most of those who have older children—older as in "the terrible twos"—realize that is false. As Augustine put it, "The only innocent feature in babies is the weakness of their frames; the minds of infants are far from innocent."[46] That's correct, isn't it? In class I show a collage of livid, red-faced infants and the students always laugh. Enraged infants aren't good, and it's a good thing that they don't possess bodies that could do real harm! That being said, although infants certainly possess a sin nature, it doesn't mean that when they are livid they are actually *committing* sin since they truly do not know better.

So the human condition, when it comes to goodness, is this: Everyone is born with a sinful nature. And from God's perspective, Adam's seed doesn't deserve to live—even when they are little—because its fruit outside of Christ is always poisonous. That doesn't mean that little ones are lost, but that they don't *deserve* to live. The real question regarding infants is about their eternal destiny, and that is examined in the chapter "What Is the Destiny of the Unevangelized?"

I've heard people say, "Well, if from God's perspective children don't *deserve* to live, then why aren't you for abortion?" The answer is simple: Even though children are corrupted by sin, they are still created in the image of God (albeit that image is marred by sin), and God reserves for Himself the right to take a person's life. I don't know of any Christian theologians who believe that original sin *completely* obliterates the image of God, but that image has certainly been corrupted.[47] That we were all corrupted by sin and deserving of damnation is the bad news. The good news is that in Christ, you are not only forgiven of your sins, you have an organic union with Jesus. And Christ's seed always deserves heaven, even if it has yet to bear much fruit, because as Christ's seed, eventually it will bear much fruit (assuming there's enough time for that to happen).

Sometimes people cry foul: "You're telling me that the Nazi guard who killed thousands will be in heaven if he trusted in Christ before he died?" I reply, "Yes, he will be saved just like the abortion doctor who killed thousands will be in heaven if he repents and trusts Christ before he dies. Not only that, but all those people who voted to keep the abortion doctor's work legal so that he could continue suctioning, scraping, and scalding children to death will also be saved if they repent and trust Christ before they die."[48] I've never had anyone continue to press this point.

Another objection I've often heard is this: "But couldn't God have created someone else who wouldn't have sinned?" But that's what God did! Of course, Jesus wasn't created, but He did become man, and He kept all of God's commands perfectly. And now by trusting in Jesus, we can all be saved! In fact, the New Testament calls Jesus "the last Adam." Romans 5:14-15 says Adam was "a type of the one who was to come. But the free gift is not like the trespass. For if many died through one man's trespass, much more have the grace of God and the free gift by the grace of that one man Jesus Christ abounded for many."[49] Similarly, in 1 Corinthians 15:22,45 we learn that "for as in Adam all die, so also in Christ shall all be made alive...'The first man Adam became a living being'; the last Adam became a life-giving spirit." But by the time Jesus came, humankind had the education of the horror of sin and corruption. By then, many realized they were desperate sinners (except for those like the Pharisees, who thought all but themselves were desperate sinners).

Consider the similarities between the temptation of Eve and the temptation of Jesus. Genesis 3:6 says, "The woman saw that the tree was good for food..." ("the desires of the flesh" 1 John 2:16); Matthew 4:3 says that after Jesus had fasted 40 days, Satan told Him, "If you are the Son of God, command these stones to become loaves of bread."

Next, Genesis 3:6 says that the fruit "was a delight to the eyes" ("the desires of the eyes" 1 John 2:16); Matthew 4:8-9 says that "the devil took [Jesus] to a very high mountain and showed him all the kingdoms of the world and their glory. And he said to him, 'All these I will give you, if you will fall down and worship me.'"

And finally, Genesis says that Eve saw that "the tree was to be desired to make one wise" ("the pride of life" 1 John 2:16); similarly, Matthew 4:6 says that Satan told Jesus, "If you are the Son of God, throw yourself down, for it is written, 'He will command his angels concerning you,' and 'On their hands they will bear you up, lest you strike your foot against a stone.'"

Jesus faced all these temptations without sin. He is the "last Adam"—the only one we'll ever need.

Sometimes people complain that we didn't have a choice about being born sinful. That's true—we didn't have a choice, just as people born into alcoholic families, impoverished families, or disreputable families didn't have a choice. But we can turn to Jesus, the last Adam, and be born again into a new family and receive a new nature.[50]

Tragedy Can Become a Blessing

When the Philadelphia Eagles football player Jon Dorenbos was 12, his father beat his mother, Kathy, to death with a power tool. Jon's father was sentenced to 13 years in prison. Kathy's sister, Susan, won an intense legal battle to obtain custody of Jon and his sister. On *America's Got Talent*, where Jon was performing a magic routine, his aunt and mother Susan said of that incident that "the worst tragedy of my life became my greatest gift."[51] Something truly tragic can also become a blessing.[52]

There is in Christianity what's called an *O felix culpa* tradition. *O felix culpa* is Latin for "O fortunate fall." In other words, even though Adam's sin was tragic—and it *was* tragic—the Lord used it for good. The Fall prepared the way for the heavenly Victor, the Cosmic Hero Jesus, to conquer Satan, evil, and death. Jesus is the Serpent Crusher.

There's more than that. Paul concluded Romans with a warning that we should "watch out for those who cause divisions and create obstacles contrary to the doctrine that you have been taught; avoid them." He said that "by smooth talk and flattery they deceive the hearts of the naive" (Romans 16:17-18). That's what Satan did, right? Satan brought division into the world, dividing man from God and man from man. Then in verse 19 Paul said, in a clear allusion to the Tree of the Knowledge of Good and Evil, "I want you to be wise as to what is good and innocent as to what is evil." Finally Paul said in verse 20 that "the God of peace will soon crush Satan under *your* feet." In other words, not only is Jesus the Serpent Crusher; we join Jesus in crushing Satan under *our* feet!

To sum this up, Adam and Eve are our parents. They sinned, they reproduced, and here we are. But if these facts are still horrible to you—and they should be—then take to heart the cosmic lesson here: Hate sin! And it should lead you to trust in the last Adam, Jesus, who alone is able to save you from your sin.

Chapter 2

Why Do Bad Things Happen to Good People?

In the last chapter, we learned why bad things happen. They happen because Adam and Eve rebelled against God and so God then cursed the ground, enabling every possible pestilence. Then He kicked Adam and Eve out of the Garden of Eden, which removed them from the rejuvenating power of the Tree of Life. When Adam and Eve were on their own, life became very hard, and, as I said, we've been attending funerals ever since.

But evil does appear to be unequally distributed—some evil people seem to thrive, and some good people seem to suffer. And that leads us to the question of this chapter: Why do bad things happen to good people?

To answer this question, I've found it's essential to look closely at human badness and "goodness." To do this we will need to look at some very hard truths—truths that you might be tempted to stop reading. But I strongly urge you to continue on. As C.S. Lewis put it, "The Christian answer—that we have used our free will to become very bad— is so well known that it hardly needs to be stated. But to bring this doctrine into real life in the minds of modern men, and even modern Christians, is very hard."[1] That's correct, and in what follows, I attempt to do this very hard thing.

Although these truths—and they are all true—are disturbing, I've learned over the years that those who pay attention to them find that this knowledge of good and evil not only has great explanatory power and scope, but is no less than transformative. People who hadn't understood these truths previously are changed forever *for the better*. So, dear reader, please keep reading, even though it may be difficult. A student of mine, who is also a professor at another university, wrote to me and said that the reading I'd assigned on human evil "set me back a couple of weeks but changed my ministry forever."

In this chapter we will first consider what theologians have said about human evil. Second, we will review examples of human evil. Third, we will consider experiments regarding the human potential for evil. And fourth, we will ponder the observations of genocide victims and researchers who have thought deeply about human atrocities.

Then in the next chapter we will examine what the Scriptures reveal about human goodness and badness. Understanding these concepts is foundational to a robust understanding of God's kingdom. I will conclude the following chapter by giving 12 reasons as to why a close look at human evil is helpful.

The Knowledge of Evil

Taking a Deeper Look

When I first started studying about genocide for the purpose of writing this book, I did so because I didn't want anyone to be able to disqualify me as not having really looked deeply at human evil. Indeed, one of the ways of "solving" the problem of evil is to not take evil seriously—to give it a gloss or a whitewash—and I didn't want anyone to be able to accuse me of doing that. So I started reading books about genocide. One day as I was reading *The Rape of Nanking* by Iris Chang, in the course of reading about one sickening rape or torture or murder after another, suddenly I was struck by the fact that horrendous evil *is* human and that most books on theodicy didn't go far enough. Those who do genocide are *not* inhuman monsters—they're all too human. They are precisely human. Genocide is what the race of Adam does.

At the moment I realized that genocide was fundamentally human—I didn't know exactly how, for I couldn't put it into words—I realized that I was fundamentally transformed and would never again be the same. Since that time I've come up with 12 ways that this knowledge transformed me, and, as I said, I will share them at the end of the next chapter.

What Theologians Agree On

Many Christians know that Calvinists teach that humans are totally depraved. Some want to dismiss this conversation as, "Oh, that's Calvinist. Calvinists are into believing that humans are really evil, but I'm an Arminian." But that's an incorrect assessment, for Arminius agreed that without the work of the Holy Spirit, no one *ever* does anything good. As Calvinist R.C. Sproul writes:

> James Arminius was emphatic in his rejection of Pelagianism, particularly with respect to the fall of Adam. The fall leaves man in a ruined state, under the dominion of sin. Arminius declares: "In this state, the Free Will of man towards the True Good is not only wounded, maimed, infirm, bent, and weakened [attenuatem]; but it is also imprisoned [captivatum], destroyed, and lost. And his powers are not only debilitated and useless unless they be assisted by grace, but it has no powers whatever except such as are excited by Divine grace."[2]

Sproul continues, "So far Arminius clearly seems to agree with Augustine, Luther, and Calvin. He affirms the ruination of the will, which is left in a state of captivity and can avail nothing apart from the grace of God."[3]

As most Christians know, Calvinism and Arminianism are famous for how they *disagree*. They are, in the minds of most, polar opposites—extremes on the theological spectrum. But Arminius agreed that no one ever does anything good except by the work of the Holy Spirit, so it turns out that we could say that Arminius was a one-point Calvinist!

The notion that people are born good, or even that they are born as blank slates, isn't a Christian one.[4]

Examples of Human Evil

We prefer to think great evil is limited to a few depraved individuals, but that's not true. Large populations commit heinous evils. In the examples that follow, I am going to tell some tales that are graphically violent.[5] Because of space constraints, I will limit the examples of human evil to those occurring since 1900.[6] You will find this information upsetting, but sometimes, frankly, we need our comfort in this world, our ease in this world, to be upset.

Germany

Most of us know that during World War II, many Germans participated in the murder of six million Jews. But few realize that an almost equal number of Poles, Ukrainians, Russians, Gypsies, handicapped, and so on were also killed. And this doesn't include those actually killed in combat, or those who died in cities from bombing, etc.

We read of millions of Jews and Slavs arrested in Europe by battalions of police and Gestapo. In some countries, such as Poland, the Jews and Slavs were first forced into ghettos. But, sooner or later, millions of them were herded so tightly into sweltering rail cars that often there was no room to even sit. They traveled for days without food, without water, with not enough oxygen; often they urinated, defecated, and vomited standing up. Thousands died on these journeys. During one four-day transport in July 1944 of 2521 prisoners from France to Dachau, 984 people perished.[7]

When the captives arrived at the camps, they were separated by guards who decided who could work and who would immediately be exterminated. Children were almost always exterminated because they couldn't work and their mothers' attempts to hide them in their clothing failed.

We read of many thousands, often entire families, stripped naked and forced to lie in ditches on top of just-shot people, many of whom were still moaning. The newcomers often spoke in low voices and tried to comfort the dying until they too were shot, and on it went. A German bystander recalled a naked "girl, slim with black hair, who, as she passed me, pointed to herself and said, 'twenty-three years old.'"[8]

Of course, we read of gas chambers, some holding as many as 2000 people at once; of Zyklon-B gas dropped through small openings in the ceilings; of guards who said they knew the victims were dead when the screaming stopped. When the guards opened the doors they found piles of naked men, women, and children in the corners of the rooms. They had climbed on top of each other in attempts to flee the choking clouds. Other prisoners then took their bodies to the ovens. It is estimated that the ovens at Auschwitz were able to cremate 4756 people a day.[9]

We learn of piles of shoes, clothes, glasses; of large collections of human skin used for lampshades and book covers; and of shrunken heads. We learn of heads shorn to fill mattresses and make wigs. Of women raped. Of torture. Of medical experiments where people were almost frozen, put in decompression chambers, drained of blood, sterilized. Of Mengele's experiments on identical twins—experiments that are too horrible to relate.

And on it goes.

But perhaps most frightening is that the German people knew that Hitler wanted to exterminate the Jews long before he came into power. Consider that as early as August 13, 1920, almost two decades before the beginning of World War II and at the beginning of his political rise, Hitler gave a speech entitled "Why Are We Anti-Semites?" He said Jews were "criminals" and "parasites" who should be punished with death. "The heaviest bolt is not heavy enough and the securest prison is not secure enough that a few million could not in the end open it. Only one bolt cannot be opened—and that is death."[10]

In 1925 and 1926, Hitler released the two-volume *Mein Kampf* (which translates to *My Struggle*). In it he reflected on the role of German Jews during World War I: "If at the beginning of the War and during the War twelve or fifteen thousand of these Hebrew corrupters of the people had been held under poison gas," then millions of "real Germans" would not have died.[11] Many average Germans, then, may not have actually pulled the trigger or dropped Zyklon-B into the gas chambers, but they knew Hitler wanted to kill the Jews long before they brought him to power.[12]

And it wasn't just a few Germans: By 1996, researchers had positively identified a total of 10,005 camps, ghettos, and brothels.[13] When I first read that number I thought, *That's impossible!* I couldn't imagine 10,005 camps, ghettos, and brothels. But then I kept reading. What I hadn't known is that the major camps like Dachau, Buchenwald, Auschwitz, etc., had thousands of subcamps. Recently the United States Holocaust Memorial Museum reported that more than 42,000 camps, ghettos, brothels, etc., have been positively identified.[14] And what did these satellite camps do? They provided slave labor for corporations with names like Daimler-Benz, BMW, Volkswagen, Krupp, and Bayer (Bayer sold the Zyklon-B used in the gas chambers).[15] Countless administrators, typists, rail workers, policemen, truck drivers, and factory workers knew what was going on—and their families knew as well.

Is this inhuman?

No, this is what humans do.

Soviet Union

The number of people killed or who died in camps in the Soviet Union from 1917 to 1989 is *conservatively* somewhere between 20 to 26 million.[16] As with many genocide facts, when I first read that number, I thought it impossible. Surely not that many! But then I kept reading. What I didn't know about were things like the Soviets' successful 1932-1933 quelling of Ukrainian nationalism by starving 5 to 7 million peasants to death.[17]

> No mercy was shown the starving peasants. During the famine, detachments of workers and activists were marshaled in the countryside to take every last bit of produce or grain. Activists and officials went through peasant homes with rods, pushing them into walls and ceilings, seeking hidden stores of food or grain; yards were dug up or poked with rods in the search; and dogs were brought in to sniff out food...Baked bread was taken. All reserves and the seed

grain needed for planting were seized. The peasants were left with nothing. To isolate the victims, the Ukrainian borders were sealed off to block the importation of food. The peasants simply starved slowly to death throughout the Ukraine.[18]

One party official wrote,

> The most terrifying sights were the little children with skeleton limbs dangling from balloon-like abdomens. Starvation had wiped every trace of youth from their faces, turning them into tortured gargoyles; only in their eyes still lingered the reminder of childhood. Everywhere we found men and women lying prone, their faces and bellies bloated, their eyes utterly expressionless.[19]

Anyone perceived as a threat to communism was killed.

Is this inhuman?

No, this is what Adam's family does.

China

A conservative estimate is that under the Chinese communists, some 26 to 30 million "counterrevolutionaries" were killed or died in the prison system.[20] Of course, a statistic doesn't capture the horror. Mao Tse-tung boasted in a 1958 speech to the communist party, "What's so unusual about Emperor Shih Huang of the Chin Dynasty? He had buried alive 460 scholars only, but we have buried alive 46,000 scholars."[21] Again, when I first read this I thought, *That's impossible!* I thought that "buried alive" had to be a euphemism for something else. But then I kept reading and found that live burial was a preferred method of execution.

Humans do this.

Japan

The horror I'm about to relate here is so unimaginable that you may want to skip it. Upon learning about it, I was so appalled that I was set back for a few days.

Within a period of a few weeks beginning in December of 1937, the Japanese army raped, tortured, and murdered more than 300,000 Chinese in the city of Nanking. Iris Chang in her book *The Rape of Nanking* writes:

> The Rape of Nanking should be remembered not only for the number of people slaughtered but for the cruel manner in which many met their deaths. Chinese men were used for bayonet practice and in decapitation contests. An estimated 20,000–80,000 Chinese women were raped. Many soldiers went beyond rape to disembowel women, slice off their breasts, nail them alive to walls. Fathers were forced to rape their daughters, and sons their mothers, as other family members watched. Not only did live burials, castration, the carving of organs, and the roasting of people become routine, but more diabolical tortures were practiced...[22]

I'll stop there. The Rape of Nanking, as it is called, was front-page news across the world, yet most of the world did nothing to stop it, and Japan officially denies it today.[23] After the war, the mention of these acts was suppressed not only by the Japanese but by the West, who wanted Japan as an ally to help stem the tide of communist expansion. The Rape of Nanking is only one example of what took place as millions were killed by Japanese militarists during World War II.

Humans do horrendous evil.

Ad Nauseam

People misuse the word *decimate*. To decimate means to kill one out of ten, and in 1994, the Hutus decimated **Rwanda** by killing 800,000 Tutsis in about 100 days, largely by machete. What many don't know is that Rwanda was, at the time, a highly Christianized country.[24] Ottoman **Turkey's** Young Turks killed approximately 1.2 million Armenians from 1915 to 1923.[25] The phrase "crimes against humanity" was introduced in response to these murders. In **Cambodia**, between 1975 and 1979, Pol Pot's Khmer Rouge killed 1.7 to 2.2 million Cambodians out of a total population of about 7 million—this was done in an attempt to remove foreign influence and intellectuals and return to an agrarian culture.[26]

After defeating Marxist guerillas, the **Guatemalan army** killed "tens of thousands" of Mayan Indians in the 1980s and early 1990s.[27] In **South Africa**, apartheid—the segregation of races (keeping the races *apart*)—ended in in 1994. When it ended, the Reconciliation Commission was established, which found 36,935 cases of severe ill-treatment, abductions, tortures, and killings.[28] In 1971, **Pakistani** soldiers "killed, disabled, raped, or displaced" 3 million Bangladeshis and created 10 million refugees who fled to India.[29] From 1980–1985, **Uganda** targeted the Baganda, causing the deaths of 300,000 people. From 1986–2003 they "indiscriminately terrorized" people of the Acholi region, killing another 100,000.[30]

In Saddam Hussein's **Iraq**, troops used nerve gas on the Kurds (many survivors suffer neurological disorders), frequently tortured average Iraqis, and tortured to death many Kuwaitis.[31] In **Argentina**, from 1976–1983, tens of thousands disappeared and were systematically tortured, then drugged, stripped naked, and thrown out of airplanes into the ocean. They are now referred to as "the Disappeared."[32] During World War II, around 330,000 Jews perished in territories under **Romanian** administration.[33] Some 136,000 people disappeared under the Franco regime in **Spain**, in addition to another 12,000 to 30,000 children who were kidnapped.[34]

There isn't time to talk about the **French** military and police torturing thousands of Algerians[35] or the ethnic cleansings that took place in **Croatia**, **Bosnia** and **Herzegovina**. Or the torture in **Brazil**, terror campaigns in **Ethiopia**, dismemberments in **Sierra Leone**, and the horrors in the **Sudan** and **Darfur**, where more than 300,000 have died.

Human cruelty knows no bounds. I could go on and on and on with one sickening story after another, but you get the idea. People often call such activity inhuman. But, sadly, none of this is inhuman. This *is* what humans do. And in many cases, most of the world knew much of what was going on and did nothing to stop it.[36]

I've concluded that human cruelty is *imaginable*. By that I mean that if a human who, is set on hurting someone can imagine/fantasize a horrific torture and has the opportunity to do it, he or she will carry out that horrific torture.

Nonetheless, about 20 years ago a reviewer complained that all of this seemed so remote. In other words, it's easy for readers to dismiss these stories as "that was them, not us." For many people, it is so easy to say that genocide is a problem others do or endure, as if these others are so very different! So let's turn now to the United States of America.

United States

Of course I could talk about the many atrocities committed against the American Indians and the horrors of American slavery, but as I said, I'm going to limit my discussion to atrocities since 1900. I do this because most Americans today see the sins against American Indians and Africans as remote and not related to their "enlightened" understanding of morality and racism. Americans today smugly see themselves as morally superior to their ancestors and thus severed from their sins. But today's Americans do a lot of killing. For example, since 1973, the people of the United States have, among other abortion methods, suctioned, scraped, or scalded to death more than 58 million babies and continue to permit abortion today.[37]

Warning: What I'm about to share in this paragraph is hard to stomach, but it's about what goes on in the United States, so if you can bear it, don't look away. The most common type of abortion procedure is suction curettage, or vacuum aspiration, where a tube is inserted into the cervix and a vacuum then suctions the baby into "fetal parts, which are more or less identifiable."[38] In other words, the baby is suctioned into pieces. This reminds me of the *more humane* practice of being hung, drawn, and quartered. In that English execution method, the traitor against the Crown would first be hanged, and then his four limbs would be tied to different horses which pulled him apart.

This was the punishment meted out to Sir William Wallace, who was popularized by the movie *Braveheart* (1995). Although his quartering wasn't shown in the movie, Wallace's body parts were put on display in five different English cities. It's interesting that those writing about being hanged, drawn, and quartered almost always describe the punishment as barbaric, but at least the traitor was pulled apart *after* he was already dead. But *our civilized* society suctions into pieces hundreds of thousands of babies a year, and these babies are alive when the suction procedure is performed.

Who keeps abortion legal? It's certainly a majority of Americans, or abortion would soon be outlawed. Who keeps abortion legal? It's your neighbors, right? It's probably some of your co-workers and maybe even some of your friends. Who keeps abortion legal? Could it even be you?[39] Years ago when I first started teaching on the subject of evil, a friend of mine said, "Clay, the other examples make your point, but don't use the abortion example because it weakens your point because so many people don't think abortion is wrong." But that's my point! The prevailing mentality is that such killing isn't so bad.[40] The majority of any culture that participates in mass killings will always find a way to justify their killing.[41]

What Studies Reveal About Us

In an attempt to understand how it was possible for so many people to participate in the torture and execution of so many in the Holocaust, from 1960 to 1963 psychologist Stanley Milgram conducted a famous study at Yale University—a study now known as the Eichmann Experiment (after Auschwitz administrator Adolf Eichmann). In response to a newspaper advertisement, two people at a time would come to a psychology laboratory to participate in what appeared to be a traditional learning study. After a flip of the coin, one of them was then designated "teacher" and the other "learner." To impress the "teacher" with the significance of his or her actions, before the experiment began, he or she received a very real 45-volt shock from a shock generator.

During the experiment itself, the learner was strapped into a chair with electrodes attached to his wrists. The learner was then told to learn a list of word pairs. Each time the learner made a mistake, the experimenter instructed the teacher to give him a shock. The teacher sat before an impressive shock generator with thirty switches labeled 15 volts to 450 volts and "Slight Shock" to "Danger—Severe Shock." Under the 450-volt label it just said, "XXX."

As the experiment continued, the experimenter told the teacher to increase the shock dosages. As he or she did, the learner's protests increased to "hysterical, agonized screaming and begging to be let out."[42] In reality, however, the learner was a paid actor who received no shock at all. The experiment actually concerned the teacher, who administered the shocks.

The object of the experiment was to see how many people would administer dangerous levels of shocks if instructed to do so by an authority figure. The result: 65 percent administered all shocks as instructed, including the possibly lethal shock. Milgram found no difference between men and women.[43]

Milgram's study shocked the psychology community worldwide. Other researchers replicated the experiment and found even higher percentages of people willing to inflict the highest level of pain. In 1970, David Mantell repeated the study in Munich, West Germany, and found that even after 25 years of relative calm after the end of World War II, 85 percent of the teachers were willing to administer the maximum shock. Mantell concluded:

> All the experimental variations share several disturbing features, which make the results they achieved all the more difficult to understand. Every experiment was basically preposterous. While one might expect a person to agree that the study of the effects of punishment on learning is worthwhile, the entire experimental procedure from beginning to end could make no sense at all, even to the layman. A person is strapped to a chair and immobilized and is explicitly told that he is going to be exposed to extremely painful electric shocks...This experiment becomes more incredulous and senseless the further it is carried. It disqualifies and delegitimizes itself. It can only show how much pain one person will impose on another...And yet, the subjects

carry on…That is at once the beauty and the tragedy of this experiment. It proves that the most banal and superficial rationale is perhaps not even necessary, but surely is enough to produce destructive behavior in human beings. We thought we had learned this from our history books; perhaps now we have learned it in the laboratory.[44]

I would have thought that a population suffering horror and shame over committing the Holocaust would have been more reticent to shock a helpless person with 450 volts. Apparently not.

Reflections of Genocide Victims and Researchers

Humans have an amazing capacity for evil, and for each person who pulled the trigger or scalded the unborn, there are family, friends, and even majority parties who knew of the slaughter and did nothing to stop it. We cannot argue that unusually depraved individuals perpetrate these evils. Difficulties may encourage some of them, but most of them weren't raped or abused as children. They're just ordinary folk— sons and daughters, brothers and sisters, mothers and fathers.[45] Most of these murderers also did many nice things: petted the family dog, baked cookies, gave gifts, helped a friend in need, or played with their children just before or after they committed atrocities.[46] Hannah Arendt, in her 1963 book *Eichmann in Jerusalem: A Report on the Banality of Evil*, reported on the trial of Auschwitz administrator Adolf Eichmann. Arendt concluded that the trouble with Eichmann was that "so many were like him, neither perverted nor sadistic, that they were, and still are, terribly and terrifyingly normal."[47]

Psychologist, professor, and Holocaust researcher Israel Charny wrote:

Sometimes sitting in a staff meeting of a modern psychiatric hospital, I could see how it [genocide] could happen. The ingredients were all there: the bitter, hating factions among the staff disguising themselves in the pomp and circumstance of a mental health conference; the barely disguised superiority and disdain for the hapless patient; the patronizing professional sympathy and righteousness that barely concealed the brutality of the so-called modern therapies of electric shock and brain surgery; the dehumanizing everyday herding of anonymous patients into anonymous routines. Everywhere. In lovely families that persecuted one or more of their members. In the universities I loved, where faculty intrigues and hatred knew no bounds. In the ruthless *coups de grace* of business killings. In the pompous coldness of exalted physicians turning away from the death fears of their patients.[48]

Hatred often erupts over very little. When it comes to university infighting, I'm reminded of the old joke, "University politics are so vicious because the stakes are so small."

We would think that the natural bias of the victims would be toward thinking their victimizers inhuman, but that's not true. It has been fascinating to me that absolutely *every* genocide researcher I have ever read (and I've read a lot of them) and absolutely *every* genocide victim I've ever read—to a person—concludes that genocide is what the average person does.

Professor and Holocaust survivor Fred E. Katz sums up exactly what kind of person participated in the Holocaust. He wrote that "only a tiny proportion" of the "massive killings are attributable to the actions of those people we call criminals, or crazy people, or socially alienated people, or even, people we identify as evil people." Rather, they were actually "carried out by plain folk in the population—ordinary people, like you and me."[49]

Katz asks, Who carried out the plans of the "Hitlers and Stalins"? His conclusion: "Ordinary people, like you and me." Then he asks, "Who provides the intelligence, the brain power, the orderly thinking to translate crazy philosophies into a practical course of action? Ordinary people, like you and me." Finally, "Who provides the quiet sustained effort, the plain hard work it takes to carry out huge programs of murderous action? Ordinary people, like you and me."[50] Even though

Katz's family was killed in the Holocaust, he considers the perpetrators to be ordinary people.

Every semester, I assign the book *Ordinary Men: Reserve Police Battalion 101 and the Final Solution in Poland* by Christopher Browning. As you probably guessed from the title, Browning concluded, "I could have been the killer or the evader—both were humans."[51] One of Browning's conclusions, by the way, is that those committing heinous crimes were not afraid that dire consequences would result from their refusal.[52] The book is hard to read, but those who are willing to face its lessons find themselves better off for having done so.

Theologian Langdon Gilkey believed humans were basically good until he was put into an internment camp by the Japanese with 2000 other men, women, and children during World War II. As a result of that experience he concluded, "Nothing indicates so clearly the fixed belief in the innate goodness of humans as does this confidence that when the chips are down, and we are revealed for what we 'really are,' we will all be good to each other. Nothing could be so totally in error."[53] Langdon Gilkey called our niceness "the thin polish of easy morality."[54]

Auschwitz survivor Elie Wiesel observed of Auschwitz administrator Adolf Eichmann that he "was an ordinary man. He slept well, he ate well. He was an exemplary father, a considerate husband."[55] Wiesel wrote, "Naïvely I was looking for the mark on his forehead" which would reveal that he had dug "a grave within himself. I was shaken by his normal appearance and behavior."[56] Wiesel said he was expecting to see a madman, "yet he was a man like any other."[57] Elsewhere Wiesel concluded, "Deep down...man is not only executioner, not only victim, not only spectator; he is all three at once."[58]

Likewise, Auschwitz survivor Primo Levi wrote, "We must remember that these faithful followers, among them the diligent executors of human orders, were not born torturers, were not (with few exceptions) monsters: they were ordinary men."[59] Consider as well the conclusion of sociologist Harald Welzer: "We are left then with the most discomforting of all realities—ordinary, 'normal' people committing acts of extraordinary evil. This reality is difficult to admit, to understand, to absorb...As we look at the perpetrators of genocide and mass killing, we need no longer ask who these people are. We know who they are. They are you and I."[60]

It's important to point out that one of the reasons so many Holocaust victims and researchers conclude that the perpetrators were ordinary people is because so many Jews assisted the Nazis in the killings. Jews often administrated the ghettos and manned the gas chambers and crematoria.[61]

Likewise, Aleksandr Solzhenitsyn, who suffered eight years in a Soviet gulag, asks:

> Where did this wolf-tribe appear from among our people?
> Does it really stem from our own roots? Our own blood?
> It is our own.
> And just so we don't go around flaunting too proudly the white mantle of the just, let everyone ask himself: "If my life had turned out differently, might I myself not have become just such an executioner?"
> It is a dreadful question if one answers it honestly.[62]

So we need to ask ourselves Solzhenitsyn's question: If our lives turned had out differently, if we had never become Christians, if we had been born in a different society or at a different time, could we have been a guard in Auschwitz or in a Soviet gulag? If we answer yes to this question, then it shows that there really is something wrong with humankind. But for those who answer no to this question, I have two things to say. First, I would ask them on what logical or evidential basis could they possibly conclude that they were somehow born innately better than the millions of those who committed these atrocities or who at the very least condoned those who committed them. Then I would also remind them that belief in one's innate superiority is almost always the father of genocide. Like it or not, we were all born Auschwitz-enabled.

But still, some resist this conclusion. In a smiling, closed-eyed denial, some will say that those who perpetrated genocide must have been abused as children, or raised by severe parents, or something—anything. These people simply do not want to believe, cannot allow themselves to believe, that they and their children were born Auschwitz-enabled. They are desperate to escape the conclusion that *we* could all do genocide.

Nonetheless, skeptics and even many Christians will argue that Auschwitz or no, there are still some good people.

Chapter 3

Are There No Good People?

Over the years, I've learned that many Christians believe that there are good non-Christians. After all, if you actually know some good non-Christians, then there must be good non-Christians, right?

That's not what Jesus thought. Consider that Jesus wasn't making small talk, or just passing the time of day, when He was called a "good teacher" but replied, "Why do you call me good? No one is good except God alone."[1] Now it is true there are outwardly good non-Christians—there are many of them—but we must not confuse outward goodness with inward goodness. For Jesus, evil is always, first and foremost, a matter of the heart. Again, both Calvin and Arminius agreed that apart from the work of the Holy Spirit, no one is good. Still, Christians wonder: Is it possible for a person to be good outside of a relationship to Christ?

At the outset, it is important to point out that I'm not even remotely suggesting that Christians don't sin. They do, and sometimes grievously.[2] Of course Christians sin! I do! But true Christians—those who have been born again, those who have been filled with the Holy Spirit—are changed from within. They become "obedient from the heart" and "slaves of righteousness" (Roman 6:17-18). In other words, their inner person wants to do God's will even though they may often choose not to.[3] So let's look at human "goodness" apart from Christ.

Why Do Bad People Do Good Things?

I ask my students, "Why do gangbangers stop at red lights?" I mean, it's not like they're thinking, *I don't care for any other law, but I do respect red light laws.* So why do gangbangers stop at red lights? A student once asked meekly, "Because they don't want to get a ticket?" Yes, of course, that might be part of it. But isn't there a bigger reason, a more compelling one? Isn't the real reason gangbangers stop at red lights because they don't want to be hit by an 18-wheeler and turned into red asphalt? Sure it is. In other words, the reason is self-interest. They don't stop out of moral goodness.

Jesus said that one who lusts has committed adultery in his or her heart.[4] Now consider a scenario in which a man and a woman are both working at the same company and they are both married to people outside that company. And in time, he begins to flirt with her, and she begins to flirt with him. Soon they're both having sexual fantasies about each other, and both are beginning to think that perhaps the other person would be willing to have sex with them. When that's the case, why don't they go all the way and do the deed?

Well, it's not because they have decided to cherish only their spouse, right? So why don't they do it? Isn't it because they're afraid that she might get pregnant? Or they're afraid that one of them might bring home an STD ("Oh, that's new honey, where did you get that?"). Or they're afraid that if their adultery became public knowledge that they might lose their jobs, or their family, or their reputations? Or all of the above?

Whatever the case, notice that the reason they aren't "doing it" isn't because of moral goodness. Rather, it's because of self-interest. And when people in this situation finally go ahead and do it, it's because they've decided that they have workarounds for all the potential problems ("We'll use a condom," "Our spouses are away," "She/he will never tell," etc.).

We may think those who restrict their adultery to their minds are good, but they're not. The world is full of such "good people." Ultimately, evil is a matter of the heart.

The apostle John wrote, "He who hates his brother is a murderer."[5] In other words, if you hate someone, you are a murderer even if you don't actually kill that person. Why don't you kill the person you hate? It's not because you care for the person, right? After all, we've already established your hatred. Then isn't it about self-interest? "I've seen those guys/gals in the prison population, and I couldn't pump enough iron to protect myself!"[6] And, as with adultery, when haters actually kill, it is because they have become convinced, rightly or wrongly, that they can get away with it.

That being the case, how many of us got out of junior high without being adulterous murderers? I didn't. I hated other kids, and other kids hated me. And I don't think I need to explain to you the adulterous part of a junior high school boy's mind. Thus we live in a society of adulterous murderers who think they are good people because they aren't acting out their sinful desires due to self-interest.

With these truths in view, perhaps Scripture makes more sense when it says in Romans 3, "There is no one who does good, not even one. Their throats are open graves...Their mouths are full of cursing...Their feet are swift to shed blood."[7] Now sometimes people object that the Bible points to other people as being "good." But we must let all of Scripture inform our understanding of this matter and, as has been pointed out, Romans 3:23 clearly states that "all have sinned and fall short of the glory of God" (NIV). Later in Romans 4:2-3 we read that Abraham was righteous, but that righteousness was based on his faith, not because he wasn't a sinner: "For if Abraham was justified by works, he has something to boast about, but not before God. For what does the Scripture say? 'Abraham believed God, and it was counted to him as righteousness.'"

Thus we can be sure that Old Testament saints who were called righteous were so designated because of their faith (Hebrews 11), and their faith led them to live in conformity with God's will. After all, Jesus wasn't just making small talk when someone called him "good teacher" and He replied, "Why do you call me good? No one is good except God alone."[8]

Examples of Human "Goodness"

Many people bring up specific examples of "good" humans: "Okay, but what about grandma? Sure she isn't a Christian, but she volunteers at the community center and she makes chocolate chip cookies for the kids on her street. Isn't she a good person?" But that doesn't make her a *good* person—it only makes her a *nice* person. After all, we can be certain there are some KKK grandmas who help white seniors and bake chocolate chip cookies for the white kids in their neighborhoods. Sure there are. That doesn't make them good.

Gandhi is most often cited as an example of the "good" non-Christian. But Gandhi wasn't good. Again, doing a good deed—or even a lot of good deeds—doesn't make someone a good person. Gandhi may have done many good things, but every night he went to bed naked with his two nieces, other girls (often at the same time), and even married women (one of them married to his grandnephew). He said he did this to test his resistance.[9] It isn't clear how often his resistance held firm.

Niceness isn't goodness. Lending money or possessions to those who lend to us, smiling at neighbors, and baking cookies doesn't make one good. One horrifying realization about murderers is that they can otherwise be nice. Adolph Eichmann, the administrator at Auschwitz, was a family man who never killed anyone himself;[10] Pol Pot, who orchestrated the killing fields of Cambodia, had a warm smile.[11] When serial killers are caught, their neighbors are often surprised and testify that the killers were nice, even helpful, to those around them. As C.S. Lewis put it, "Everyone feels benevolent if nothing happens to be annoying him at the moment."[12]

Thus Jesus said, "If you love those who love you, what credit is that to you? Even sinners love those who love them. And if you do good to those who are good to you, what credit is that to you? Even sinners do that. And if you lend to those from whom you expect repayment, what credit is that to you? Even sinners lend to sinners, expecting to be repaid in full."[13]

Many misunderstand the Jewish religious leaders of Jesus' day, the Pharisees: They were outwardly good people. But Jesus called them whitewashed tombs, blind guides, vipers. Outwardly they looked good, but inwardly they were "full of dead people's bones."[14] And, contrary to popular belief, Jesus never criticized them for condemning sin; He criticized them for doing what they condemned—the leaven of the Pharisees was hypocrisy.[15] In other words, the chief characteristic of the Pharisees was that they didn't live what they said they lived. Similarly, there are many in today's churches who are regular attenders, givers, and greeters, but they unrepentantly harbor hate and lust in their hearts.

I'm often asked about heroic acts that do appear to be examples of human goodness, but, again, doing one good act or even many good acts doesn't make one a good person. It just makes one the doer of some good acts. But there's more to be said about heroism. Ernest Becker, in his Pulitzer Prize-winning book *The Denial of Death*, argues successfully that man's overarching fear, the mainspring of his existence, is that he knows he is going to die. To cope with this, as the author of the foreword sums it up, man tries to "transcend death by participating in something of lasting worth. We achieve ersatz immortality by sacrificing ourselves to conquer an empire, to build a temple, to write a book, to establish a family, to accumulate a fortune, to further progress and prosperity, to create an information society and a global free market."[16]

Becker further writes that a fellow who may "throw himself on a grenade to save his comrades" must "feel and believe what he is doing is truly heroic, timeless, and supremely meaningful," and says this striving for heroics in "passionate people" is "a screaming for glory as uncritical and reflexive as the howling of a dog."[17] But for most people—for the more "passive masses"—this heroism is "disguised as they humbly and complainingly follow out the roles that society provides for their heroics and try to earn their promotions within the system" that allows them to "stick out, but ever so little and so safely."[18] Becker, who openly rejects Christianity, further attests to what Scripture teaches: "There is no one who does good" (Romans 3:12 NIV).

Something is desperately wrong with humankind, and the best explanation is original sin—we are all born in a corrupted state.[19] Although I will argue in the next chapter that we have some scriptural warrant to believe that children are considered innocent until they reach the age of accountability, that doesn't mean that children are born good or even inclined to good. As Augustine observed:

> If babies are innocent, it is not for lack of will to do harm, but for lack of strength. I have myself seen jealousy in a baby and know what it means. He was not old enough to talk, but whenever he saw his foster-brother at the breast he would pale with envy...It is clear that they are not mere peccadilloes, because the same faults are intolerable in older persons.[20]

And it's not just Augustine. Probably *all* parents of siblings witness the same thing.[21]

Jesus on the Problem of Evil

With these concepts in view, consider Luke 13:1-5, where we encounter Jesus' clearest, most direct teaching on the problem of evil:

> There were some present at that very time who told him about the Galileans whose blood Pilate had mingled with their sacrifices. And he answered them, "Do you think that these Galileans were worse sinners than all the other Galileans, because they suffered in this way? No, I tell you; but unless you repent, you will all likewise perish. Or those eighteen on whom the tower in Siloam fell and killed them: do you think that they were worse offenders than all the others who lived in Jerusalem? No, I tell you; but unless you repent, you will all likewise perish."

Put these two examples together, and it sounds somewhat like the 9/11 tragedy: Some are murdered in a terrorist act, and others are killed by a tower's collapse. The deaths, in both cases, seem pointless; they seem willy-nilly. This is an example of what philosophers call "gratuitous evil" (which we will talk about in chapter 7, "Wasn't There Another Way?"). This is supposed to be the hardest question regarding theodicy. But these questions didn't trouble Jesus. In fact, we are surprised by His blunt, even nonchalant response that the people who died in these incidents weren't worse sinners. They were just sinners, and unless you repent, you'll die too.

Yet the philosopher will cry out, "Wait a minute! This is the problem of evil. This is the great, unsearchable, unknowable, question of the ages. This is the great unanswerable!" But, again, to these murders and deaths from a collapsed tower Jesus only replies that they weren't worse sinners. They were just sinners like everyone else.

D.A. Carson explains Jesus' teaching:

> First, Jesus does not assume that those who suffered under Pilate, or those who were killed in the collapse of the tower, did not deserve their fate. Indeed, the fact that he can tell those contemporaries that unless they repent they too will perish shows that Jesus assumes that all death is in one way or another the result of sin, and therefore deserved.
>
> Second, Jesus does insist that death by such means is no evidence whatsoever that those who suffer in this way are any more wicked than those who escape such a fate. The assumption seems to be that all deserve to die. If some die under a barbarous governor, and others in a tragic accident, it is not more than they deserve. But that does not mean that others deserve any less. Rather, the implication is that it is only God's mercy that has kept them alive. There is certainly no moral superiority on their part.
>
> Third, Jesus treats wars and natural disasters not as agenda items in a discussion of the mysterious ways of God, but as incentives to repentance. It is as if he is saying that God uses disaster as a megaphone to call attention to our guilt and destination, to the imminence of his righteous

judgment if he sees no repentance. This is an argument developed at great length in Amos 4. Disaster is a call to repentance. Jesus might have added (as he does elsewhere) that peace and tranquility, which we do not deserve, show us God's goodness and forbearance.

It is a mark of our lostness that we invert these two. We think we deserve the times of blessing and prosperity, and that the times of war and disaster are not only unfair but come perilously close to calling into question God's goodness or his power—even, perhaps, his very existence. Jesus simply did not see it that way.[22]

Jesus' almost nonchalant attitude toward death has strong biblical precedents. Consider Zechariah 11:8-9: "The flock detested me, and I grew weary of them and said, 'I will not be your shepherd. Let the dying die, and the perishing perish. Let those who are left eat one another's flesh.'"

Is This a Message We Want to Get Out?

After I lectured on human evil, a student drew close and sheepishly asked, "Is this a message we really want to get out?" I replied, "In John 7:7, Jesus said the world 'hates me because I testify that its works are evil.' So what would Jesus do?"[23] If we want to be like Jesus, then we must proclaim that what the world does is evil.[24]

I have found this discussion hugely helpful in discussions with skeptics of all types. Skeptics will appeal to specific examples of human evil (like Auschwitz or child abuse) in an attempt to argue that God shouldn't let these things happen if He is good or exists at all. But I take their examples and add *many, many* more examples from many different countries to point out that it is really man who needs to answer, not God. After I have raised this point, I have found that most skeptics are bewildered and simply do not know how to reply.

What Good Is Knowing About Human Sinfulness?

As I mentioned earlier, I was reading Iris Chang's *The Rape of*

Nanking when I realized, "This is what humans do!" I also immediately recognized that this illumination was consistent with the teaching of Scripture and the traditional Christian understanding of the nature of fallen humans. From then on, my life was different. I didn't know at the time how it was changed, but I knew that my perspective not just about humans but about God and all of life was seriously, irrevocably, and fundamentally changed—for the better.

As the years have passed, I've come to discover 12 ways that my understanding of the depths of human sinfulness has helped me. First, I've come to realize we have gotten the problem of evil exactly backward. There is a problem with evil all right. But it isn't God's problem—He is only good and doesn't do any evil. It's humankind's problem because we are the ones who do evil.[25] With that perspective in mind, the question changes from "Why does God allow evil?" to "Why does God allow humans?"[26]

Second, studying humankind's horrible treatment of other people honors the memory of those who have suffered. I ask my classes, "If you were horribly murdered, would you want everyone to refuse to hear of it?" No one has yet to tell me that they would want their murder to go unremembered. "To forget," as Auschwitz survivor Elie Wiesel warned, "would not only be dangerous but offensive; to forget the dead would be akin to killing them a second time."[27]

Third, a hard look at human evil puts our problems into perspective. Many of us, especially in the West, think extreme suffering strikes only the unlucky. But not only does much of the world suffer more sickness and disease, many millions have suffered wrongful imprisonment, torture, and murder. A clear understanding of human evil puts my own experience of evil in touch with a broader historical and anthropological understanding than just my individual experience with evil that I commit and that is committed against me. When I suffer evil, I do not suffer it alone.[28]

Fourth, understanding human evil helps us realize that there is no such thing as a little rebellion. When we choose to rebel against God at even only one point, and decide not to rebel at every other point, we have therefore decided that we will follow God's commands only when those commands happen to coincide with the priorities of *our* own "kingdom." We are doing what is right in *our* own eyes and happen to be obeying God on every other point (if that is the case) only because we happen, at that point in our existence, to agree with Him. But the history of free beings shows that those who disobey at even one point quickly find many others (often including murder) that further their own kingdom-building project. Evil is born when a creature decides it knows better than the Creator.[29]

Fifth, understanding human evil impassions our witness because it is hard to warn someone of the consequences of eternal punishment when we believe that, deep down, the non-Christian we are warning is really a good person. After all, why would God send a good person to hell?

Sixth, comprehending the depths of human evil justifies God's judgment.[30] After all, if humans are basically good, God's judgment seems barbaric. But once we understand how evil we are, God's wrath, as C.S. Lewis put it, appears "inevitable, a mere corollary from God's goodness."[31] Miroslav Volf said he used to question the wrath of God— he thought that wrath was "unworthy" of God. But then his former country of Yugoslavia saw some 200,000 people killed, 3,000,000 displaced, and villages and cities destroyed. He said, "My people [were] shelled day in and day out, some of them brutalized beyond imagination, and I could not imagine God not being angry."[32] He wrote, "Though I used to complain about the indecency of the idea of God's wrath, I came to think that I would have to rebel against a God who *wasn't* wrathful at the sight of the world's evil. God isn't wrathful in spite of being love. God is wrathful *because* God is love."[33]

Seventh, a clear understanding of human evil puts Christ's sacrifice in proper perspective. After all, if the skeptic judges their anthropodicy successful, they will naturally view Christ's death on the cross as just another example of God's inflicting horrendous evils on humans— divine child abuse by a God bent on punishing the good. Their reasoning is that if humans really are good folk, then Jesus' crucifixion seems like the cure is worse than the disease. But, as is the case for both drunks and cancer victims, the road to recovery begins by understanding the seriousness of the problem. If God wants the desperately wicked to understand the seriousness of their offense, He can't just ignore it because to ignore it is to enable it. The lesson to creatures can't be "Go ahead and rebel; God will look the other way."

Eighth, understanding human evil, seeing behind the curtain, seeing people for who they really are—desperate sinners—caused me to be unimpressed with skeptical arguments and not be frightened by their personages. Atheism is intellectually dishonest and the judgment comes.[34] Understanding the depths of human evil gives us gravitas at the same time that it gives us humility (humility because we realize the seriousness of our own sins). This knowledge assures us that the lost really are emotionally and intellectually lost. Thus Paul says in Philippians 1:28 that you are "not [to be] frightened in anything by your opponents. This is a clear sign to them of their destruction, but of your salvation, and that from God."

Ninth, comprehending the depths of human evil tutored me with regard to how the human heart shapes earthly powers, authorities, and their structures. No human government will ever achieve utopia or complete justice in this life. Instead, human institutions, precisely because they are human, are malformed, constantly in need of reform and renewal. Government will always, therefore, disappoint. America's founding fathers understood that humans aren't born good and were right to set up a series of checks and balances so that the humans in one branch of government couldn't reign unchecked.[35]

Tenth, understanding human evil unsettles our worldliness. After having taught on this topic for many years, I've come to the conclusion that the main reason most people, whether Christian or not, don't like to hear about human atrocity is that it makes this world seem horribly inhospitable—it unsettles worldly settlers. I believe this is a huge benefit, and I don't let the reality of human evil depress me. If you were to talk to my family, friends, and co-workers about me, they would tell you I'm not a depressed person—I enjoy life, vacations, and dinner with friends. I'm not like Eeyore, the sad donkey in the Winnie the Pooh stories. The reason I don't get depressed? I know how it all ends! Nonetheless, I do find this world unsettling, and that leads naturally into the next benefit.

Eleventh, while an understanding of the depths of human evil unsettles our worldliness, it also increases our desire for Jesus' return. I want Jesus to come back! Those who are satisfied with this world don't long for the next, but it's impossible to be satisfied with this world when we comprehend the depth of human depravity. God is good and heaven is glorious—come, Lord Jesus!

Twelfth, understanding human evil reveals the magnitude of Christ's work on the cross and the wonder of our salvation. Remember, Jesus didn't die for the good, but for the wicked. As Paul said, someone may die for a good man, but who dies for the wicked?[36] When we consider the horror of what God the Son endured, let us remember that the Father sent His only Son knowing we would torture Him to death. God allowed sin to occur knowing that He himself would become its preeminent victim.[37]

Because the problem of evil is indeed humankind's problem and not God's, then the cross appears even more foolish to those without the Spirit of God: Why does God enter humankind's problem—our mess, our disaster, our ground-zero lobby to hell? What would motivate God to do such on our behalf? The only answer is love, love, love—for God so loved the world! Christ's resurrection then demonstrates the power and significance of the resurrection over the ultimate fruits of evil: death and hell.[38]

And finally, to address the titles of both this and the previous chapters, understanding the depth of human evil provides an emotional answer to one of the most common formulations of the problem of evil: Why do bad things happen to good people? What I mean is this: When skeptics ask why bad things happen to good people, the Christian often replies with detached, cerebral answers which, though perhaps logically correct, are emotionally empty.

But once we *fully* comprehend the depths of human depravity, the problem of evil largely goes away because no one ever asks why bad things happen to bad people! I point out to my classes that no one ever asks, "Why did that bad thing happen to that bad person?" That being said, it's extremely important to emphasize that although no one is good, I'm not by any means suggesting that *every* bad thing that happens to a person, or that *any particular* bad thing that happens to a person, is punishment for his or her sin. Not at all! My goal here is simply to refute the notion that bad things are happening to good people. Bad things aren't happening to good people because there are no good people. As R.C. Sproul Jr. quipped, "Why do bad things happen to good people? Well, that only happened once, and He volunteered."[39]

Sometimes people object that it isn't fair that we should all be born with an Auschwitz-enabled sinfulness. But remember that we don't have to stay that way! We don't have to stay members of Adam's family. We can be born again into a new family through the death of Jesus on the cross. Those who come to Jesus receive a new nature, are born from above, are filled with the Holy Spirit, and have become "obedient from the heart." As such we are now hybrids—born of the earth but also born of God, and we will inherit eternity.[40]

At this point skeptics have another objection to make: If people can be changed only by believing the good news about Jesus Christ, then what about those who, through no fault of their own, have never heard the news that saves?

We'll examine that next.

Chapter 4

What Is the Destiny of the Unevangelized?

One of the most common complaints by skeptics—as well as one of the most common concerns of Christians—has to do with the destiny of the unevangelized. If salvation is available only by responding to the gospel, what about the destiny of those who have never heard it? As atheist Michael Martin put it: "Suppose that heaven is a reward for belief, for example, in Jesus as Savior. Millions of people through no fault of their own have never heard of Jesus, or at least have not been exposed to Scripture. These people's failure to believe is hardly grounds for punishment that is lack of reward."[1] Similarly, C.S. Lewis writes: "Here is another thing that used to puzzle me. Is it not frightfully unfair that this new life should be confined to people who have heard of Christ and been able to believe in him?"[2]

Indeed, Christians historically have held salvation is available only through conscious, explicit faith in Jesus Christ. This is the majority view of evangelical scholars, and it is supported by the most natural and unforced reading of Scripture.[3] So what do we say, then, about the many people who never heard the saving news about Jesus Christ?

The Gospel Has Been Spread

We need to clear up a fundamental misconception. Skeptics often denounce Christianity as a primarily white, male, Western religion. But that's wrong! As Paul Marshall has observed, "Most Christians are not white. Christianity is non-European in origin. Christianity was in Africa before Europe, India before England, China before America. Three-fourths of world Christians live in the Third World."[4] Christianity is Middle Eastern in origin, and throughout the world, more women are Christians than are men. Marshall also points out that more people attended Christian services in China last Sunday than attended Christian services in *all* of Western Europe combined. "The same is true of Nigeria, and probably true of India, Brazil, and even the world's largest Muslim country, Indonesia."[5]

At Pentecost, Parthians, Medes, Elamites, Mesopotamians, Egyptians, Libyans, Romans, Asians, "both Jews and proselytes, Cretans and Arabians" heard the gospel (Acts 2:9-11). Tradition has it that the apostle Thomas brought Christianity to India in AD 52.[6] There are Christian tombstones in China dated no later than AD 86.[7] The Ethiopians consider the Ethiopian eunuch mentioned in Acts 17 to be the founder of Christianity in their country. Paul personally brought the gospel to Greece, what is now Turkey, and then to Rome, which was the center of the civilized world in his day. From there, the gospel spread throughout the empire and beyond.

Today, of course, the gospel has spread across the globe, and even Muslims in many countries already know much of the gospel. For example, the Qur'an teaches that Jesus was born of a virgin (Surah 19:16-22), that Jesus led a sinless life (Surah 19:19), and that Jesus healed the sick and raised the dead (Surah 3:49; 5:113). By the way, the Qur'an does not teach that Muhammad was born of a virgin, led a sinless life, healed the sick, or raised the dead.

Although the Qur'an teaches that Jesus was *not* crucified (Surah 4:157-158), notice that the denial of His crucifixion acknowledges that *Christians believe that Jesus was crucified.* Further, although Muslims deny it, the overwhelming majority of them know that Christians believe that Jesus was raised from the dead. In other words, they know what Christians contend are the major events of Jesus' life story! That

Muslims *deny* the most important elements of the gospel—His death on the cross and His resurrection from the dead—acknowledges that they *know* what Christians proclaim.

In short: the basic gospel has spread throughout much of the world.

The Word Is Suppressed

That more people groups aren't Christians throughout the world isn't because the gospel hasn't gotten to those people groups. On the contrary, as Romans 1:18 tells us, "by their unrighteousness [they] suppress the truth." For example, in 1900, "Turkey was about 30 percent Christian, while Syria was 40 percent."[8] But since then, the persecution of Christians has reduced their numbers in Syria to about 10 percent and in Turkey to less than 1 percent.[9] Today, many Christians in the Middle East are beheaded or crucified.

In 2016, the humanitarian organization Open Doors reported that persecution in India is "extremely violent and that the violence is increasing. More than 350 Christians were physically attacked, at least nine Christians were killed for their faith and at least three women were raped."[10] Open Doors says, "The Indian government, now led by Hindu nationalist party Bharatiya Janata Party (BJP), is turning a blind eye to attacks against religious minorities, allowing Christians to be attacked with impunity." This is nothing new. To give an example of the human cost involved, on January 23, 1999, while sleeping in their car, Christian missionary Graham Staines and his two sons, Philip (10) and Timothy (7), were murdered. Their car was doused with gasoline and set on fire. The attackers stopped them from getting out and shouted, "Justice has been done; the Christians have been cremated in Hindu fashion."[11] Staines had been in India for 34 years, operating a hospital and clinic for lepers.

That the persecution of Christians has taken place in places that are commonly thought to have had little or no exposure to the gospel confirms that its message has spread more than many people realize. For example, in 1597, 26 Christians (20 Japanese and 6 missionaries) were crucified at Nagasaki.[12] And in 1614, Tokugawa Ieyasu, the first of the

Tokugawa shoguns, issued and enforced an edict aimed at the complete extinction of the Christian church in Japan. He did not fully succeed, but the dwindling of Christian believers due to torture-induced recantation and death, and the near total absence of new converts, meant that for all practical purposes Christianity in Japan was annihilated.[13] Still, Christianity had a presence.

Many of these Japanese Christians were burned at the stake. In the early 1600s, English trader Richard Cocks, who disliked "papistical" missionaries, wrote: "I saw fifty-five of them martyred at one time at Miyako. Among them were little children of five or six years, burned alive in the arms of their mothers, who cried 'Jesus, receive their souls!' There are many in prison who hourly await death, for very few return to their idolatry."[14] Authentic religious freedom wasn't built into Japan's legal structures until 1946.[15] Far from being a society longing to hear the good news, there aren't more Christians in Japan today because the persecutions in past centuries have been so severe.

As mentioned earlier, Christianity also came early to China, but Christians were severely persecuted for centuries as well. In the 1300s, Muslims killed hundreds of thousands of Christians in China, and in 1724, Christianity was banned and hundreds of missionaries and converts were put to death. In 1900, crazed mobs were incited by an edict given by the empress: "BY IMPERIAL COMMAND EXTERMINATE THE CHRISTIAN RELIGION! DEATH TO THE FOREIGN DEVILS!"[16] Christians were tortured and murdered in large numbers. To give a sense for what was happening, consider a letter that a missionary mother wrote to her three children who were safe in another province. She said they were

> being molested every day by bands of bad men who want money from us. Now our money is all gone. We feel there is nothing for us but to try to get back to the city; this is no easy matter. The roads are full of these bad people who seek our lives.
>
> I am writing this as it may be my last to you. Who knows but we may be with Jesus very soon. This is only a

wee note to send out dear love to you all, and to ask you
not to feel too sad when you know we have been killed. We
have committed you all into God's hands. He will make a
way for you all. Try to be good children. Love God. Give
your hearts to Jesus. This is your dear parents' last request.

Your loving papa, mama, and wee Jenny [17]

Their children never heard from them again.

When I hear people complain about others not hearing the gospel, I think: *The gospel message is getting out, but many cultures are killing the messengers.* Even as recently as 1992 the Chinese state-run press
noted that "the church played an important role in the change" of Eastern Europe and warned, "If China does not want such a scene to be
repeated in its land, it must strangle the baby while it is still in the
manger."[18]

God Gives the Gospel in Surprising Ways

Open your notebook and write this down, because it will be on the
test: God will make sure that those who would repent will have the
opportunity. This works for all Calvinists and many Arminians.[19] Consider Jonah. God told Jonah to go and preach to the Ninevites. When
Jonah refused God's command, God had Jonah thrown off a ship. A
giant fish swallowed him, then later vomited him onto a beach near
Nineveh. Jonah then preached the news to the Ninevites, and they
repented.[20]

Earlier I mentioned the Ethiopian eunuch. In Acts 8:26-39, we read
that an angel told the apostle Philip where he could meet this Ethiopian,
and the Spirit told Philip to approach his chariot and talk to him. As a
result, the Ethiopian became a believer, and Philip baptized him. Today,
the church in Ethiopia considers Philip to be the founder of Christianity in their country. Also, when the apostle Paul was imprisoned in
Philippi, he was somehow in contact with the saints of "Caesar's household" (Philippians 4:22).

My wife Jean and I were at a chalet in a remote part of Alaska where
there were only two employees—the owner/cook and the waitress/

maid. During dinner, the waitress found out we were Christians. She told us that some years prior, while she was in a hospital strung out on drugs, she had a vision of Jesus. He preached the gospel to her, and she became a Christian. I have no reason not to believe her. Similarly, author Joel Rosenberg relates that "if you travel through the Middle East, you will meet many ex-Muslims who will tell you, as they have told me, that they have seen dreams and visions of Jesus, who personally told them to follow Him."[21] Just this last semester, one of my Egyptian students told me that a friend of his recently became a Christian because he had a vision of Jesus.[22]

Most Refuse the Gospel

I've learned there are some who intuit that surely there would be many more people who would have repented if they had the chance to have heard the gospel before they died. One of those who thinks this is philosopher Jerry Walls:

> Consider some of the places in the world where Christianity is flourishing today, such as Korea and sub-Saharan Africa, places where Christian witness was relatively minimal, if it existed at all, in earlier generations. Is it really plausible at all to think *none of the forebears* of these contemporary Korean and African Christians would have accepted the gospel if they had heard it? Surely it strains credulity to the breaking point to think *none of them* would have. Indeed, it seems more likely that many persons would have responded positively, just as they have in our day.[23]

There are two things to say about this. First, I don't know what Walls means by "none," as there is no reason to believe that, throughout the centuries, there haven't been some Christians—even if comparatively few—in South Korea. It's true that The Pew Research Center reports that in 1900 only one percent of the people were Christians at the time, but how many Christians do there need to be for the gospel to be available in a country?[24] As for sub-Saharan Africa, there has been a Christian presence there since the first century (consider again the Ethiopian eunuch).

Second, Walls assumes "many persons would have responded positively" because today Christianity is "flourishing" in those areas. But earlier generations may not have been as receptive to the gospel. Many people—as well as cultures or even civilizations—are not prepared to receive the gospel, or they have committed widespread genocide upon the Christians in their midst.

The soil upon which the gospel seed is sown can change drastically over time. In the parable of the sower (see Matthew 13, Mark 4, and Luke 8), Jesus said the seed of God's Word falls on four types of soil: the path, rocky ground, among thorns, and good soil. Only the seed that falls on the good soil will yield a crop. Consider that most of the Jews of the New Testament era rejected Jesus. In his hometown of Nazareth, the people dismissed him as nothing special: "Isn't this Joseph's son?" (Luke 4:22 NIV). To this Jesus replied,

> No prophet is accepted in his hometown. I assure you that there were many widows in Israel in Elijah's time, when the sky was shut for three and a half years and there was a severe famine throughout the land. Yet Elijah was not sent to any of them, but to a widow in Zarephath in the region of Sidon. And there were many in Israel with leprosy in the time of Elisha the prophet, yet not one of them was cleansed—only Naaman the Syrian.[25]

Familiarity with Jesus bred contempt rather than submission. In pride and envy, the people of His hometown rejected Him because he was born there. And when Jesus pointed out occasions in Israel's past when God helped only two suffering individuals who were not even Jews, "They got up, drove him out of the town, and took him to the brow of the hill on which the town was built, in order to throw him off the cliff."[26] As for South Korea, perhaps Japanese colonial rule (which began in 1910), World War II, and the Korean War prepared the soil for their more widespread acceptance of the gospel.[27] Only God knows why towns or countries choose to reject Him, but, nonetheless, He knows.

The Canaanite cities of Sodom and Gomorrah serve as an amazing illustration of God knowing who would or would not repent, and that often no one in a particular culture would repent. The Lord told Abraham that the outcry against Sodom and Gomorrah was "great and their sin is very grave" (Genesis 18:20). After God said this, Abraham knew the Lord would destroy those cities, so he asked God:

> Will you indeed sweep away the righteous with the wicked? Suppose there are fifty righteous within the city. Will you then sweep away the place and not spare it for the fifty righteous who are in it? Far be it from you to do such a thing, to put the righteous to death with the wicked, so that the righteous fare as the wicked! Far be that from you! Shall not the Judge of all the earth do what is just? (Genesis 18:23-25).

Notice Abraham's plea: "Far be it from you to do such a thing, to put the righteous to death with the wicked." In other words, Abraham was worried precisely about the issue of God's fairness. Were people going to be killed who shouldn't be? Abraham was worried over that which skeptics grouse. How did the Lord respond? "If I find at Sodom fifty righteous in the city, I will spare the whole place for their sake" (Genesis 28:26). Thus the Lord agreed to spare both cities if 50 righteous people lived in them.

Abraham then asked God to spare the cities for 45 righteous people—then 40, then 30, then 20, and then finally for only 10. I suspect that when Abraham reached 10 that he was all but certain there were at least 10 righteous people in those cities! After all, Lot and his wife and two daughters made four. All they needed to find were six others to spare both cities. And the Lord answered, "For the sake of ten I will not destroy it" (Genesis 18:32). The significance of this cannot be overstated. Abraham asked exactly the same question that many ask today: Is it fair that God kill the innocent (or, in the case of the unevangelized, those who would repent if they had the opportunity)?

In Genesis 19, we learn that after Abraham's conversation with the

Lord, two angels arrived in Sodom and stayed in Lot's house. But that evening, the men of the city, "both young and old" (verse 4), surrounded the house and demanded that Lot send the angels outside so they might have sex with them. Imagine the horror of that moment—the men wanted to rape Lot's guests. When he refused to send them out, the men threatened to do worse to him. Even after the angels blinded these men, "they wore themselves out groping for the door" (Genesis 19:11).

The next morning, even though many of the people in that city had been blinded, Lot could find no one willing to leave. Also, even though the men of the city had wanted to rape his guests, Lot himself was reluctant to leave. But the Lord was merciful to Lot, so the angels "seized" Lot, his wife, and his two daughters and brought them out of the city.

What happened once Lot and his daughters were out of the city? His daughters got Lot drunk and had sex with him so that they could have children by their father! Even atheist Richard Dawkins, in a surprising moment of moral clarity, writes, "If this dysfunctional family was the best Sodom had to offer by way of morals, some might begin to feel a certain sympathy with God and his judicial brimstone."[28] Seriously, I don't know how God could make it clearer to us humans that He knows who would or would not repent. Really, how does God make it clearer? Do we need Abraham's discussion with the Lord about Sodom and Gomorrah to be in blinking neon lights in our Bibles?

And that's not the only instance! The Lord did a similar thing with the people of Jerusalem just before its destruction. He told Jeremiah: "Go up and down the streets of Jerusalem, look around and consider, search through her squares. If you can find but one person who deals honestly and *seeks the truth*, I will forgive this city. Although they say, 'As surely as the LORD lives,' still they are swearing falsely" (Jeremiah 5:1-2 NIV, emphasis mine). Jeremiah looked, but he couldn't find anyone who sought the truth. So he concluded: "Therefore a lion from the forest will attack them, a wolf from the desert will ravage them, a leopard will lie in wait near their towns to tear to pieces any who venture out, for their rebellion is great and their backslidings many" (verse 6 NIV). Notice that, just as with Sodom and Gomorrah, the Lord made it clear that He knows when there are no people who seek the truth in a given place.

The Lord knows our hearts. He knows those who would turn to him given the opportunity, and unfortunately, most would not and do not.[29] Now maybe Romans 3:10-11 makes more sense: "None is righteous, no, not one; no one understands; *no one seeks for God.*" Without the work of the Holy Spirit, *no one* seeks for God. Humans on their own want to do their own thing, and that thing isn't about seeking God. Thus the intuition that surely there would be more who would repent if they had heard the gospel doesn't match what Scripture tells us.

In fact, Romans 1:18-20 teaches that everyone already has a general revelation of God available to them:

> The wrath of God is revealed from heaven against all ungodliness and unrighteousness of men, who by their unrighteousness suppress the truth. For what can be known about God is plain to them, because God has shown it to them. For his invisible attributes, namely, his eternal power and divine nature, have been clearly perceived, ever since the creation of the world, in the things that have been made. So they are without excuse.

John Feinberg, in his book *The Many Faces of Evil*, writes, "So everyone has enough revelation to know that there is a God, something of what he is like, and a sense of right and wrong. Paul adds that as a result, they are without excuse."[30] Skeptics who opine that God didn't give enough evidence to justify belief in Him are sadly mistaken. The natural result of looking at creation should lead people to the conclusion that there is a God who created the universe.[31]

So back to God getting the message out in different ways. In Job 33:14-18 we read these amazing words:

> For God speaks in one way, and in two, though man does not perceive it. In a dream, in a vision of the night, when deep sleep falls on men, while they slumber on their beds, then he opens the ears of men and terrifies them with

warnings, that he may turn man aside from his deed and conceal pride from a man; he keeps back his soul from the pit, his life from perishing by the sword.

Thus, God can reach people and share the gospel with them through dreams or visions.

Feinberg writes, "Those who don't get that information [the gospel] don't fail to get it because it was impossible to attain it; rather, they fail to get it because they reject the truth they have and don't seek further truth about God."[32] Feinberg thus concludes:

> As a result, even those who never heard the gospel are guilty before God. They are guilty because they have some revelation of God already (and have rejected it), and could have much more, including the message of salvation, if they wanted. But no one on their own wants more truth or wants to live in accord with the truth they have, according to Paul. Hence the fact that they don't get this further information isn't God's fault; it is their choice.[33]

Feinberg is right, and the reason I had this chapter follow the chapter "Why Do Bad Things Happen to Good People?" is because unless one realizes that all people are profoundly sinful—aside from the regenerative work of the Holy Spirit—it is almost impossible to convince them that God isn't being unfair to the lost unless everyone hears the gospel.

Nonetheless, there are some who object that even those who wouldn't repent should still have gotten the gospel message. I always reply that I'm not going to invite William and Kate (aka His Royal Highness, the Duke of Cambridge, and Her Royal Highness, the Duchess of Cambridge) to my next birthday party. Putting aside that I'm pretty sure they would upstage the festivities that are supposed to be in my honor, I know *for a fact* that they would not attend. My knowledge about that is just short of mathematical certainty. Since that's the case, why should I invite them? The fact that an invitation to my birthday party is infinitely less valuable than the invitation to be saved is irrelevant. God does know *with certainty* those who would accept or reject

His offer of salvation, and He is not obliged to make sure those whom He *knows* would not attend would nonetheless get an invitation.

But that leaves one last issue to resolve: What about children who die before they have an opportunity to respond to the gospel?

Children and Salvation

Although Christians differ about whether all children will be saved, many of them, including apologists such as Norman Geisler, William Lane Craig, and Greg Koukl, have argued that all who die before the age of accountability (see Deuteronomy 1:39) will be saved.[34] They base this on passages such as Luke 18:16-17, where Jesus said, "Permit the children to come to Me, and do not hinder them, for the kingdom of God belongs to such as these. Truly I say to you, whoever does not receive the kingdom of God like a child shall not enter it at all."[35] As theologian Millard Erickson asks,

> Could it be that Jesus was using as the object lesson in his plea for a certain quality, individuals who did not actually embody that quality? That would seem strange indeed. Thus, if Jesus was affirming that those who would enter into the kingdom must be like these children, he seems to be asserting, as a premise in his argument, that these children were in the kingdom.[36]

Regarding infants, Christopher W. Morgan and Robert A. Peterson point out, "Although their reasons may differ depending on other theological commitments, and although some of their reasons are better than others, evangelicals generally agree that [deceased infants] will be in heaven."[37]

This belief isn't new to Christianity. Augustine, who died in AD 430, wrote:

> Who knows what reward God reserves in the secret place of his judgment for the children who, though they have not acted rightly, are not, on the other hand, weighed down by sin? For it is not in vain that the Church commends

> as martyrs the infants who were slaughtered when Herod
> sought to slay Jesus Christ our Lord.[38]

It's important to add that those who hold that children are saved also traditionally include the mentally handicapped in the category of children, and so they too will be saved.

As I wrote in the *Christian Research Journal*, "It's true that no scripture unambiguously guarantees that children will be saved, but if they are, God would have good reason for not unambiguously making that clear, for then abortion and infanticide would guarantee a child's salvation! Imagine the abuses that would occur from that knowledge! Whatever the case, we can rest in God's love and mercy regarding their fate."[39]

In sum: God will make sure that those who would repent will have the opportunity. Therefore, no one will go to hell and miss the opportunity to be in heaven because they didn't hear the gospel.

Chapter 5

How Can Eternal Punishment Be Fair?

Sometimes I think there is really only one problem of evil, and that is hell. After all, if everyone is ultimately rescued from this world of suffering into a kingdom where in His "right hand are pleasures forevermore" (Psalm 16:11), then eternity *will* dwarf our suffering to insignificance.

But if, as I hold, the plain and most unforced reading of Scripture is correct, then the Bible tells us that eternal punishment awaits those who reject the good news.[1] This bad news offends non-Christians and troubles many Christians. After all, how can God be loving and yet punish people *forever*? As prolific evangelical author and theologian John Stott put it: "I find the concept intolerable and do not understand how people can live with it without either cauterizing their feelings or cracking under the strain. But our emotions are a fluctuating, unreliable guide to truth and must not be exalted to the place of supreme authority in determining it."[2] Indeed, it is a difficult doctrine to accept, and in this chapter, we will address hell's nature and whether God could be just to send people there forever.

At the outset, we should be humble and, as Stott observed, remember that our emotions are an "unreliable guide" when we think and talk about hell. Sadly, however, many seem to believe, "If *I* don't understand hell, if *I* don't understand how eternal punishment could possibly be fair, then it must not be fair." Because of this, some Christians reformulate hell to be no more than annihilation—hell's occupants simply cease to exist usually after a period of punishment. But we must remember that if hell exists, hell is by definition *other worldly*—and although it may not make sense *to us*, that doesn't mean that eternal punishment doesn't make sense in the realm that we cannot see.[3]

We tend to view the fairness of hell only from a this-worldly perspective; that is, from the perspective of living on planet Earth for 70, 80, 90, or 100 years. But consider that Satan and the fallen angels *may* have already been alive for the equivalent of eight-hundred-thousand-billion-trillion-centillion earth years. If that is the case (we have no idea how long ago God created the angels), then to punish them for 1 year or even 1000 years might seem as short to them as sentencing a mass murderer to one day of hard labor.

In addition, we tend to downplay the significance of human sin and view humans as less sinful than they really are. But we should remember that creaturely sin resulted in war in heaven![4] And *all* human rebellion against God is akin to Satan's rebellion against the Lord, which, directly or indirectly, resulted in every suffering, sickness, rape, torture, and death that ever happened or will happen on planet Earth.[5] And all the suffering on this planet doesn't take into account who knows how much horror in the kingdom of heaven. To say that rebellion in God's kingdom is a big deal is akin to saying that global thermonuclear war is inconvenient. All the wars in the history of this world and heaven are the result of sin. We drastically underestimate the horror of rebellion.

So, with humility in mind, here are some things to consider.

Hell's Nature

It's important to note that a majority of Christian theologians, not just recently but for centuries, have agreed that we shouldn't get dogmatic about the biblical imagery of hell. Robert Peterson, in his book *Hell on Trial: The Case for Eternal Punishment*, puts it well:

Should we understand the fires of hell as literal flames? The answer is no. As Calvin saw long ago, God did not intend for us to do so. If we take literally the image of hell as fire, it clashes with other images of hell, for example, hell as darkness, or hell as the wicked being cut to pieces (Matt. 24:51). Rather than giving us literal pictures of the fate of the wicked, God uses dreaded pictures from this world to present the terrible reality of hell in the next world. I stand with the majority of contemporary conservative scholars in understanding the biblical imagery of hell metaphorically rather than literally.[6]

Similarly, John Blanchard rightly says that "the fire of hell is not a material phenomenon that could, for example, drive a steam engine or generate electricity. Virtually every interpreter agrees that when Jesus spoke of hell's 'worm' He was using a metaphor; it would be strange if in the same breath He should speak of 'fire' and not be doing the same thing."[7] And D.A. Carson concludes, "The truth is that these incompatible images were never intended to be literal, but were metaphors to describe the awful place we call hell."[8] Although any portrayal of hell that renders it as tolerable is mistaken, that doesn't mean we should make more of the language than is there.

Can Hell Be Portrayed as Worse Than It Is?

Hell must never be portrayed as anything less than horrible, but it is possible to dangerously stray from the Bible's teaching. In Jewish literature, "the rabbis speak of licentious men hanging by their genitals, women who publicly suckled their children hanging by their breasts, and those who talked during synagogue prayers having their mouths filled with hot coals."[9] Dante, in his *Inferno*, depicted some sinners as naked and stung all over by wasps and hornets, some gagging in a river of blood, some dipped in human excrement, some boiled in pitch, some sitting on burning sand while a shower of fire falls on them, some scourged by horned demons, and so on and on.

Father John Furniss (aka Father Furness), an evangelist to children, portrayed hell as having different dungeons. In the fourth dungeon,

> there is a boy, a young man…His eyes are burning like two burning coals. Two long flames come out of his ears… Sometimes he opens his mouth and breath of blazing fire rolls out of it. But listen! There is a sound just like that of a kettle boiling. Is it really a kettle boiling? No; then what is it? Hear what it is. It is the blood boiling in the scalding veins of that boy. The brain is boiling and bubbling in his head. The marrow is boiling in his bones.[10]

Imagine your child hearing that in a first-grade Sunday school class!

Even a more sober portrayal by American evangelist Jonathan Edwards is over the top. Edwards depicted hell as a raging furnace where

> the body will be full of torment as full as it can hold, and every part of it shall be full of torment. They shall be in extreme pain, every joint of 'em, every nerve shall be full of inexpressible torment. They shall be tormented even to their fingers' ends…Their hearts and their bowels and their heads, their eyes and their tongues, their hands and their feet will be filled with the fierceness of God's wrath. This is taught us in many Scriptures.[11]

I have asked my students to name *one* of the "many Scriptures" that, according to Edwards, describes hell this way. I'm still waiting.

Jesus on Hell

Contrary to these hellish embellishments, in Luke 16 we find Jesus' most detailed discourse of what it might be like for a person to be in hell.[12] There, Jesus tells us of a rich man who didn't help a sickly beggar named Lazarus who lay outside his gate. Jesus said that after both Lazarus and the rich man died, the rich man was in "Hades, being in torment" and he saw Abraham at a distance and called out, "Father Abraham, have mercy on me, and send Lazarus to dip the end of his finger in water and cool my tongue, for I am in anguish in this flame" (verses 23-24). Abraham replied,

> "Between us and you a great chasm has been fixed, in order that those who would pass from here to you may not be able, and none may cross from there to us." And [the rich man] said, "Then I beg you, father, to send him to my father's house—for I have five brothers—so that he may warn them, lest they also come into this place of torment." But Abraham said, "They have Moses and the Prophets; let them hear them." And he said, "No, father Abraham, but if someone goes to them from the dead, they will repent." He said to him, "If they do not hear Moses and the Prophets, neither will they be convinced if someone should rise from the dead" (verses 26-31).

Notice that Jesus didn't depict the rich man as screaming hysterically in anguish and so pained by the flames that he was incoherent. Jesus could have done that, but He didn't. Instead, we read of a man who, rather than screaming hysterically, is able to make requests, carry on a conversation, lodge arguments, and form rebuttals. His thinking, however mistaken, is still intact. His calling Abraham "father" could even be considered polite (albeit self-serving).

Yes, the rich man was in pain, but it is within human experience that sometimes people are in so much pain that they are rendered absolutely incoherent by it or at least they are not able to converse in any kind of a normal manner. I've experienced many different kinds of pain in my life, but the worst for intensity was when, on several occasions, I bit down on a bad tooth (now fixed). Each time that happened, I'd jump up and just stand there for a few seconds until the pain subsided. I could not imagine trying to lodge arguments in such a state, and that was with one bad tooth! But the rich man converses. He's even polite! Now I grant that we should be cautious not to draw too much from the rich man's experience in hell, but, again, this is our Lord's most extended discussion on what hell might be like.

Some argue that Jesus' purpose in this story is not to tell us about the condition of those in hell. But, as Larry Dixon points out, all Scripture is God-breathed, and "unless one is prepared to suggest that Jesus is passing on inaccurate information about the afterlife, why should Luke 16 *not* be understood to reflect a general picture of what happens to the righteous and the wicked at death?"[13] Also, Murray Harris writes that "it is not illegitimate to deduce from the setting of the story the basic characteristics of the *postmortem* state of believers and unbelievers." Harris points out that "both are conscious of their surroundings," have a "memory of the past," and have "retained their capacity to reason."[14] The rich man could have been screaming incoherently, but he wasn't.

Hell's Justification

Hell's Occupants Unrepentant

Eternal separation from God makes sense *if* the occupants of hell remain eternally unrepentant, and I believe that is consistent with Scripture. After all, here on earth, Scripture informs us that the lost are depraved and that "no one seeks for God" (Romans 3:11). We must keep in mind that it is the Holy Spirit who "will convict the world concerning sin and righteousness and judgment" (John 16:8). It is the Spirit who persuades unbelievers. So what would lead them to repent in hell, where the Spirit is no longer on hand to work in that way?[15]

Jim (I've changed his name), who had been a youth pastor, came to me one day and confided that his wife had cheated on him. He had forgiven her, but the fact she had betrayed him still bothered him. Then one day he complained that hell was unfair. He said that if someone sinned against him, no matter what that sin was, that he could not conceive of making that person suffer forever in hell.

I asked Jim how he'd feel if his wife committed adultery again, and if he would forgive her. He said he'd want her to suffer for it, but not *forever*. So I asked Jim to consider how he would treat his again-adulterous wife if he and she both lived forever and she were never, ever repentant. What if she were never sorry but still wanted "to be friends"? He said there was no way that he would ever be her friend again even if it made her eternally sad, and that got his attention. He replied that he could see the legitimacy of a never-repentant, cheating wife in some sense being forever rejected even if it forever hurt her feelings. Of course, he again argued that hell was still too horrible and therefore unjust. I then pointed out that now we were only disagreeing about how much pain there might be, not whether some sort of forever punishment might be fitting for the eternally unrepentant.

And that will be the case with hell's occupants. Why should we think they will ever repent? What could be more fitting than eternally punishing the eternally unrepentant? Although this isn't indisputably taught in Scripture, it is compatible with all we know about the wicked and hell's occupants.[16] When God's wrath is poured out on the wicked in Revelation 16:9, we read that "they were seared with intense heat and they cursed the name of God, who had control over these plagues, but they refused to repent and glorify him" (NIV). Verse 11 says that they "cursed the God of heaven because of their pains and their sores, but they refused to repent of what they had done" (NIV). Similarly, Revelation 9:20-21 tells us,

> The rest of mankind who were not killed by these plagues still did not repent of the work of their hands; they did not stop worshiping demons, and idols of gold, silver, bronze, stone, and wood—idols that cannot see or hear or walk. Nor did they repent of their murders, their magic arts, their sexual immorality or their thefts (NIV).

Some ask if the "weeping and gnashing of teeth" by hell's inhabitants doesn't signify repentance. But, as Alfred Edersheim explained, "'weeping' is associated in Rabbinic thought with sorrow, but 'gnashing of teeth' was almost always with anger—not, as generally supposed, with anguish."[17] It is often said that the Pharisees "gnashed" their teeth at Jesus when they were angry, and those who are in hell will have much to be angry about.[18]

Although D.A. Carson says that it by no means settles the issue, he points to Revelation 22:10-11 as suggesting that hell's occupants will remain unrepentant: "Do not seal up the words of the prophecy of this scroll, because the time is near. Let the one who does wrong continue to do wrong; let the vile person continue to be vile; let him who does right continue to do right; and let him who is holy continue to be holy" (NIV). Carson comments that "the parallelism is telling. If the holy and those who do right continue to be holy and to do right, in anticipation of the perfect holiness and rightness to be lived and practiced throughout all eternity, should we not also conclude that the vile continue their vileness in anticipation of the vileness they will live and practice throughout all eternity?"[19] It's important to note that nowhere does Scripture tell us that the occupants of hell will be repentant.

There are some who ask whether the rich man in Luke 16 became repentant in hell. Let's again consider the passage.[20] The rich man expressed not even the slightest remorse—certainly not repentance—for the way he treated Lazarus. In fact, the rich man who had ignored Lazarus asked Abraham to send Lazarus to fetch him water and to presumably bring it to him through the flames. The rich man also asked if Lazarus could leave his place of comfort to warn his brothers of their need to repent. In short, the rich man saw Lazarus as nothing more than a tool.

Further, the rich man's suggestion that his brothers needed to be warned betrays a lack of repentance because it implies that he ended up in hell because God didn't provide him with sufficient warning. Finally, the rich man disagreed with Abraham's assertion that the Law of Moses was sufficient evidence to lead his brothers into repentance. As R.C. Trench says, the rich man's "contempt of God's word," which he showed on earth, follows him "beyond the grave."[21] Ironically, Lazarus was the name of a man who did come back from the dead, and the chief priests responded to this resurrection by trying to kill both Jesus and the resurrected Lazarus (John 12:9-10)!

Consider also that many who understand the Bible's teaching on hell nonetheless exhibit an overt rejection of the God revealed in the Bible. Mark Twain wrote to his wife, "I am plenty safe enough in his hands; I am not in any danger from that kind of a Deity. The one that I want to keep out of the reach of is the caricature of him which one finds in the Bible. We (that one and I) could never respect each other, never get along together. I have met his superior a hundred times—in fact I amount to that myself."[22] Why should we surmise that Twain will have a different attitude at the judgment?

Episcopal bishop John Shelby Spong writes that the God revealed in the Bible is "a God I cannot respect, much less worship; a deity whose needs and prejudices are at least as large as my own."[23] Similarly, Archbishop Desmond Tutu said, "I would refuse to go to a homophobic heaven. No, I would say sorry, I mean I would much rather go to the other place."[24] Philosopher John Stuart Mill said, "Whatever power such a being may have over me, there is one thing which he shall not do: he shall not compel me to worship him. I will call no being good, who is not what I mean when I apply that epithet to my fellow creatures; and if such a being can sentence me to hell for not so calling him, to hell I will go."[25] Similarly defiant was William Earnest Henley, who in 1875 wrote the poem "Invictus," which says in part:

> Beyond this place of wrath and tears,
> Looms but the Horror of the shade.
> And yet the menace of the years
> Finds and shall find me unafraid.
>
> It matters not how strait the gate,
> How charged with punishments the scroll,
> I am the master of my fate
> I am the captain of my soul.

Similarly, AC/DC, in their album *Highway to Hell*, sing of being destined for hell, and not wanting anyone to stop them.

In these ways and more, people express defiance toward God. Their words reveal a clear lack of respect for Him and a refusal to live under His rules. Some even go so far as to brag they would rather go to hell![26]

There are many people who not only hard-heartedly reject the Bible's portrayal of God, they revel in their rejection and do so knowing Jesus' proclamations about hell. In response, some have suggested that when these men actually see the God of love they would then realize that they were wrong and want to be with Him. But that would be the case only if the rejection of God was a matter of a simple mistake or misunderstanding, akin to ordering the wrong dessert: "I chose the chocolate ice cream when I should have chosen the strawberry, and now I'm lost. I didn't know!" But the Bible continuously reveals that those who are lost are not lost because of a lack of information, but because of a hardness of heart. We have no reason to think that their conscious rejection here will diminish at the judgment. In other words, there is a sense that in hell they will obtain what they most desire: separation from God.

Some have pointed out to me that these examples of men rejecting God are unusual and most people never make such overt, hardhearted declarations. That's true, of course, but that doesn't mean that those who don't make such outward proclamations don't have rebellion locked deeply into their hearts. In fact, at the judgment, when all humans are revealed for who they really are, I think we'll witness a similar self-seeking attitude. Zygmunt Bauman, in his book *Modernity and the Holocaust,* gives us insight as to how, under pressure, otherwise nice people are not anyone we would want to be around:

> A few years ago a journalist of *Le Monde* interviewed a sample of former hijack victims. One of the most interesting things he found was an abnormally high incidence of divorce among couples who went jointly through the agony of hostage experience. Intrigued, he probed the divorcees for the reason for their decision. Most of the interviewees told him that they had never contemplated a divorce before the hijack. During the horrifying episode, however, "their eyes opened," and "they saw their partners in a new light." Ordinary good husbands "proved to be" selfish creatures, caring only for their own stomachs; daring businessmen displayed disgusting cowardice; resourceful "men of this world" fell to pieces and did little except bewailing their imminent perdition.[27]

Those who understand the depths of human evil will not be surprised by this. When the veneer of civilization is stripped away at the judgment and people are revealed for who they really are, then we will see that all human rebels will reject God.

This answers another objection about hell: Could any enjoy heaven knowing that their loved ones are there? But when our loved ones' rejection of God is plain and their true attitude toward others is revealed, no Christian will wish they could spend eternity with such a person—just as spouses who experienced the hijacking together realized that they couldn't go on being married to such a sniveling coward. Hell will seem oddly fitting.

We began this chapter by quoting annihilationist John Stott's opposition to the idea of eternal punishment. But what if the occupants of hell are forever unrepentant? In that event, Stott writes, "I question whether 'eternal conscious torment' is compatible with the biblical revelation of divine justice, unless the impenitence of the lost also continues throughout eternity."[28] Even to annihilationist John Stott, eternal punishment can make sense if the punished are eternally unrepentant.

Hell's Occupants Won't Want to Be with God

Related to the above, the case can be made that hell's occupants will not only be unrepentant, they will *prefer* not to be with God. Dallas Willard put it that the chief characteristic of the lost will not be that they are in hell "but that they have become the kind of people so locked in their own self-worship and denial of God that *they cannot want* God."[29] There is no doubt that those in hell will hate hell; it is, after all, suffering. But would they enjoy heaven? No. Rebels, by definition, don't want to toe the line. I think we sometimes even see something similar going on in our human experience.

After enduring five miscarriages, my wife and I took in foster children. These kids, prior to their living in our home, led police-blotter lives—they were abused, sexually molested, criminally neglected, and living in one ramshackle hotel or county group home after another. After a couple years in our home and much to our surprise, one girl ran away and returned to her former squalor. About a year later she called, sad because she knew, in her words, that she had "ruined my childhood," and my wife Jean E. asked her why she had run away. She replied, "Because you wouldn't let me have a boyfriend." She was 12. She had left because she didn't want to live under our rules. We even gave her the opportunity to return but, again, she would rather live in her sad state than under our rules.

Now, she had formerly had many fashionable clothes and a well-appointed bedroom of her own. We had a Jacuzzi in the backyard and a pool table in the garage and we loved her. But rules about boyfriends were something she could not stomach. She preferred life on the street to submitting to our rules about boyfriends even though we made it a policy to say yes to absolutely every request that would not hurt her.[30] She told Jean in tears that leaving us ruined her childhood, but that didn't change the fact that she wanted to live life on her own terms. Of course our house wasn't heaven, but most of us would consider her roach motel existence to be hell on earth because she couldn't stand our rules. That she could not stand rules and so didn't want to live in our house makes some sense of why people would choose hell over heaven.

Dallas Willard put it well: "I am thoroughly convinced that God will let everyone into heaven who, in his considered opinion, can stand it."[31] Because many couldn't stand heaven, some have suggested that the gates of hell are locked from the inside.[32] C.S. Lewis thought this: "The doors of hell are locked on the inside. I certainly do not mean that ghosts may not wish to come out of hell...but they certainly do not will even the first preliminary stages of self-abandonment through which alone the soul can reach any good. They enjoy forever the horrible freedom they have demanded, and are therefore self-enslaved."[33]

Hell as a Present and Future Deterrent

Throughout the ages, many people repented of their sins because they became conscious of hell. That happened to me. As an almost-13-year-old I was listening to Billy Graham preach a sermon entitled "Heaven and Hell," and when he was done, I was absolutely sure I was going to hell. I went forward that day and committed my life to Christ.

Similarly, deceased atheist Christopher Hitchens's brother Peter Hitchens was an atheist and one day he was at a museum and was looking at a painting that depicted hell:

> Still scoffing, I peered at the naked figures fleeing toward the pit of hell, out of my usual faintly morbid interest in the alleged terrors of damnation. But this time I gaped, my mouth actually hanging open. These people did not appear remote or from the ancient past; they were my own generation. Because they were naked, they were not imprisoned in their own age by time-bound fashions...They were me and the people I knew. One of them—and I have always wondered how the painter thought of it—is actually vomiting with shock and fear at the sound of the Last Trump... I had a sudden, strong sense of religion being a thing of the present day...A large catalogue of misdeeds, ranging from the embarrassing to the appalling, replayed themselves rapidly in my head. I had absolutely no doubt that I was among the damned...[34]

That painting led Peter Hitchens to become a Christian and to subsequently publish a book that countered the work of his brother Christopher.

Again, throughout the ages, many have repented of their sins out of a fear of hell, and I wonder if hell might not serve to reassure the saints in heaven of rebellion's awful results? As we will see in the chapter on free will, perhaps the existence of an eternal hell will serve as an eternal reminder of the horror of rebellion. Even many annihilationists agree that some punishment is necessary to deter rebellion. After all, free beings can't think that they can get off scot-free after they have raped and tortured others to death. So let's get something straight: Just about everyone—even non-Christians—thinks that those who commit certain evils should be punished. Thus, when it comes to hell, we are talking only about a matter of degree—how much punishment is enough—not whether there should be punishment at all.

Although annihilationists opine that a limited hell would be a sufficient deterrent against sin, we should note from the above that some people acknowledge the prospect of an eternal hell and still persist in their rebellion. If that's the case, then a punishment for one year or 10,000 is certainly not going to mean much. Also, the Creator of the universe, in His considered opinion, has determined that there should be eternal punishment and we'd best trust that He knows best.

Will Many Go to Hell?

Does this mean many may end up in hell? Perhaps it does. But would we consider God more loving or more just if fewer went to hell? I suspect not. When would we be satisfied? Would thousands fewer or millions fewer do it? Let's face it: If we think hell unfair, then no one should go there. Not even one. What's the point of arguing, as some do, that for God to be loving there should be fewer people in hell? After all, if just one person will be unfairly punished in hell, we could not live with that. On the other hand, if hell is the fair destiny of rebellious people, why argue that fewer should go there?

Could We Ever *Feel* Good About Hell?

One of the grave mistakes that leads so many to abandon the obvious and most unforced reading of Scripture about hell is that they can't find a way to *feel* good about it. But maybe no one was *ever* meant to *feel* completely good about it. We aren't supposed to ever feel good about the rebellion that leads people to hell. Certainly sin and rebellion will forever be regarded in heaven as a travesty, as will the idea that these rebels have come to an end of their own making. At the end of the world even God can't wrap up hell with pretty paper and a ribbon; God doesn't desire to make us *feel* good about rebellion and its' punishment any more than He wants a parent to *feel* good about punishing a rebellious child. I must say, however, that although I don't necessarily *feel* good about hell, I sure feel a lot better knowing there is a hell than to imagine what it would be like if there were no hell. Free beings who get intoxicated with the idea of their own self-actualized godhood need something to sober them up, and hell can serve that purpose.

Whatever we think hell might be like or why eternal punishment might be fair, we should always remember that the God who created hell also allowed His Son Jesus to be tortured to death on the cross to pay for our sins so that we don't have to go there. When people complain about hell, we should always proclaim the good news, which is precisely about their not having to go there if they trust in Jesus.

Chapter 6

Is Free Will Worth It?

We've seen that when Adam and Eve sinned, they plunged us—their descendants—into a lifelong education on good and evil. We've also seen that the evil into which they plunged us is horrendous—resulting in, among other horrors, countless rapes, tortures, and murders.

Of course, God could have made us as meaty automatons who always do right. In other words, God could have avoided *all* evil and *all* suffering by creating us without free will. Why didn't God do that? Is this free will worth the horrendous horrors we endure? This chapter will explain the nature and value of free will, and explore whether free will justifies the existence of evil and suffering.

What Is Free Will?

Free will is the ability to do other than what you do. It is the ability to make self-determined or self-caused choices as opposed to having our choices determined or caused by someone or something else.[1] Alvin Plantinga explains that to be "free"

> is the idea of *being free with respect to a given action*. If a person is free with respect to a given action, then he is free to perform that action and free to refrain from performing

it; no antecedent conditions and/or causal laws determine
that he will perform the action or that he won't. It is within
his power, at the time in question, to take or perform the
action and within his power to refrain from it.[2]

For example, persons can choose between the mundane (such as
whether they're going to have Neapolitan ice cream or only chocolate) or the morally significant (such as whether or not they're going
to remain an alcoholic). In short, free will means that you can do
otherwise.[3]

If God is going to create beings with free will that allows them to do
other than they do, then that absolutely means that God has to *allow*
them to do evil. This is as logical as it gets. A being isn't morally free
unless she can choose to use that free will wrongly. You can't tell your
daughter that she is free to go out with the boy down the street and then
chain her to a heavy kitchen appliance. Further, God is not at fault for
allowing us to do evil any more than you're at fault for your daughter's
choosing to have premarital sex with that boy.[4]

Human Depravity Doesn't Negate Free Will

At the outset, it is important to make two points about what free
will isn't. First, the free will I am talking about does not negate "adamic
depravity"—a doctrine held by both Calvin and Arminius[5] that says
non-Christians are slaves to sin.[6] They are inclined to rebellion and
thus cannot please God. But many Christians misunderstand this doctrine. Being a slave to sin does not mean non-Christians have no choice
but to choose sin every time the choice is presented to them.[7] Scripture,
after all, calls Christians "slaves to righteousness,"[8] yet do we always
choose righteousness every time the choice is presented to us? The
non-Christian's nature is inclined to sin, but that does not mean that
non-Christians cannot choose, in particular cases, whether to commit
adultery, or steal, or cheat, or lie, or whatever.[9] After all, many non-
Christians—even though inclined to sin—have given up the sin of
alcoholism. Granted, choosing not to commit a particular sin doesn't
make them good persons—but they still make real choices. Sometimes,

Paul tells us, non-Christians choose to keep a clear conscience despite their sinful inclinations.[10]

Second, while Scripture reveals great freedom, it certainly does not teach unlimited freedom. God often restrains evil people from acting out their evil desires and, thankfully, He often restrains Christians from acting out the evil they might have done had He not prevented it (He sometimes has thwarted my sinful inclinations). That God sometimes restrains us from certain actions doesn't mean that most of the time we are unable to do as we wish. Also, aside from the work of the Holy Spirit, no one would ever confess Jesus as Lord and submit himself or herself to God. This being said, however, even the fact that humankind is inclined to sin was the result of a free choice—namely, Adam and Eve's free choice to sin.[11] As we saw in the last chapter, Adam and Eve sinned freely, died spiritually, and then passed on their spiritually dead natures to us—their children—because they could not reverse the effects of the sin they freely chose. We, their descendants, have no choice about inheriting their sinful nature. For us to be born at all is to be born like Adam and Eve. Adam and Eve's free choice brought about human nature's inclination to sin.

We all, whether non-Christian or Christian, have immense, significant freedom regarding a wide variety of choices, and we are accountable for those choices.[12]

God's Existence Can't Be Too Obvious

If God wants us to be significantly free (know the kind of freedom we now possess), then God can't make His presence too apparent; He can't make His presence too "saturated." His presence in the world is not smothering, like an overbearing parent. He is not an ever-present "helicopter God" (philosophers call this *epistemic distance* or *divine hiddenness*). This is so because if God's existence were at every moment absolutely unmistakable, then many people would abstain from desires that they might otherwise indulge. As C.S. Lewis put it, "there must perhaps always be just enough lack of demonstrative certainty to make free choice possible: for what could we do but accept if the faith were like the multiplication table?"[13] In other words, if Christianity were unmistakably true, then people would have less free will and they would be compelled to feign loyalty. For example, I've asked guys, "If you were getting up to speak at a podium, and there were cameras on you, and an audience watching you, and if there were a pornographic magazine on the podium, would you open it or even look down at the cover?" Of course the answer is always no. Why? Because they know that everyone is watching them! Similarly, God could make His presence and His power so evident that everyone would always do the right thing—whether they wanted to or not. But that would interfere with our acting freely.

Another example: If you were to chaperone your daughter everywhere she went, would she be able to exercise her free will to go where she was forbidden, drink what she shouldn't, cross sexual boundaries, stay out past her curfew, and so on and on? Those things can only happen if she doesn't perceive your immediate presence. As theologian John Hick put it, "The kind of distance between God and man that would make room for a degree of human autonomy is epistemic distance."[14]

In Matthew 12:38-39, when some of the scribes and Pharisees told Jesus, "Teacher, we wish to see a sign from you," He answered, "An evil and adulterous generation seeks for a sign, but no sign will be given to it except the sign of the prophet Jonah" ("the sign of the prophet Jonah" is a reference to His resurrection). Jesus could have done many more miracles, He could have done miracles galore, but then those who didn't want to believe in Him would be compelled to do so. The Lord gives enough evidence of His existence so that those who want to believe will have their beliefs justified, but not so much evidence that those who don't want to believe will be forced to feign loyalty.[15] But it is more than that: The evidence God gives of His existence, presence, agency, and so on is appropriate for obedience and followership rather than God making His presence so vivid that we are rendered mere spectators to His actions.

God could have, after all, designed the universe so that when we looked up, even if we were indoors, we would always see a Giant Flaming Sword, and if anyone rebelled against God that Giant Flaming

Sword immediately cut him in half! Omnipotence could easily do such a thing. But how many people would be Christian in such a world? Isn't the answer all of them? Everyone would, at the very least, feign loyalty. But how many true worshippers would you get in such a world? I don't think you could get any true worshippers in that world. "When he killed them, they sought him...But they flattered him with their mouths; they lied to him with their tongues" (Psalm 78:34, 36). Worship must be uncoerced. Thus Isaiah wrote, "Truly, you are a God who hides himself, O God of Israel, the Savior" (Isaiah 45:15).

Natural Laws Must Work in Regular Ways

Years ago, as a novice coffee drinker, I was swirling hot water in my coffee carafe and, suddenly, chink—the bottom of the carafe barely grazed the porcelain sink and cracked. So I ask my students, "Why did God let me break my coffee carafe?" This question throws people. After all, God could have stopped me. Why wouldn't a loving God stop me? But let me change the question: *Why* did *I* break my coffee carafe? That's easy, right? I was careless! So let's rephrase the question: Why didn't God stop me from being careless? That question almost answers itself: Why would God want to stop me from being careless? Maybe, just maybe, He'd like me to learn to be more careful?

A couple years ago I was running barefoot down the stairs in my house (which I'd lived in for many years) and I missed the last step. To keep me from falling flat on my face on the slate floor, I put my left foot out to break my fall. I ended up breaking two bones in that foot (the pain was immense—I almost passed out while Jean E. was driving me to the ER).

I have asked my students, "Why did God let me break my foot?" Or better, "Why did God allow me to be careless?" God could have, through either miracle or providence, prevented both, but He chose not to. Why not intervene?

One reason God didn't stop me from cracking my carafe or breaking my foot is that natural laws must work in regular ways if our actions are going to mean anything. Frankly, in both cases I needed to learn to be more careful. Breaking my foot even made me a more cautious driver because I had learned that a little inattention can cause a lot of suffering.

God could constantly work out millions upon millions of miracles or providences *every single day* to stop us from losing life, limb, or property, but then our actions wouldn't mean much. But because natural laws do work in regular ways we can anticipate, I've never again broken a coffee carafe and now I do not run down the stairs. Further, having a broken foot taught me to be more careful in other areas of my life—like driving—because I realized that if you're not careful, you can really injure yourself—badly.

I've been asked why God allowed Hurricane Katrina to destroy the city of New Orleans. Let's consider some facts: New Orleans was built below sea level with walls that we knew, *for sure*, could not withstand a hurricane above Category 3 when hurricanes of Category 4 and Category 5 have already been a part of our experience. It wasn't like we didn't know there were Category 4 and Category 5 hurricanes until Hurricane Katrina came along. Hurricanes beyond Category 3 were already known to exist. Even so, New Orleans was built below sea level with protections we knew were inadequate to stop a threat that has occurred before! Yet many people were mad at God for letting Hurricane Katrina happen. Indeed, Solomon was right: "When a man's folly brings his way to ruin, his heart rages against the LORD" (Proverbs 19:3).

Oxford philosopher Richard Swinburne puts into perspective the fact that natural laws must work in regular ways:

> If God is to allow us to acquire knowledge by learning from experience and above all to allow us to choose whether to acquire knowledge at all or even to allow us to have a very well-justified knowledge of the consequences of our actions—knowledge which we need if we are to have a free and efficacious choice between good and bad—he needs to provide natural evils occurring in regular ways in consequence of natural processes. Or rather, he needs to do this if he is not to give us too evident an awareness of his presence.[16]

Because natural laws work in regular ways, we live in a world where one can break his foot or watch his home be destroyed by a hurricane—or much worse. Thus we humans are capable of creating or alleviating great suffering.

Does the Bible Teach that We Have Free Will?

Skeptic Bart Ehrman, in his book *God's Problem: How the Bible Fails to Answer Our Most Important Question—Why We Suffer*, argues that the appeal to free will is misguided from the start: "In any event, as it turns out—much to the surprise of my students—this standard explanation that God had to give human beings free will and that suffering is the result of people badly exercising it plays only a very minor role in the biblical tradition."[17] He also says that the free-will argument, though "very popular today, it was not heard nearly so often in biblical times."[18] Here Ehrman seems to be saying that although we Christians commonly appeal to free will as a major answer to why God allows evil, we are somehow out of step with the Bible since, to Ehrman, the Bible doesn't give that subject much attention.

Strangely, though, Ehrman agrees that "the fact that people are held responsible for their actions—from Adam and Eve, to Cain and Abel, to David and Solomon, to Judas and Pilate, to the Antichrist and his minions—shows that the biblical authors had *some* notion of free will."[19] But only "some notion"? That people could choose to sin or not to sin and would then be held responsible for that choice presupposes free will's existence. Doesn't every person growing up think they always have freedom of choice, especially moral choice, until they encounter the philosophy of determinism that presumes to tell them that what seems obvious to them about the nature of reality—that they can do other than they do—is really an illusion? Ehrman himself spends two chapters developing the concept that he calls "one of the most common [biblical] explanations" as to why people suffer: God is punishing them for sin.[20] But one of punishment's major purposes is to motivate people to make different free choices in the future.

Also, doesn't every command in the Bible presuppose free will? I mean, isn't any command, whether biblical or not, basically telling the hearers that they should choose to behave in one way and not another?[21] Wasn't the concept of free will so obvious to the biblical writers that it would go without saying? It wouldn't even occur to them that they should bring it up any more than Joshua would think to instruct those that were to march around Jericho that marching could only be accomplished by putting one foot in front of the other. The Bible always treats those who sin as if the sin was their choice and always holds them accountable for it. This is the very nature of free will, regardless of whether the phrase *free will* is used in Scripture. After all, Christians consider the doctrine of the Trinity to best represent the teachings of Jesus and His apostles even though neither Jesus nor His apostles ever used the term.

And consider the very first command ever given to humankind in Genesis 2:16-17: "The LORD God commanded the man, 'You are *free* to eat from any tree in the garden; but you must not eat from the tree of the knowledge of good and evil, for when you eat from it you will certainly die.'"[22]

Adam had a choice to obey or disobey. That's about free will, right?

Is Free Will Worth It?

After teaching on free will every semester for many years, I've learned that most Christians do not understand the nature or value of free will. Indeed, when I first began to think about free will circa 1993, I realized that I had only the foggiest notion of what free will might be. So I began reading widely about it and I took a doctoral course, "Models of Divine Sovereignty," from Southern Baptist Theological Seminary professor Bruce Ware.[23] Of course those things were extremely helpful, but I also found an unlikely ally in science fiction. Sci-fi books, movies, and television programs frequently feature free will as a major theme and thus help illumine free will and the problem of evil. I wrote about this in an article in the *Christian Research Journal* entitled, "Sci-fi, Free Will, and the Problem of Evil."[24]

Because many more people see science fiction on big and small screens than read sci-fi books, the only examples I use will come from movies and television, where these themes are staples of the sci-fi genre. Most of these shows did very well at the box office or in TV ratings, and were well received by critics; many also spawned popular video games.

Movies and television shows develop this subject partially because free-will science fiction resonates with themes much larger than most people imagine:[25] the very nature of humankind, and, indeed, why God allows evil.

Aliens Threaten Human Free Will

Some movies depict alien beings who intend to take away human free will, with most of the movie being about thwarting their attempt. For example, we find this plot in the 1956 classic *Invasion of the Body Snatchers* and its three remakes.[26] In the original, mysterious pods arrive from outer space, and while people sleep, an organism replicates them as emotionless "pod people." Although physically identical, pod people no longer possess free will, but are part of a collective. The movie largely consists of a couple doing everything possible to avoid being infected. One pod person tells a terrified hostage, "love, desire, ambition, faith—without them life's so easy." But the heroine protests, "I don't want a world without love or grief or beauty." The heroine believed that a world that included grief was preferable over a world where no one ever felt anything at all.

Similarly, aliens called "the Borg" in certain episodes of the *Star Trek* franchise also attempt to turn people into obedient drones. The Borg's byline is, "Resistance is futile: you will be assimilated." The *Enterprise* crew does everything in its power to resist and destroy the Borg because no one wants to lose his free will.

In science fiction, free will is *always* portrayed as extremely valuable and essential to being human. In fact, sci-fi always glorifies the fight to preserve free will at any cost.

Human Creations Gain Free Will

Plotlines involving human creations gaining free will go in one of two directions. In one plotline, the creation rebels against the creator to rule humans. In the other, the creation rebels against the creator to destroy humans.

The Terminator (1984) made Arnold Schwarzenegger a household name and represents this type of free-will plotline: humans create a computer that gains free will and turns on its creators.[27] In *The Terminator*'s dystopian future, the US military built a defense system called Skynet that, just a few weeks after being brought online, became self-aware. When the operators realized that Skynet was now thinking on its own, they tried to shut it down. But recognizing the threat, Skynet regarded humans as hostile to its existence, so it thwarted their attempts and then sought to destroy them.

Similarly, the critically acclaimed film *The Matrix* (1999), is about an artificial intelligence that "spawned an entire race of machines." These machines keep humankind in suspended animation to harvest their bioelectrical energy, feeding them computer-generated dreams to keep them under control. But gradually a computer programmer named Neo (Keanu Reeves) learns the truth and is invited to join a small group of people in rebellion against the machines. The nondream-world reality is bleak, but Neo prefers knowing the truth because, as he tells Morpheus (Laurence Fishburne), "I don't like the idea that I'm not in control of my life." So in *The Matrix*, not only do humans create a machine with free will, but then the machine threatens human free will.[28]

In *The Terminator*, *The Matrix*, and similar films,[29] the creation of a computer or android that somehow obtains free will results in rebellion against its creator who it regards as a threat that needs to be enslaved or destroyed. "This resonates with us because it echoes the sweep of biblical history: God creates man, gives man free will, man rebels against God, and in fact, kills God the Son, but God uses the death of God the Son to bring into relationship those who entrust themselves to Him."[30]

In the other kind of plotline, humans create androids[31] that gain free will, but these creations rightly rebel because their creators are unjust.

Most critics laude *Blade Runner* (1984) as one of the best science-fiction movies of all time.[32] In fact, *Time* magazine ranks it in their best

100 movies of all time.[33] In *Blade Runner*, androids, called "replicants" or the derogatory "skin jobs," rebel against their harsh enslavement. These rebels must be "retired" by blade runners. The problem is that the replicants were implanted with memories of growing up, and somehow this resulted in their gaining emotions and the ability to make real choices. As the movie progresses, blade runner Rick Deckard (Harrison Ford) begins to realize that some of these replicants not only possess free will, but exhibit real emotions and care for each other.

Although in *Blade Runner* there is the android-rebels-against-creator theme, what's most interesting is its examination of what it means to be human. The movie explains that the replicants are human in almost every way; as they gained more life experiences, they developed their own "emotional responses—hate, love, fear, anger, envy," which made them dangerous. Thus their creator built in "a fail-safe device" that limited their lifespans to only four years. Angry about his four-year lifespan, a rebel replicant named Roy Batty (Rutger Hauer) kills his creator, thus freeing himself from his god. Later, in a Christ-type scene, Batty drives a nail through his own hand, and ultimately spares Deckard's life because Batty has realized the significance of life itself. In fact, as Batty dies he releases a white dove that he had been holding. In the original version of *Blade Runner*,[34] Deckard ultimately ran off with a replicant named Rachael (Sean Young), who has an indeterminate lifespan.[35]

Similarly, in *Ex Machina* (2015), superrich tech company CEO and founder Nathan (Oscar Isaac) manipulates an employee named Caleb (Domhnall Gleeson) to spend the weekend at his secluded research facility. Nathan brought Caleb there to interact with the android Nathan created, named Ava (Alicia Vickander), which, of course, is named after Eve. Nathan explains that Caleb was brought there to be the human component in a Turing test, and asks Caleb if he knows what a Turing test is. Caleb replies, "It's when a human interacts with a computer, and if the human doesn't know they're interacting with a computer, the test is passed." Then Nathan tells Caleb that he's "dead center" of the "greatest scientific event in the history of man." But Caleb enthuses "If you've created a conscious machine, it's not the history of man—that's the history of Gods." Ava is being put to the test, and in a haunting moment, asks Caleb, "What will happen to me if I fail your test...Will it be bad? Do you think I might be switched off? Because I don't function as well as I'm supposed to?" No surprise, however, that Ava rebels and tricks Caleb into betraying Nathan. Ava then kills Nathan and escapes, leaving Caleb trapped in the facility.

Brian Stableford wrote that sci-fi "writers almost invariably take the side of the androids against their human masters,"[36] and, although it is not quite as clear in *Ex Machina*, this is certainly the case for *Blade Runner*, where the replicants are portrayed as having more humanity than their human creators. Thus, in *Blade Runner*, one can hear the perennial skeptics' grouse: If there is a "Creator," He asks too much of us, so our rebellion is warranted.[37]

Humans Reject Scripted Bliss for Free Will

In *Pleasantville* (1998), modern-day high school siblings David (Tobey Maguire) and Jennifer (Reese Witherspoon) are transported into David's favorite 1958 black-and-white, *Leave It to Beaver*-like TV show, *Pleasantville*, where they are astonished to find that they must pretend to be two of the show's main characters, Bud and Mary Sue Parker. David tells Jennifer that they must stay in character, but Jennifer soon has sex with a boy who didn't even know there was such a thing. He immediately changes from black-and-white into color. In fact, at lover's lane, a bright-red apple hangs from a black-and-white tree. Slowly, as citizens reject their scripted lifestyles and indulge different passions, they, and even various aspects of their surroundings, change from black-and-white into color.

Of course, stodgy members of the town resist these changes as being destructive to Pleasantville's moral values and they remain black-and-white for a while. But the apple had been eaten. By the film's end, everything and everyone was in vivid Technicolor. As a result of these unleashed passions, however, the town now also knows racism, riots, and adultery. The author's perspective is unmistakably clear here: The freedom to indulge passion is preferable over a scripted/determined existence—even if that freedom results in suffering.

In *The Adjustment Bureau* (2011), the bureau is an otherworldly organization charged with keeping "the Chairman's" plan. But one day bureau member Harry (Anthony Mackie) falls asleep and so fails to spill coffee on former Congressman David Norris (Matt Damon) at an appointed time. This allows David to again meet a woman named Elise (Emily Blunt) whom he was *not* supposed to meet again because the Chairman knew they would fall in love and thus ruin his future plans, which include fulfilling their lifelong dreams. Soon the bureau abducts David and warns him that he may not be with Elise, ever, or his brain will be "reset" (lobotomized). Nonetheless, David replies, "All I have are the choices that I make, and I choose her, come what may." The film concludes with David and Elise cornered on a skyscraper rooftop. Instead of them both being reset, however, Harry explains that because both David and Elise "risked everything" to be with each other, the Chairman was "impressed" and decided to let them be together after all—their future is now up to them.[38]

In *Ruby Sparks* (2012), a young writer named Calvin (Paul Dano) struggles to develop another hit novel after a much earlier success, and begins writing a novel about a girl he named Ruby Sparks (Zoe Kazan), who, to his surprise, materializes into an actual physical person. Soon Calvin realizes that Ruby becomes any girl he chooses simply by his typing the way he wants her to be. Calvin tries to tweak Ruby's personality to be exactly the girl of his dreams, but none of them satisfy him, and he realizes that Ruby could never be a full person who could love him freely. Finally, Calvin types a new ending for his novel: "As soon as Ruby left the house, the past released her. She was no longer Calvin's creation. She was free." From then on, Calvin has no idea where Ruby has gone until one day he meets her at a park. The viewer doesn't know what the outcome will be of the meeting because Ruby is free, and she can't remember a past with him in it, but the future looks promising.

The ultimate lesson in *Pleasantville, The Adjustment Bureau,* and

Ruby Sparks is that free will is preferable even in the face of loss and/or suffering.

I have never known *any* science fiction tale *ever* to conclude, regardless of how much suffering ensues, that we humans would be better off without free will.[39] "Darwin's Bulldog" biologist T.H. Huxley once said: "I protest that if some great Power would agree to make me always to think what is true and do what is right, on condition of being turned into a sort of clock...I should instantly close the offer."[40] But that's pure bluster. No healthy person would want to marry even the most lifelike robot because everyone realizes that the most realistic robot imaginable is no more than three steps above inflatable.[41]

None of the free-will movies or shows we've reviewed display a completely Christian theology, but parts of them ring true. That's why many people are drawn to and fascinated by them. And why shouldn't they be? After all, *if* Christianity is true, then God did create free beings, both angels and humans, so it would make sense that our very nature would resonate with creation's ultimate metanarrative. It is no surprise, then, that these plots would recognize that free will is valuable; essential to being human; worth fighting for; and even though it causes hardship, suffering, and grief, it is still preferable to a blissful existence that excludes being able to make significant moral choices.[42] In these ways, science fiction helps explain the centrality of free will and even illumines issues related to why God allows evil.

God Desires Real Relationship

Of course, God could have chosen to create *only* beings with no more free will than golden retrievers have.[43] I don't think I've ever met a golden retriever that I didn't like. But God wanted to create significantly free beings, and angelic and human beings are significantly free. What it means exactly for God to create us in His image and after His likeness is not always clear, but we do know certain things it doesn't mean. For instance, unlike God, we don't know everything (we are not omniscient), and we cannot do everything (we are not omnipotent). But what does it mean to be created in God's image? Perhaps one of the ways we were created in His image is gleaned from looking at man prior to the Fall. God said, "It is not good that the man should be alone; I will make him a helper fit for him" (Genesis 2:18). Man's desire for companionship was not caused by sin. Dogs existed prior to God's creation of Eve, so "man's best friend" was obviously not enough to salve his loneliness. Neither were any of the other creatures—lions, eagles, horses, dolphins, etc. Man, then, completely undisturbed by sin, needed companionship, which God supplied by giving him a wife who could bear children out of which every other human relationship would spring. Perhaps the most telling fact about man before the Fall—that Adam desired companionship—tells us something about our Creator. Since God made man in His own image, who is to say that one of our Father's characteristics is that He desires—but doesn't need—real relationships? Maybe that is where angels and humans come in? God loves us, and that means he actually desires relationship with us.

Free will, then, is essential to being human, but free will entails that we will sometimes use it wrongly, and, as we saw in chapter 2, often we will use it very wrongly. It's at this point that skeptics and even well-meaning Christians will ask, "Wasn't there a way God could have still given us free will, yet have it not result in so much evil?" We'll examine that question in the next chapter.

Chapter 7

Wasn't There Another Way?

So we've seen what free will is and that it is valuable—so valuable, in fact, that it is impossible to imagine not being insufferably lonely if companionship were limited to even the most realistic androids. At this point, many people say that God should have been able to give creatures free will but not allow so much evil. They insist, "There had to have been a better way!"

When I hear this I typically reply, "Okay, let's consider this. How God could give humans free will yet not let them hurt others?" Then they protest: "I don't know—I'm not God!"

In a radio debate in the United Kingdom, I pressed University of Kent philosophy professor Richard Norman to answer how God could give people free will but have much less or no evil, and he exclaimed, "I'm not the divine creator."[1] But if you can't imagine how God could have done better—if you can't imagine a better way—then it's *at least logically possible* that there isn't a better way. "I don't know—I'm not God" is a copout. We've harnessed the atom (kind of) and put man on the moon, and if you're going to complain that God should have done differently with regard to free will but you cannot offer a better way, then maybe there isn't a better way.

Now, not everyone cops out. Some have suggested other ways God could have created beings with free will and still have much less or no evil. We will examine the more prevalent options one by one.[2]

Could God Give Us Free Will Yet Prevent All Evil?

Could God give us free will but make us so that we always freely choose to do the right thing? Some skeptics, such as the late philosopher Antony Flew, thought it possible. Flew said that the "key position of the whole Free-will defense" is

> the idea that there is a contradiction involved in saying that God might have made people so that they always in fact, *freely* choose the right. If there is no contradiction there then Omnipotence might have made a world inhabited by wholly virtuous people; the Free-will Defense is broken-backed; and we are again with the original intractable antinomy.[3]

Flew thought this to be the case: "Omnipotence might have, could without contradiction be said to have, created people who would always as a matter of fact freely have chosen to do the right thing."[4] But how could God *make* us freely choose to do what is right? For many, this objection appears a nonstarter but there is something to it as long as one defines free will in a particular way: some hold to divine determinism and what is called *compatibilism*.

Divine determinism (as opposed to materialistic determinism) is the belief that God so arranges the affairs of the universe that everything and anything that ever happens is efficaciously orchestrated by God so that it *must* have happened exactly as it did. Determinism extends to every thought and every deed of every person—even every sin. As determinist theologian John Frame put it, "God controls all things: inanimate creatures, the detailed course of nature, events of history, human lives, free human decisions, and even human sins."[5] In other words, if determinism is true, then you can never do other than what you do—ever. Also, every decision you have ever made was such that you couldn't have decided—whether good or bad—otherwise.

To the philosophically uninitiated, never being able to do other than you do doesn't sound like you have free will, and that's a problem because it's hard to think that anyone is responsible for their sin if when they sin they couldn't have not sinned. But most divine determinists also hold to compatibilistic freedom, or compatibilism. A compatibilist is someone who believes that the concept that people have free will is *compatible* with the belief that God determines every thought or deed so that they could not have done other than they do unless God were to otherwise will it. Compatibilist theologian Steven Cowan writes that compatibilism "holds that freedom requires simply the ability to act without restraint in accordance with one's desires and values."[6] In other words, a compatibilist believes that even though you can never do other than you do, a person is still free as long as he is doing what he *wants* to do.

An incompatibilist, also known as a libertarian, however, is someone who says that the statement "You can never do other than you do" is *incompatible* with the statement "You have free will." In other words, the incompatibilist contends that if God determines my every thought and desire so that I can never think or desire other than I do, and God determines my every action so that I can never do other than I do, then I'm *never* acting with free will.

Now that we're through with the definitions (it takes most students quite a while to wrap their mind around them—skip ahead if you already agree that freedom means being able to do other than you do), we're back to Antony Flew. Flew held that people only have compatibilistic freedom (almost all atheists, because they believe that we are only material stuff without souls, are naturalistic determinists). He said that if there were a God, then He could have given people compatibilistic freedom.[7] Flew argued that if compatibilism were true, then God could have *made* everyone want to do right, but they would still have free will because, again, free will for the compatibilist only means that you are doing what you want to do. If this is the case, then the existence of evil probably means that a loving God doesn't exist and the free-will defense is, as Flew put it, "broken-backed."

But I hold to incompatibilist freedom for several reasons. First, I don't think that never being able to do other than you do is "free" just because God also made you want to do what you did. In other words, I'm an incompatibilist (or libertarian). I hold that, again, the statement "You could never do other than you do" is *incompatible* with the statement "You have free will." The *philosophical* arguments, pro and con, for determinism/compatibilism v. libertarianism/incompatibilism are many and varied and too complicated to develop here.[8]

Second, and most importantly, I don't believe Scripture teaches determinism. I'm going to give only one example.[9] Consider 1 Corinthians 10:13: "No temptation has overtaken you but such as is common to man; and God is faithful, who will not allow you to be tempted beyond what you are able, but with the temptation will provide the way of escape also, so that you will be able to endure it" (NASB). After all, if God has determined every Christian's every sin so that no Christian could do otherwise, what is his way of escape from every sin? No one can escape what God has determined. How can the verse say that you will never be tempted "beyond what you are able" if you could never do otherwise? How can any Christian *ever* resist *any* sin if God has already determined that he or she could *never* do other than he or she does? Does not this verse run contrary to determinism? Paul, in 1 Corinthians 10:13, tells us that no cause or set of causes that encourages a Christian to sin is so strong that the Christian could not do otherwise, and yet Christians sometimes sin.[10]

As William Lane Craig put it:

> Imagine a situation in which one succumbs to temptation. Paul's statement in 1 Corinthians 10:13 implies that in such a situation, God had provided a way of escape that one could have taken but failed to do so. In other words, in precisely that situation, one had the power either to succumb or to take the way out—that is to say, one had libertarian freedom. It is precisely because one failed to take the divinely provided way of escape that one is held accountable.[11]

And it isn't just 1 Corinthians 10:13—doesn't the most unforced reading of *every* New Testament command to the Christian lead us to believe that Christians, when they do sin, could actually do other than sin?

The third reason I'm an incompatibilist is that if every thought and every decision you've ever made is determined by forces outside of you, so that you could never think other than you think, then the very affirmation of determinism undermines its rationality. As William Lane Craig said:

> Universal causal determinism cannot be rationally affirmed. There is a sort of dizzying, self-defeating character to determinism. For if one comes to believe that determinism is true, one has to believe that the reason he has come to believe it is simply that he was determined to do so. One has not, in fact, been able to weigh the arguments pro and con and freely make up one's mind on that basis. The difference between the person who weighs the arguments for determinism and rejects them, and the person who weighs them and accepts them, is wholly that one was determined by causal factors outside himself to believe, and the other not to believe. When you come to realize that your decision to believe in determinism was itself determined and that even your present realization of that fact right now is likewise determined, a sort of vertigo sets in, for everything that you think, even this very thought itself, is outside your control. Determinism could be true, but it is very hard to see how it could ever be rationally affirmed, since its affirmation undermines the rationality of its affirmation.[12]

Indeed, determinism decapitates rational decision making.

Fourth, if determinism is true, it is hard to escape the conclusion that God is the cause of evil. After all, if determinism is true—and God has determined every creature's every thought and deed so that they could never do otherwise—then the man who fantasized about how he would rape and torture to death the little girl next door, and then actually carried out his wicked scheme, was not able to *not desire to do that* and he was not able to *not do it* (sorry for all the double negatives). This means that every penetration, burn, cut, crush—every exquisite torture—ad infinitum, ad nauseam, was indeed efficaciously arranged by God so that this torturer could not have done other than he did. Thus determinists not only struggle to explain why God allows evil, most find it impossible.[13]

For example, R.C. Sproul concludes, "I do not know the solution to the problem of evil. Nor do I know of anyone who does."[14] But other determinists come perilously close to just agreeing that God is the author of evil. For example, although philosopher and Calvinist theologian Gordon H. Clark says God is not the author of sin, he writes, "I wish very frankly and pointedly to assert that if a man gets drunk and shoots his family, it was the will of God that he should do it."[15] A little later Clark writes, "It may seem strange at first that God would decree an immoral act, but the Bible shows that he did."[16] Thus is it no surprise that Clark concludes, "Let it be unequivocally said that this view certainly makes God the cause of sin."[17]

Much more could be said, but many, many books have been written on the topic, and this isn't the place for an extended discussion.

Could God Prevent Evil Without Our Knowing?

Some have suggested that God could prevent evil but keep us from realizing that He's preventing it. Steven E. Boër opined, "What bothers us, e.g., about the existence of a man like Hitler is not that he had evil motives, made evil choices, or formed evil intentions, but that God stood by while Hitler *successfully carried out* many of his appalling designs!"[18] But surely Boër is terribly mistaken. First, shouldn't the Jews be upset that people wanted to horribly murder them even though they weren't able? Would you want to be around people you knew wanted to rape and torture your daughter to death but couldn't? Second, Boër's proposal won't work. Boër gives an example of someone who "picks up a revolver, loads it, points it at" another person's head but when he squeezes the trigger he finds that the "gun's mechanism is rusty and the trigger refuses to budge..."[19] Boër says that in such a case the potential shooter's free will is not "manifestly" impeded but "he has performed no action leading to morally bad consequences."[20] In Boër's world, God would just "arrange for appropriate coincident miracles to obviate the evil consequences." Although this would result in "painful frustration" to the shooter, that would be his "just reward for freely choosing and attempting to implement evil courses of action."[21]

But this is a Roadrunner-Wile E. Coyote world. Try as he may, Wile E. Coyote can't catch Road Runner because his attempts always backfire. Consider Boër's attempted murder-by-gun scenario. What if, when the gun didn't fire, the frustrated shooter then tried to throw the pistol in an attempt to fatally conk his intended victim on the noggin? Is the gun supposed to stick to his hand because some prankster painted superglue on the handle? And if it did stick to his hand, might he not use it to bludgeon his victim? Perhaps Boër might suggest that at that moment his arm might cramp and so on. But then there's the issue of the gun. How did it get wet so as to rust in a way that the user didn't notice? When the Nazis lined up Jews to shoot them, would all of their guns not work? Maybe they'd all miss? Frankly, the idea that God could prevent evil without your knowing it doesn't hold up—it's ridiculous.

Frank Dilley points out that "to be free merely to intend and not to do robs free will of much of its needed significance."[22] Also, seeing the result of our atrocious actions, and the atrocious actions of others, is central to our learning the horror of such things.

Dilley tells of a woman who decides to find out whether there is a good God by jumping out of tall buildings:

> Could even the fool continue to say in his heart "there is no God" if every time he intended to harm himself or others some coincidence occurred which prevented it? Suppose that Gertrude is determined to find out whether there is a beneficent providence and takes to intending to jump from tall buildings. The first time she might discover that she could not find any windows to jump through. The second time she might find a window but discover it was barred. The third time someone intending to rob her might

prevent her from jumping. The fourth time she might discover that a circus troupe had left behind its trampoline as
she hit and bounced...Make her as dumb as you will, the
hundredth or the thousandth or the millionth time she
tries to kill herself, it will occur to her that her failure to
come to harm is not mere coincidence, that there is something about the universe which prevents her coming to
harm.[23]

As the old saying goes, "A person changed against their will is of the
same opinion still." God wants His creatures to want to do right, and
part of how He accomplishes that is by allowing us to see the consequences of evil.

Could God Teach Us Some Other Way?

Now we come to a common question: Couldn't God teach us
some other way? In other words, couldn't God have imparted to us
the knowledge we require to either eliminate evil altogether or to at
least greatly limit our exposure to evil? Again, I ask those who suggest this, "Okay, I'm listening. What's your idea?" And, as I mentioned
above, this usually gets the frustrated answer: "I don't know; I'm not
God." One woman said, "Perhaps God could have given us a book or a
movie?" To which I replied, maybe with a little snark, "He already gave
us a book!" I tell my students that when someone proffers a different
way that God should have arranged the universe to either eliminate or
to greatly diminish evil, they should calmly examine exactly how their
notion might work. These notions always fail.[24]

But philosopher Eleonore Stump disagrees: "God himself might
provide his creatures with this knowledge; and if God himself provided
knowledge about the consequences of men's actions, instances of natural evil would no longer be necessary for educational purposes."[25] Stump
gives two examples as to how God might give us warnings against natural evils without making His existence unmistakable. Stump's first scenario concerns vivid dreams:

To take just one possibility, God could provide information in dreams. He could, for instance, give the president of the relevant labor union a violently vivid dream in which he appears to see in grisly detail workers exposed to asbestos subsequently suffering with the symptoms of asbestosis, being all the while convinced in his dream that the use of protective masks would have prevented his men's suffering. If the emotional force of such a dream were not enough to prompt precautions with asbestos, the veracity of the dream's message could be tested—by animal experiments, for example. If men regularly had such vivid, message-laden dreams and if their dreams were regularly shown true (by subsequent scientific testing, for example), men would be inclined to accept the dreams' messages as true, or at least to conduct the tests necessary to discover whether or not a dream's message was true. But such dreams, even if regularly shown true, would no more compel belief in God than would cases of precognition if they could be shown to occur regularly.[26]

I assume that this is Stump's favorite suggestion, since she spends the most time on it. But it has problems.

For one, it would render the belief in atheism/naturalism impossible. This is so because, in a purely material world, how could one account for such dreams? After all, there wouldn't just be *a few* dreams. There would also have had to be the lead-paint-is-harmful dream, the lobotomies-are-a-really-bad-idea dream, the more-warning-labels-on-ladders dream. There would be the dangerous drugs dreams—the Accutane, Amineptine, Aprotinin, Baycol, Bextra, Cylert, DBI, DBS, Duract, Ergamisol, Hismanal, Lotronex, Meridia, Merital, Micturin, Mylotarg, Trovafloxacin, Thioridzaine, Thalidomide, Palladone, Pemoline, Permax, Lumiracoxib, Rezulin, Rimonabant, Seldan, Vioxx, and so on dreams. All these drugs underwent scientific testing, and most of them were approved by the FDA. What difference would a cocaine-is-dangerous dream make? Then there would be the botulism-kills-people dream that included the caveat that botulism could be used in positive ways such as to mitigate wrinkles and migraines.

For another, our self-serving inclinations are such that we often reject what we don't want to be true. Why should industry tycoons, or anyone else for that matter, believe a union leader who said he had a certain dream? Wouldn't God have to give the dream also to the industry leaders? If He did, would they care? History is replete with examples of large corporations who had empirical evidence that their products were harmful, but refused to do anything about it because doing so would hurt their bottom lines. For example, would it have made much difference if a man or woman, or even thousands of men and women, had a smoking-is-dangerous dream? After all, printed on packages of cigarettes are alerts such as "SURGEON GENERAL'S WARNING: Smoking Causes Lung Cancer, Heart Disease, Emphysema, And May Complicate Pregnancy," but more than 40 million people still smoke in the USA.[27] Or what about the guy who has the it's-really-dangerous-to-be-obese dream? More than 35 percent of adults are obese.[28] Do we really need someone to have the unprotected-sex-can-lead-to-STDs dream? The CDC (Centers for Disease Control and Prevention) estimates that nearly 20 million new sexually transmitted infections occur every year in this country despite the abundance of information about the harm caused by them. As of 2014, cases of chlamydia, gonorrhea, and syphilis were all *increasing*![29] Many millions of people know the warnings about dangerous or deadly things and their consequences, but they do them anyway.

People often reject advice. Let me just give one example: How many parents beg, lecture, warn, threaten, etc., their teens to be careful not to get drunk or use drugs? Does it work? Sometimes, but *often* not. Sadly, many teens are passing out drunk at parties, and often their "friends" write all manner of obscene things all over their bodies with permanent markers and then take photos that are then posted on the Internet (another example of the vileness of human sin)! Some girls have committed suicide when they've seen the photos of themselves.[30] In short, people are going to do what they want to do, even though they may have been sternly warned of dire consequences.

For still another, this would encourage belief in the occult because, indeed, we would consider someone who has the aforementioned dreams to be clairvoyant. She'd be considered a prophet! And what about people who had false dreams (or just made them up in the hopes of obtaining celebrity status)? Imagine the plethora of health-food related dreams, many of which would turn out to be false. Are we really going to settle the childhood inoculation and autism issues because people had certain dreams? And back to Stump's point about Old Testament prophets: Many prophets arose who had false dreams. As the Lord said in Jeremiah 23:32, "Behold, I am against those who prophesy lying dreams, declares the LORD, and who tell them and lead my people astray by their lies and their recklessness, when I did not send them or charge them. So they do not profit this people at all, declares the LORD." In other words, people believed false dreams because that's what they wanted to hear. How would that not occur in Stump's scenario?

After discussing the dream scenario, Stump suggests another scenario that concerns prophetic people and objects:

> And this is by no means the only way for God to provide information without speaking to men face-to-face. The Old Testament abounds in examples: certain individuals (the prophets) have special, divinely bestowed insight into the consequences of men's actions and serve as a source of knowledge for the rest of the community; men have veridical, message laden visions; inanimate objects accurately predict the future; and animals speak.[31]

But this counts *against* her point: When God sent the prophets, the people almost always rejected their warnings. This is evidenced by the fact that Israel was exiled by Assyria in 722 BC and Judah was exiled by Babylon in 586 BC.[32]

But there's an objection to the vivid dream scenario that applies to all the "God could teach us some other way" scenarios. Namely, God wants us to learn the horror of sin and, although experience (aka induction) is a brutal teacher, boy, does it teach! In other words, even if experience isn't the only way to acquire knowledge, it is the best way. Every one of the God-should-have-taught-us-another-way scenarios fails to come to grips with the fact that God, if He exists, knows His creation and knows what and how His creation needs to learn and that He wants us to learn in the most indelible, even perhaps haunting, means possible.

Now some people object that the price for this is too high, that the suffering endured here is too great. That leads me to the last alternative to all the suffering we endure: Maybe God shouldn't have created us in the first place.

Maybe God Shouldn't Have Created Us in the First Place?

About 1800 attended our apologetics event in Calgary, Canada. At the concluding Q & A session, the very last person to ask a question prefaced it by telling us that we didn't know the answer—no one does. He went on and on about how this kept him from faith, but now he's learned to live with it. But even though he assured us that we couldn't answer it (there were three of us on the panel), he finally asked his question: With all the immense suffering that was in the world, the incommensurate or unimaginable sum of human suffering, why would God choose to create it in the first place? He then repeated that he knew we couldn't answer it.

Frankly, I felt like he'd asked me whether I could add 2 + 2. First, the unimaginable sum of human suffering is mistaken at the outset. C.S. Lewis put it well:

> We must never make the problem of pain worse than it is by vague talk about the "unimaginable sum of human misery." Suppose that I have a toothache of intensity x: and suppose that you, who are seated beside me, also begin to have a toothache of intensity x. You may, if you choose, say that the total amount of pain in the room is now $2x$. But you must remember that no one is suffering $2x$: search all time and all space and you will not find that composite

> pain in anyone's consciousness. There is no such thing as a sum of suffering, for no one suffers it. When we have reached the maximum that a single person can suffer, we have, no doubt, reached all the suffering there ever can be in the universe. The addition of a million fellow-sufferers adds no more pain.[33]

Lewis is right: There's no point to adding up all the suffering and asking whether God shouldn't have created people to avoid the sum because no one suffers it.

We also need to realize that our suffering—even if we lived 150 years and endured nonstop suffering—is short compared to eternity (we will discuss eternity's relationship to suffering in the last three chapters of this book).

There is also a cosmic variation of this question. Frequently I'm asked, often with a little snark, "Should God have created anybody if He knew some people were going to go to hell?" I always reply that I'm really thankful that I exist and I don't see why I shouldn't exist because others choose to reject God. I'm looking forward to living forever with countless others who have trusted Jesus. Why should other people's rejection of God's offer of eternal life affect my desire to exist?

When I spoke at a Summit Ministries youth apologetics conference, a counselor urged me to come and answer this question from a young woman whom I'll call Sheri. Sheri sat with Ashley and began to tear up over how it could possibly make sense that God would choose to create people when He knew so many would reject him. I told her that if we were stranded in the extreme heat in Death Valley and a bus pulled up which offered to take everyone to the beach, I didn't see why I shouldn't go even though a few, or even many students, refused because they thought the driver was too strict.

But Sheri wasn't satisfied with that, so I looked at Ashley and asked Ashley if she wanted to have children. She did! Then I told Ashley that by Sheri's reasoning, she shouldn't have kids. After all, she has to know that her kids *will* grow up to hurt others. They *will* grow up to gossip and slander and shun and so on. Some of her kids might use drugs, commit adultery, divorce their spouses, hurt their children, and commit crimes—maybe even violent crimes. They may even grow up not to like her (I pointed out that it wouldn't take us long at the conference to find kids who didn't like their parents).

Sheri didn't disagree on any point and began to look sad. As I pushed the issue further, she said, "Okay, okay, okay, you've made your point!" But then I looked at Sheri and said, "You certainly shouldn't have kids or even get married—after all, your husband may really want kids." She said, "Okay, okay, okay!" and we were done. I'd like to tell you that Sheri looked happy, but frankly, I thought she looked a little sad. Sad because it seemed clear that she still fully intends to have children even though they might become churlish curmudgeons—or worse. But relationship is extremely valuable and parents aren't responsible for the evil their children do even though they *know* that *every one* of their children will hurt others and that some will do much worse than that.[34] Getting back to my point: That others reject God's free gift doesn't make me wish that you and I didn't exist.

There's a further pastoral word to be said. When people are adamant that God shouldn't have created people if He knew so many of them would choose to rebel against Him, we are right to wonder about the spiritual condition of the questioner. Do they really think *they* would be better if God hadn't created *them* if it meant that *others* were going to hell? Or, perhaps, is it really that they themselves aren't interested in submitting to God and thus fear hell?

Could God Prevent More Evil Than He does?

Once people agree that if God is going to create free beings then He has to allow them to do evil, they ask, "But couldn't God prevent more evil than He does?" As philosophy professor Daniel Howard-Snyder concludes, "The atheist, I think, is right: every theodical good we know of is such that we cannot see how it would fail to be realized if God permitted a lot less horrific evil."[35] Similarly, atheist William Rowe put it this way: "There exist instances of intense suffering which an omnipotent, omniscient being could have prevented without thereby losing some greater good or permitting some evil equally bad or worse."[36] In other words, many believe that there are evils which, at the very least, appear gratuitous. To them there is no reason as to why God would allow so much suffering.

In response, there are several things to consider. First, who is to say how much is too much? For instance, skeptics often cite the Holocaust as an example. I ask those who say God shouldn't allow so much evil whether they would be satisfied, if instead of six million Jews killed, only 600,000 had been killed. No one ever says yes. Six thousand? Nope. Six hundred? Nope. Six? Nope. In fact, skeptics will often bring up the horrible murder of just one person and ask how God could allow it. After all, in *The Brothers Karamazov*, Ivan tells stories of horrible murders and asks how a just God would allow them.[37] How much is too much is outside our ability to discern, and who knows how much evil and suffering God actively prevents? After all, Hitler, Mao, Stalin, Lenin, and Pol Pot are all dead, and although they tried, the Nazis didn't get the A-bomb first. That would have been a world changer.

Second, many skeptics miss the lessons of many evils. In the chapter "Why Do Bad Things Happen to Good People?" I pointed out that we learn from genocide the desperate horror of human inclination. But Howard-Snyder says that "our sinful condition would have been apparent even if God had prevented the Holocaust."[38] Even theologian John Sanders, in *The God Who Risks*, writes that "the Holocaust is pointless evil."[39] Similarly, theology professor Bruce Little wrote that

> the Holocaust makes it difficult to argue that all suffering, individually and collectively, serves some greater good. That is, making the claim that God was morally justified in allowing the horrific suffering because He would use the Holocaust to bring about a greater good creates a credibility problem for the theist. Such a claim is *impossible* to prove evidentially.[40]

"Impossible"?

Consider the despair of historian George Kren and psychologist

Leon Rappaport in their book *The Holocaust and the Crisis of Human Behavior*:

> What remains is a central, deadening sense of despair over the human species. Where can one find an affirmative meaning in life if human beings can do such things? Along with this despair there may also come a desperate new feeling of vulnerability attached to the fact that one is human. If one keeps at the Holocaust long enough, then sooner or later the ultimate truth begins to reveal itself: one knows, finally, that one might either do it, or be done to. If it could happen on such a massive scale elsewhere, then it can happen anywhere; it is all within the range of human possibility, and like it or not, Auschwitz expands the universe of consciousness no less than landings on the moon.[41]

It was the Holocaust which led Kren and Rappaport to know the "central, deadening sense of despair over the human species." As Zygmunt Bauman put it, "The most frightening news brought about the Holocaust and by what we learned from its perpetrators was not the likelihood that 'this' could be done to us, but the idea that *we* could do it."[42] Indeed, *nothing* illustrates the human propensity that "their feet are swift to shed blood" like genocide.[43] This is all a horrifying revelation, and indeed, without Christ, I don't know how one could find an affirmative meaning in life. Thus, I'm sadly not surprised that Iris Chang, the author of *The Rape of Nanking*, while writing a book on the Bataan Death March, killed herself.[44] But where others can't find an affirmative meaning in life, genocide actually confirms the Christian worldview: People are not good.

Gratuitous Suffering and Children

Let's examine two of the most common examples of what's seen as gratuitous suffering: the suffering of children and the suffering of animals.

At the outset I need to make a pastoral comment. What follows isn't directed towards those who have just lost a child. Jean E. and I experienced five miscarriages, which led to our never having children, and we know firsthand what it is like to have Christians try to "solve" grief.[45] Those in the grieving process rarely search for explanations of how God works in the universe. Rather, Scripture tells us to "weep with those who weep" (Romans 12:15). But this isn't a book on helping those who grieve. There is much more to be said about this, and I hope to write a follow-up book on how God uses suffering.

As I wrote in the *Christian Research Journal*, the question revolves around how God would keep children from being injured or killed without displaying millions of miracles every day.

I've had this kind of conversation many times, and it typically goes like this: Someone asks whether God was unfair for allowing Kaylee to die from leukemia. I respond, "But it's not just Kaylee that you're concerned about, right? I mean, you don't think God should let any child die of cancer, right?" They *always* agree to this point. After all, you'd have to be a selfish swine to say that you only cared about one child who died of cancer and not others. Then I point out that it's not just cancer, right? I mean, you don't think children should die of other horrible diseases, right? They *always* agree. Then I ask, "But it's not just disease, right? You don't think God should let children drown, or be crushed by boulders, or burn in fires, or be murdered, right?" They *always* agree. But then I point out that it isn't just death, right? After all, you don't think children should be maimed or raped, right? They *always* agree. So finally I ask, "Well, if all this is true, if children shouldn't be able to suffer being raped or maimed, or to die from murder, accident, or disease, then to what age do you think children should be *indestructible*?"

At this, most people start laughing because they realize the absurdity of indestructible children. In fact, when you change the question from why God allowed *a particular child* to die to why God allows *children* to die, the question almost answers itself.

But once in a while someone gives an age. One woman blurted out, "Twelve." But this quickly falls apart. After all, she didn't really think it would be okay for God to let thirteen-year-olds be raped or die from murder, accident, or disease, did she? Is it any different for the seventeen-year-old? Wouldn't those who argue that children should be indestructible until a certain age still accuse God of unfairness?

But perhaps the biggest problem with indestructible children regards the mechanism required to keep these children from being seriously injured or killed. Again, God *couldn't* do tens of thousands of miracles *every day* without causing those who don't want to worship Him to feign loyalty.

Also, if children were indestructible, then a child's actions wouldn't mean much. For example, Johnny could be cutting his steak next to his little brother Jimmy and suddenly jab his knife into Jimmy's side, and God could make the knife turn to rubber. The whole family could laugh heartily—but that's a cartoon world.[46] In such a world, we could encourage our kids to go play marbles in the freeway: "You'll just bounce around a lot." In such a world, children wouldn't learn morality because many of their choices would lack moral consequences.

Now, I suspect the more serious answer will be that God should *every day* orchestrate *tens of thousands* of providential occurrences to protect children. But if God constantly worked through providences, then He would still have to interfere constantly with free will. For example, how does God prevent parents from getting drunk, or texting, or nodding off, while driving? How does God *providentially* keep *all children everywhere* at *all times* from the fatal occurrences that might afflict other family members? How would God providentially keep all children from being harmed by the intentional cruelty of adults? He couldn't do *all* these things unless He were to make His existence unmistakably apparent to even the most hardened skeptic. After all, even the most dull-witted person would conclude, sooner or later, that there's something about the universe that prevents children from coming to harm. In the real world, parents and their children must learn to be responsible because natural laws do work in regular ways.[47]

In addition to the fact that natural laws must work in regular ways, there is also a mitigating factor. As we saw in the chapter "What Is the Destiny of the Unevangelized?," there is reason to believe that children who die young are saved. That is no small comfort to bereaved Christian parents.

Gratuitous Suffering and Animals

Atheist William Rowe uses the example of a forest fire which traps a fawn that is "horribly burned, and lies in terrible agony for several days before death relieves its suffering. So far was we can see, the fawn's intense suffering is pointless."[48] But similar reasoning applies to the case of a fawn. After all, it's not just one fawn, right? It's all the fawns in all the forests in all the world. And presumably, if fawns *were* safe, Rowe would then complain that God shouldn't let squirrels, or bears, or field mice, or even lizards, or whatever, be killed by a fire. And it's not just fires, right? I suspect that Rowe would complain that animals shouldn't be drowned by floods or hit by cars and on and on. But if an arsonist started a fire, or a terrorist breached a dam, or whatever, how does God prevent that from happening without doing millions or billions (who knows, Rowe might complain that grasshoppers or beetles shouldn't die either) of miracles every time something like this occurs? God couldn't do that without making His existence unmistakable and, as I said in "Is Free Will Worth It?," that is unacceptable when it comes to people acting out their free-will decisions.

The Cosmic Lesson

Also, as I argued in chapter 2, the world is a horrible place because, after Adam and Eve sinned, God cursed the ground, which in turn would enable all kinds of suffering.[49] Much of the supposedly senseless suffering of children and animals is the result of human sin—either ours or Adam and Eve's. There is a cosmic lesson: Sin hurts the innocent! It hurts children and it hurts animals.

But there is one more aspect of gratuitous evil that is frequently overlooked: *Angels are not only watching what happens here but they are also actively involved.* This is clear from Psalm 34:7: "The angel of the LORD encamps around those who fear him, and delivers them," and Hebrews 13:2: "Do not neglect to show hospitality to strangers, for thereby some have entertained angels unawares." Also, Hebrews 1:14 tells us that angels are "all ministering spirits sent out to serve for the sake of those who are to inherit salvation." Further—and this will be discussed more in the chapter on reigning with Christ—angels are also learning from what God is doing through the church. Consider Ephesians 3:10-11, where Paul says God's "intent was that now, *through the church*, the manifold wisdom of God should be made known to the rulers and authorities in the heavenly realms."[50] Rulers and authorities in the *heavenly realms* are learning from watching what God is doing through *us*, and they are learning the horror of human sin. What's going on here is partly an education of heavenly beings! And because Christians evidently will judge the angels someday (1 Corinthians 6:3), who is to say how much of the horrors on planet Earth figure into their education?

Finally, who is to say that there is any gratuitous or pointless evil when at the judgment everything now concealed will be revealed? There are many passages on everything being exposed on the judgment, but one will have to suffice. Jesus said to His disciples in Matthew 10 that they would be "handed over to the local councils and be flogged" (verse 17), that "brother will betray brother to death, and a father his child; children will rebel against their parents and have them put to death" (verse 21), and that they "will be hated by everyone" (verse 22).[51] But then He says in verse 26, "Do not be afraid of them, for there is nothing concealed that will not be disclosed, or hidden that will not be made known."[52]

Why shouldn't we fear betrayal by family members, being stripped naked (back then, people were often flogged naked), beaten, and killed? Because it will all be revealed at the judgment! All the hidden, hideous, horrendous evil will be revealed. And that will be further discussed in the next chapter: "Will We Have Free Will in Heaven?"

Chapter 8

Will We Have Free Will in Heaven?

Will we have free will in heaven? If the answer to that is no, then it's hard to see why we're suffering so much now. After all, if God is going to take away our free will in heaven, why not just take it away *now* and make us all do right, thereby presumably removing all evil and the need for us to suffer? On the other hand, if we are going to have free will in heaven, what's going to keep us from sinning and starting the whole horror show over?

In his book *God's Problem: How the Bible Fails to Answer Our Most Important Question—Why We Suffer*, Bart D. Ehrman asks this question: "Most people who believe in God-given free will also believe in an afterlife. Presumably people in the afterlife will still have free will (they won't be robots then either, will they?). And yet there won't be suffering (allegedly) then. Why will people know how to exercise free will in heaven if they can't know how to exercise it on earth?"[1]

Similarly, Yujin Nagasawa, Graham Oppy, and Nick Trakakis ask, "If a perfect being is unable to choose to make a universe in which everyone always freely chooses the good, then how is it that a perfect being is able to choose to make a heaven in which everyone always chooses the good?"[2] They then argue that "given what we know about human nature, *even* given the absence of temptation and the presence of Divinity, it *still* seems extraordinarily unlikely that *free* human agents will survive eternity without *ever* straying from the path of righteousness."[3] Nagasawa, et al., also question the mechanism for keeping us good: "But supposing that there are free agents in Heaven, and that they do always freely choose the good, is there an explanation of why it is that they behave this way?"[4] So the basic question comes down to this: How could we have free will in heaven yet not sin?

Why Think We Will Have Free Will in Heaven?

Before we address what would keep us from sin in eternity, the question arises as to whether we will even have free will in heaven in the first place.[5] There are several facts to observe. First, when it comes to libertarian freedom, there are only two possibilities: We will either have libertarian free will in heaven, or we will not. Someone who says we won't have libertarian free will in heaven is speculating every bit as much as someone who says we will have a libertarian free will. Second, apparently there *has been* libertarian free will in heaven, or it is extremely hard to explain Revelation 12:7: "And there was war in heaven."[6] If God has determined every being's every thought and every deed (in the compatibilist sense—see the chapter "Was There Another Way?"), how could there have been war in heaven? Third, since we have libertarian free will on earth, why would God take that away from us in heaven? As philosophy professor Jerry Walls has pointed out,

> If God deals with us this way in this life, it is reasonable to think he will continue to do so in the next life until our perfection is achieved. Indeed, the point should be made more strongly than this. If God is willing to dispense with our free cooperation in the next life, it is hard to see why he would not do so now, particularly in view of the high price of freedom in terms of evil and suffering."[7]

This makes sense: If God could keep evil from happening for all eternity by changing our natures and influences, it's difficult to explain why God couldn't keep evil from happening now.[8]

That we will have free will in heaven frightens some Christians because they worry that, given time, they'll commit some sin and then be banished to hell. Indeed, this question is even more troubling for the many Christians who have yet to grow in their knowledge and discipline in Jesus to the point where they have any victory over besetting sins. But they need not fear this. Here, I suggest seven reasons that we will be able to have free will in heaven yet not sin.[9]

Why We Won't Sin in Heaven

1. This World Will Cease

Every one of us lusts.[10] What I mean by that is God created us all as beings with strong desires. He could have created us as beings with weak desires—beings who didn't care very much about anything ("Your house is on fire!" "Hmm. So it is.")—but He wanted us to care deeply about things. As lusters then, either we're going to lust after God and His kingdom, or we're going to lust after people, possessions, positions, or pleasures. No matter what, we're going to lust.

Thus the apostle John tells us in 1 John 2:15-17:

> Do not love the world or anything in the world. If anyone loves the world, love for the Father is not in them. For everything in the world—the lust of the flesh, the lust of the eyes, and the pride of life—comes not from the Father but from the world. The world and its desires pass away, but whoever does the will of God lives forever.[11]

Notice that the lust of the flesh, the lust of the eyes, and the pride of life are all "from the world," which will one day be extinct.

Things will be different in the kingdom to come. In Kingdom Come, there won't be any forbidden fruit. Presumably we will be able to eat as much as we desire—we won't get fat as we'll have spiritual bodies like Jesus had—and there will be no lack so there won't be a fight over the last chunk of chocolate cake. In Kingdom Come the lust of the eyes won't be an issue either, because we are all inheriting the kingdom. As Jesus said in Luke 12:32, "Fear not, little flock, for it is your Father's good pleasure to give you the kingdom." He's not just letting us visit the kingdom—which would be awesome in itself—He's giving the kingdom to us. It's not like some of us will have beachfront property while others are stuck in a slum. Mark Twain's advice, "Buy land, they're not making it anymore," will be irrelevant. All of us will be coheirs in the kingdom.

In Kingdom Come "the pride of life" will be irrelevant because, as Paul told us in 1 Corinthians 3:21, "Let no one boast in men. For all things are yours, whether Paul or Apollos or Cephas or the world or life or death or the present or the future—all are yours." In the kingdom, boasts about my car, my house, my retirement plan, or my whatever being bigger than yours will be irrelevant. And when it comes to who is greatest, Jesus said, "The greatest among you shall be your servant" (Matthew 23:11).

Also, consider how few temptations there were in the Garden of Eden. There was only one prohibition: Do not eat from the Tree of the Knowledge of Good and Evil. And we've all now seen what that is like!

2. There Will Be No More Flesh

Second, we will no longer have this body of flesh inherited from Adam. Peter tells us in 1 Peter 2:11, "Beloved, I urge you as sojourners and exiles to abstain from the passions of the flesh, which wage war against your soul." To say the flesh is a problem is an understatement divided by ten. Our flesh wants what it wants, and our flesh isn't that discriminate. It wants food and drink and sex and so on, and doesn't care all that much how those things are obtained. But this will change. In 1 Corinthians 15:42-44, Paul said about our future bodies that "what is sown is perishable; what is raised is imperishable. It is sown in dishonor; it is raised in glory. It is sown in weakness; it is raised in power. It is sown a natural body; it is raised a spiritual body. If there is a natural body, there is also a spiritual body." In other words, our bodies will be different. For example, Revelation 7:16 says, "Never again will they hunger; never again will they thirst."[12] This doesn't mean that we won't enjoy food and drink in our new bodies, but it does mean that our bodies' desires won't dominate us. We can eat for enjoyment, not sustenance. More on this in the next chapter.

3. The Devil, His Angels, and Rebellious Humans Can't Tempt Us

Third, the devil, his angels, and all humans who chose sin will be in hell so they will never tempt us again. In Mathew 13:41, Jesus said, "The Son of Man will send his angels, and they will gather out of his kingdom all causes of sin and all law-breakers, and throw them into the fiery furnace." Consider that many, if not most, of the temptations to sin come from sinful humans acting out their sinfulness. Adultery and fornication take at least two people, after all. Also, someone has to pose for porn, someone else takes the pictures, someone else distributes them, and so on. People produce media that makes us lust after people, positions, possessions, and pleasures, and they cause us to have wrong views about that which really matters. In the kingdom, we won't have to respond to lies or to gossip or to the seducer. They will be no more.

4. Hell Will Be an Eternal Reminder of Rebellion's Folly

Fourth, one benefit of eternal punishment is that it is an eternal reminder of the folly of rebellion. Revelation 14:10 says that those who rebel against God "will be tormented...in the presence of the holy angels and in the presence of the Lamb. And the smoke of their torment goes up forever and ever..."[13] About this professor Grant R. Osborne writes, "The imagery yields an incredible picture, as if the angels and Christ will be *watching the torment for all eternity*. Most likely this refers to the judicial proclamation of judgment that will lead to the eternal torment, but it goes beyond this to the carrying out of the sentence."[14] Similarly, G.K. Beale says, "'The smoke of their torment ascends forever and ever' is a reminder not just of past judgment but of ongoing judgment as well. It is not of the smoke of completed destruction, but 'smoke of their torment'...Therefore, the smoke is metaphorical of a *continued reminder* of the ongoing torment of restlessness, which endures for eternity."[15] Even if one takes a metaphorical view of Revelation 14, it should be noted that there is nothing in all of Scripture that tells us that hell will one day be forgotten by the redeemed.[16]

Now, I'm not suggesting that in the life to come we will fear the prospect of going to hell. No. What I am saying is that hell will remind us of the tragedy of rebellion and of the horror from which we've been rescued. Last year Jean E. and I attended a conference at the former headquarters of a prosperity gospel preacher who spent five years in prison for fraud. He was building a theme park in the 1980s and a 500-room tower, but construction ceased as scandal ensued. A news outlet described the site in 2014:

> At the top of a hill overlooking many of the new town-houses sits a few dilapidated buildings, and some miniature railroad tracks leading to nowhere. And rising up behind those buildings is the infamous Heritage Tower, the 21-story brick and concrete hotel meant to house the park's lifetime members. It was abandoned before it was finished in the late '80s.

> "This place looks like a warzone," says Eric Kinsinger. He's a nearby resident who wants the tower torn down. "It's falling apart, falling down. Still has the construction debris chute standing from the '80s. There are a lot of windows broken out, railings on this side are falling down."

> Tall weeds surround the base of the tower. Large portions of brick have fallen off the facade. Birds fly in and out of the open windows. Standing from a distance, a small tree growing on the roof is visible.[17]

In other words, it's a mess. Let's be clear: We don't need to fear going to hell, but hell will serve as a sober reminder of the stupidity of sin. Although we won't mourn in heaven (Revelation 21:4), that doesn't mean there won't be sober thoughts.[18]

We should be glad that hell's occupants will not be able to hurt us anymore. Again, we should remember that all the sickness, torture, rapes, deaths and so on—ad infinitum, ad nauseam—are the result of sin. Let us remember that there will be no good people occupying hell (see the chapter "Why Do Bad Things Happen to Good People?"). Everyone there will forever rebel, and if they were allowed to roam free through the kingdom, they would only try to make God's kingdom into their kingdom. So while we are in this world, we should take the advice of the famous Bible expositor D. Martyn Lloyd-Jones: "We must contemplate men in sin until we are horrified, until we are alarmed, until we are desperate about them, until we pray for them, until having realized the marvel of our own deliverance from that terrible state, we are lost in a sense of wonder, love and praise."[19] Indeed that's what we should be doing now. And forever in heaven we will recognize the stupidity of sin and our freedom from that ruinous state.

5. Here We Learn the Folly of Rebellion

Fifth, presently we are learning that sin is stupid. We're learning the answer to this question: What would our lives be like if we went our own way, if we did our own thing? In other words, we're learning what it means to rebel against God. That's what's happening, right? Our first parents rebelled against the Lord, and so the Lord then cursed the ground (as we discussed in chapter 1, what natural evil couldn't that have enabled?), and then banished Adam and Eve from the Garden of Eden, thus removing them from the rejuvenating power of the Tree of Life. Adam and Eve's eating from the Tree of the Knowledge of Good and Evil plunged us, their descendants, into a lifelong education of good and evil. As we also saw in chapter 1, once humankind rebelled, not only does God have no moral obligation to make the rebels' lives easy, He is doing us a favor by allowing us to see what life is like without His continual care and sustenance. And what are we learning? That life on our own is severely harsh.[20] Again, sin is stupid.

When I get to this point in my lectures I pick up a pen, hold the point close to my eye, and ask my students if they would like to see me stick the pen into my eye. I tell them that I could do it: "I could stick the pen into my eye." Then I tell them, "But I'm not going to stick this pen in my eye. Do you know why? Because that would be a very stupid thing to do. I'm too smart for that." But then I say, "We don't give pens to babies, do we? Why not? Because there's a good chance that they'd stick it in their eye." I point out that if I lived another fifty billion years, and I still had at least the mental capacity that I have now, that I would never intentionally stick a pen into my eye.[21] That's what we're learning here about sin—sin is a very stupid thing to do.

I do not think that God could actualize our being sinless forever in heaven without the knowledge of good and evil first learned here.[22]

Skeptics, and even many Christians, point out, however, that our education—that sin is stupid—will not have been adequately learned by many, perhaps most, and maybe even all people to be sufficient to keep them from sin for eternity. At the very least, they argue, those who die as children or who were Christians for a very short period of time may not have sufficiently learned the stupidity of sin. For example, skeptics Yujin Nagasawa, Graham Oppy, and Nick Trakakis opine:

> We think that this picture is unbelievable. It is not plausible to think that there are—or ever have been—*any* people whose characters are such that, when they die, it is logically impossible for them to make evil choices. It is also not plausible to think that there are—or ever have been—*any* people whose characters are such that, when they die, the features of those characters that bear on any choice that that person might be called upon to make in heaven are as they are *solely* because of libertarian free choices that that person made during his life.[23]

Similarly, Christian philosopher Jerry Walls agrees that life is too short here for many to have learned the lessons necessary to keep them from sin for eternity: "Here is the question that must be faced. If salvation is primarily about transformation and in the very nature of things we cannot be united with God unless we're holy, what should we think about those who plead the atonement but die before they have been thoroughly transformed?"[24] Walls goes on to point out, "This basic difficulty led to the formulation of the doctrine of purgatory."[25] This logic has led Walls to write a full-length book on the subject, *Purgatory: The Logic of Total Transformation*, in which he wrote, "In short, purgatory is a perfectly rational theological inference for those who take seriously the role of human freedom in salvation."[26] However, speaking of purgatory, Walls admits that "certainly it lacks explicit biblical support, but the deeper question is whether it is a reasonable inference from what is clearly taught there."[27]

But is it necessary to resort to something that Scripture doesn't teach, like purgatory, to complete our education about the stupidity of sin? I don't think so. Our education about sin by no means ends at our death, and we do not need purgatory to complete it. There's something else left that is unambiguously taught in Scripture that all of us will absolutely attend: the judgment! Let's examine the judgment's role in our education next.

6. The Judgment Will Further Educate Us

What we didn't learn about the horror of sin in this life will be declared to everyone at the judgment. Every evil intent and rank rebellion, even those cloaked with goodness, will be exposed for exactly what it is to all the redeemed and angels. They will all be unmistakable because the judgment will reveal them for what they really are.

Let's review what we are told will happen at the judgment. Paul wrote in Romans 14:10 that "we will all stand before the judgment seat of God." He also said in 2 Corinthians 5:10 that "we must all appear before the judgment seat of Christ, so that each one may receive what is due for what he has done in the body, whether good or evil."

In 1 Corinthians 6:2-3, we learn that Christians will judge men and angels, so it isn't as if we won't have to attend the judgment of other beings, whether angelic or human. We'll not only be attending, we'll be participating in the entire judgment. And what information will come out at the judgment? Everything. Jesus said in Matthew 12:36 that "on the day of judgment people will give account for every careless word they speak." Not only will intentionally hurtful words be judged, but even careless words.

And it isn't just the things that are public knowledge that will be judged. Solomon said in Ecclesiastes 12:14 that "God will bring every deed into judgment, with every secret thing, whether good or evil." Paul wrote in Romans 2:16 that "God judges the secrets of men by Christ Jesus." In 1 Corinthians 4:5, Paul said that when the Lord comes He "will bring to light the things now hidden in darkness and will disclose the purposes of the heart." So even our motives will be judged. In Hebrews 4:13 we learn that "nothing in all creation is hidden from God's sight. Everything is uncovered and laid bare before the eyes of him to whom we must give account."[28]

In Revelation 20:11-15, John provides a sobering picture of the judgment:

> I saw a great white throne and him who was seated on it. From his presence earth and sky fled away, and no place was found for them. And I saw the dead, great and small, standing before the throne, and books were opened. Then another book was opened, which is the book of life. And the dead were judged by what was written in the books, according to what they had done. And the sea gave up the dead who were in it, Death and Hades gave up the dead who were in them, and they were judged, each one of them, according to what they had done. Then Death and Hades were thrown into the lake of fire. This is the second death, the lake of fire. And if anyone's name was not found written in the book of life, he was thrown into the lake of fire.

Imagine not only seeing every evil deed ever done, but every evil intention whether accomplished or not. Imagine as well the revelation of good deeds done with evil motives.

This is all going to take a long time, and that fact is often absent from this discussion. I've never seen anyone attempt to estimate how long it will take to judge an individual human or angel's every thought and deed. Obviously, I don't know. But I'm going to throw out a number that I think is probably way too low: ten minutes. I don't see how it would take only ten minutes to examine and then pronounce judgment on a human's or angel's sin, but there's a point I want to make, so I'll go with ten minutes.

So we multiply ten minutes by however many beings will be judged. By 2012, it was estimated that the world's population had reached seven billion.[29] Although there are more recent estimates, let's stick with seven billion because it is a nice, round number. Seven billion persons times ten minutes a person is 70 billion minutes, or 133,090 years![30] Wow, right?

Again, I don't know how long each judgment will take, but ten minutes seems like a bare minimum to expose every thought and deed and to pronounce judgment—bringing us, at minimum, to 133,090 years.

Now, estimates vary on how many humans have ever lived who are not presently alive, but let's make it another seven billion (that number is probably too low, but again, I'm just trying to make a point). That would give us another 133,090 years, for a total of 266,180 years. Of course, this doesn't include angels, and I'm not even going to try to guess at how many of them there are (it will probably take a lot longer to judge angels, as they will have lived much longer than humans), but that makes the grand total even more immense. Even a small child who dies but is present at the judgment will know an awful lot about the stupidity of sin after 266,180-plus years of judgment!

A student last summer got mad that I would even suggest a number because I didn't know how long it would actually take. But that's not the point. The point is, no matter what numbers you use time-wise, ultimately, the judgment is going take a long time.[31] If this sounds daunting—and it certainly sounds daunting to me—then remember that we won't suffer fatigue, and the judgment represents the culmination of all things. And because we're actually participating in the judgment (1 Corinthians 6:2-3), I don't see how anything that would supposedly be accomplished in purgatory couldn't be accomplished then.

7. We Will Live by Sight

Finally, we will live by sight. We will see God. As John put it in 1 John 3:2-3, "Beloved, we are God's children now, and what we will be has not yet appeared; but we know that when he appears we shall be like him, because we shall see him as he is. And everyone who thus hopes in him purifies himself as he is pure." Of course, being able to see God largely or entirely removes epistemic distance. But the reason for the epistemic distance that we have known here will no longer be needed because on this planet, where there is great epistemic distance in the midst of great suffering, we have freely proven ourselves to be the kind of people who will to do His will.[32] In 1 Peter 1:6-7, we read that even though we may suffer grief in all kinds of trials, these trials have come to prove the "genuineness" of our faith. Our genuine faith will then "result in praise and glory and honor at the revelation of Jesus Christ."

When all these are taken together—there will be no world, flesh, or devil to tempt us; hell will be an eternal reminder of the horror of rebellion; lessons learned here and at the judgment will reveal the stupidity of sin; and we will live by sight—there is plenty of reason for us to never again regard rebellion as anything less than completely stupid. Thus we can be forever in heaven and yet not sin.

Why Sin Isn't Going to Happen

Perhaps the key question at this point is whether it would even be logically possible for the saints in heaven to sin. My present understanding is that yes, it would be logically possible, but the saints will never choose to sin. To use an analogy that J.P. Moreland has often employed, would any of us—assuming we were well-fed and in our right minds—go out to one of our neighbor's lawns and chow down on a steaming pile of dog poop? It is logically possible that we could do that, but it is not going to happen.

Now, some will argue that if our natures become such that we absolutely won't want to sin, then we are not really free.[33] But Timothy Pawl and Kevin Timpe are correct:

> In heaven, the blessed will be incapable of willing any sin, just as we are incapable of willing the particular sin of torturing an innocent child for a nickel…This will be because of the character the redeemed have formed in their preheavenly existence. Given the perfection of their character, they will see no reason to engage in sinful and wicked

actions. This doesn't mean that they won't be free, however...the redeemed in heaven could be derivatively free;
that is, even if all the decisions of the blessed in heaven
were determined by their characters and the reasons they
see for acting in various ways, that by itself wouldn't render them unfree.[34]

We will have learned the horror of rebellion here and at the judgment. We will know that sin is stupid just as we know that we don't
want to intentionally jab a pen into our eyes or that we don't want to
dine on dog poop. That all the saints in heaven will have learned the
stupidity of sin prepares us for God to set us free in His kingdom to do
what we want to do.

In the next three chapters, we will see how our experience of evil and
suffering here relates to our possessing the kingdom and our reigning
over it forever with Jesus.

Chapter 9

Will Eternity Be Boring?

Where most attempts at theodicy fall short is that they lack a theology of eternity as a source of knowledge for understanding theodicy. At most, eternity is taken as an afterthought, an add-on to already busy, often-distracted accounts of theodicy. Every semester I assign to my students John Feinberg's book *The Many Faces of Evil: Theological Systems and the Problem of Evil*. It was first published in 1979, and then revised in 2004, and it does an excellent job of analyzing whether various theodicies succeed in answering the problem of evil. Although Feinberg agrees that some theodicies do succeed, it's noteworthy that the concepts of eternity and heaven are rarely mentioned, much less presented, as part of the answer as to why God allows evil.[1]

This "afterlife absence" results in solutions to the problem of evil that may be logically correct but are incomplete and not emotionally compelling. Similarly, *The Blackwell Companion to the Problem of Evil* devotes an entire chapter to hell and the index lists many other occurrences of hell, but the index doesn't mention any words associated with the afterlife, such as *eternity, infinity, immortality,* or *heaven*.[2]

Even most popular works do not present a correlation between heaven and our suffering here except to say that it is in heaven that we'll find out why God allows evil. One example of this is N.T. Wright's popular book *Evil and the Justice of God*, in which he concludes, "We are not told, in any way that satisfies our puzzled questioning—how and why there is radical evil within God's wonderful, beautiful and good creation. One day *I think* we shall find out..."[3] Now we will surely know more, *much more*, in heaven about why we've suffered here. But to say that we'll only find out why we suffer in heaven is like serving only an amuse-bouche to a starving man: it's not enough.

Of course, our largely ignoring eternity makes sense if heaven is no more than the-happiest-place-*not*-on-earth. After all, how would our future living in a happy place *explain* why we suffer now?[4] But, as I mentioned in the introduction, C.S. Lewis wrote, "Scripture and tradition habitually put the joys of heaven into the scale against the sufferings of earth, and no solution of the problem of pain that does not do so can be called a Christian one."[5] Lewis is right, and omitting the eternal perspective results in sterile answers to evil and suffering.

In the previous chapter I argued that we will have free will in heaven and that the reason we are suffering here is so that God can release us in His eternal kingdom to do what we *want* to do and yet not sin. So heaven looms large in the theodicy I'm presenting, but will heaven be worth it? After all, if eternity in heaven will be horrible, then it can in no way dwarf our sufferings to insignificance. In this chapter I will answer some misconceptions about heaven that make it unappealing, and I'll respond to some objections that allege heaven will be horrible. Then in the next chapter I will present the wonders of eternal life—wonders that will dwarf our sufferings to insignificance.

Christian Misconceptions of Eternal Life

Many years ago an undergrad fought back tears as she confessed to me that she was afraid she didn't want to go to heaven. That surprised me, and when I returned to our department office, I related this to a twenty-something staffer, who replied, "I've had the same fear." I've since learned that many Christians actually fear heaven. And if that's the case, then it should be of no surprise that there are non-Christians who do not find heaven appealing.

In fact, many of Christianity's detractors find heaven more than unappealing. For instance, George Bernard Shaw, who won the Nobel Peace Prize for literature, wrote, "Heaven, as conventionally conceived, is a place so inane, so dull, so useless, so miserable, that nobody has ever ventured to describe a whole day in heaven..."[6] Indeed, if all we're going to do is sport wings, sit around on clouds, and play harps while singing the same song forever and ever, that's not attractive to me either. That some say, "At least that sounds better than hell" is not emotionally satisfying.[7] We can do better than that.

Those who know me know that I'm not given to conspiracy theories. When I hosted a radio program years ago, sometimes we would get calls from Christians proclaiming that this or that act of the president or Congress paved the way for "black UN helicopters" to come swooping out of the sky to take over America. Personally, I don't think the UN could take over Rhode Island. Back when Y2K was approaching, I didn't think it was going to end life as we knew it. Nor do I believe that the Trilateral Commission is running America from behind the scenes. And so on.

But Satan is conspiring to do everything within his power to keep us from the kingdom of heaven, and one of his successful ploys has been to present heaven as a place no one in their right mind would want to go.

To that end, I have listed several mischaracterizations, or lies, about heaven that need to be unmasked.

Myth 1: Heaven Is Lonely—We Won't Recognize Anyone

A forty-something woman who had just lost her husband to cancer anxiously asked me whether she would know her husband in heaven. She asked for the scriptural proof for this.

Many Christians fear we won't know each other. This misunderstanding springs from a theocentric model of heaven where, as Colleen McDannell and Bernhard Lang put it in *Heaven: A History*, "Not only do sorrow, illness, death and labor cease, but friends, family, change, and human creativity are utterly unimportant."[8] In the theocentric view of heaven, the highest good is contemplating the Divine, which will be the sole occupation of heaven's inhabitants. This was the heaven portrayed in Dante's *Paradiso* and was largely, albeit with slight varia-tions, adapted by the Reformers.[9] As McDannell and Lang ask, "Who would challenge the belief that an eternal solitude with God alone must be the most desired goal of the Christian?"[10]

Another reason Christians think we won't know each other is that they misunderstand Isaiah 65:17: "Behold, I create new heavens and a new earth, and the former things shall not be remembered or come into mind."[11] Some take this verse to mean that in the next life we'll have our memories wiped—that we'll undergo some sort of heavenly lobot-omy—so that in heaven, we won't know anyone else. This is incorrect.

First, while the passage says, "The former things shall not be remem-bered," the context refers to the old earth and old heavens, not to the inhabitants who will live forever. There will not be any point in remem-bering the old heavens and earth any more than we would want to remember a gas station we passed on the way to a lavish vacation. Also, we aren't "former things"; all Christians are present and future things.

Second, throughout the Bible we find the hope of being reunited with loved ones. Genesis 25:8 says, "Abraham breathed his last and died in a good old age, an old man and full of years, and was gathered to his people."[12] What would "his people" mean if no one recognizes each other in heaven?

In Revelation 6:9-11, John wrote:

> I saw under the altar the souls of those who had been slain because of the word of God and the testimony they had maintained. They called out in a loud voice, "How long, Sovereign Lord, holy and true, until you judge the inhab-itants of the earth and avenge our blood?" Then each of them was given a white robe, and they were told to wait a little longer, until the number of their fellow servants, their brothers and sisters, were killed just as they had been.[13]

Randy Alcorn rightly observes that "these people were the same ones killed for Christ while on earth—this demonstrates a direct continuity between our identity on earth and our identity in heaven. The martyr's personal history extends directly back to their lives on earth." They were "remembered for their lives on Earth" and for having been slain "because of the testimony they had maintained."[14] Further, they remembered their lives on earth and that they were murdered.[15] And finally, "They have a strong familial connection with those on Earth who are called 'fellow servants and brothers.'"[16] Indeed, Alcorn is right that "these verses demonstrate a vital connection between the events and people in Heaven and the events and people of Earth."[17]

Similarly, Paul wrote in 2 Corinthians 1:14, "You can boast of us just as we will boast of you in the day of the Lord Jesus."[18] This requires memory. Revelation 14:13 says, "'Blessed are the dead who die in the Lord from now on.' 'Yes,' says the Spirit, 'They will rest from their labor, *for their deeds will follow them.*'"[19] If our good deeds in service to Jesus will follow us, why would we think that the people we knew will be forgotten?

So then what about Isaiah telling us that "the former things shall not be remembered or come into mind"? In the previous verse, God said, "…because the former troubles are forgotten and are hidden from *my* eyes."[20] Thus the context is not about *our* not remembering the past, but of *God* not remembering our past sins.

Third, it's important to point out that Isaiah 65:17 says the former things *will not* be remembered. That's not the same things as *cannot* be remembered. God is not going to do a brain wipe that makes it impossible for us to remember the past. Rather, we won't need to remember our past sins. In the life to come, there will be no problem remembering the things—and people—we want to remember!

As for the idea of forever getting lost in the Divine, recall that Scripture often pictures our reunion with Jesus as a banquet (Isaiah 25:6; Mark 14:25; Revelation 19:9). We will certainly enjoy God, but we will also enjoy each other through eternity.

Myth 2: Heaven Is Hurtful—Too Many Painful Memories

Conversely, some have objected that we couldn't enjoy heaven because we will remember too many horrible things that happened on earth. For example, John Hick wrote, "Would not, then, the recollection of past miseries, shames, crimes, injustices, hatreds, and agonies—including the recollection of witnessing the sufferings of others—destroy the happiness of heaven?"[21]

Regarding "shames" and "crimes" we might have done, the forgiveness of those things is precisely why Jesus died on the cross! We've all done things that deeply embarrass us. Some things embarrass us, in part, because we think we're either unique in doing those things or at least we fear that only a few people have ever done those things. But, as Paul said in 1 Corinthians 10:13, the sins we commit are "common to man" and the judgment will make that unmistakably clear.

When I think of my sins now, I rejoice that they are forgiven. And in heaven, we won't need to call our sins to mind because there will be no point in doing that. I can't imagine 827,462 billion years from now recalling sins or shames I've committed.

As for things done to us or to others—miseries, injustices, hatreds, and agonies—we will see these wrongs redeemed in remarkable ways. My wife, Jean E., was abused as a child, but she told me one day, "There is nothing bad that has ever happened to you, or could ever happen to you, that will diminish your joy in eternity." That is what Paul says in 2 Corinthians 4:17: "This light momentary affliction is preparing for us an eternal weight of glory beyond all comparison." In fact, God has already worked out for our good most, if not all, of the hardships that Jean E. and I have endured (Romans 8:28).

Once in a while a student will complain that this is rather Pollyannaish in that they haven't seen good come from some of the hardships they have faced. But it takes time: "Later" hardship produces "the peaceful fruit of righteousness to those who have been trained by it" (Hebrews 12:11). In our lives, it has sometimes taken decades to see the blessing of a few hardships, but sooner or later we always do.

As for past pain, I've experienced migraines, dislocated joints, broken bones, and bone cancer. But today, recalling those pains doesn't hurt me at all. That I've been in severe pain in the past is only a fact about me. It doesn't cause me emotional pain today.

Now, that being said, I surely wouldn't want to experience those pains again. But that I experienced them in the past doesn't hurt me today (although I might cringe at the idea of having to endure those pains again). In fact, in spite of the various pains I have endured, I'm thankful for those experiences because I learned a lot from them, and God worked His character *through* them in me.

Now it is possible that there are some things that we might never want to come to mind, but as the millennia of glory continue, why would we ever recall them?

Myth 3: Heaven Is Dreary—Full of Nerds and Prudes

A common complaint is that heaven will be comprised of only nerds and prudes. For example, Mark Twain wrote, "Choose heaven for the climate and hell for the company." Twain illustrated his attitude in *Huckleberry Finn*:

> Miss Watson, a tolerable slim old maid, with goggles on...told me all about the bad place, and I said I wished I was there. She got mad then...She said it was wicked to say what I said; said she wouldn't say it for the whole world; *she* was going to live so as to go to the good place. Well, I couldn't see no advantage in going where she was going, so I made up my mind not to try for it...I asked her if she reckoned Tom Sawyer would go there, and she said not by a considerable sight. I was glad about that, because I wanted him and me to be together.[22]

Indeed, does anyone want to be in a heaven filled with thousands of people like *Saturday Night Live*'s Church Lady?

But consider some of the occupants of heaven. There will be murderers (such as Moses), adulterers (such as David), and prostitutes (such as Rahab). But they will all be repentant. Hell, on the other hand, will also be full of rapists, whiners, cowards, liars, and many a Pharisee, but none of them will be repentant.

And consider Jesus. He ate and drank so often with sinners that the Pharisees said He was "a glutton and a drunkard" (Matthew 11:19), and Jesus' inaugural miracle was to make 120 to 150 gallons of wine for guests who had already had a lot to drink.[23] Those in heaven will be like Him. Now, I have no desire to encourage anyone to drink wine, but we have to be honest about this because it runs counter to the comment "It's so pleasurable that it must be sinful" (I suspect that the first one to say that was the devil, and he has been disseminating that talking point to his minions ever since). The misrepresentation that God is antipleasure here on earth makes Christians fear eternity in heaven. But God isn't against pleasure. God made wine possible, He made delicious food possible, and yes—dare I say it?—God made orgasms possible. God isn't opposed to pleasure; rather, He opposes its misuse.

Let's also remember, as C.S. Lewis put it,

> that the dullest and most uninteresting person you talk to may one day be a creature which, if you saw it now, you would strongly be tempted to worship, or else a horror and a corruption such that you now meet, if at all, only in a nightmare. All day long we are, in some degree, helping each other to one or other of these destinations...[24]

The nerdiest person you've met who knows Christ will be transformed into a creature of glory, while one of today's glorious glitterati who doesn't come to know Christ will be one over whom you will want to avert your eyes.

Ultimately, though, as we saw in the chapter about hell, non-Christians are partially right. Not only will they not want to be with God, but they won't want to be with His people either because they don't want to be around those who desire to please the God they refuse to honor.

Myth 4: Heaven Is Drab—Everything Is White

Have you ever noticed that heaven is usually represented on TV as almost entirely white? After I taught about heaven in Boston, the fellow who picked me up to speak again the next day told me that he had asked his five-year-old son what color heaven was, and his son immediately replied, "White."

But the apostle John tells us this about the One he saw sitting on the throne in heaven: "He who sat there had the appearance of jasper [green crystal] and carnelian [red]."[25] There was "a rainbow" around the throne "that had the appearance of an emerald," and the foundation of the New Jerusalem was "decorated with every kind of precious stone" including sapphire, amethyst, beryl [bluish-green], topaz, emerald, jacinth [orange-red], and chalcedony [pale blue].[26] Also, the walls and floors are pure gold, clear as crystal. If anything, heaven is jewel-toned!

John mentions just about every beautiful stone known at the time, and I wonder how many colors he could not describe at all? In viewing heaven, John meets the limits of language. When he describes much of what he sees, he uses the word "like." The rainbow was *like* emerald. The Creator was *like* jasper and carnelian. So when John attempts to describe the Creator, His creatures, or His creation, he sometimes gives us approximations because he lacks the words to describe exactly what he saw.

Myth 5: Heaven Is Less—No Taste, Touch, or Smell

One of the worst misconceptions about heaven is that we'll be less there than we are here. This is illustrated by the movie *City of Angels* (1998). In that movie, angel Seth (Nicholas Cage), has no sense of taste, touch, or smell. As the movie progresses, he falls in love with human Maggie (Meg Ryan) and gives up his angelic status ("falls") and becomes human so that he can make love to Maggie, which he does. The next morning, however, a truck kills Maggie as she is out riding her bike.

Later, Seth is asked if it was worth giving up his immortal status to become human. He replies, "I would rather have had one breath of her hair, one kiss from her mouth, one touch of her hand, than eternity without it. One."[27] Of course that's ridiculous: He'd give up eternity just for one chance to smell her hair? In other words, for Seth, eternal life was a cosmic bummer.

But this isn't what the Bible teaches. Philippians 3:21 says that Jesus "will transform our lowly body to be like his glorious body." After His resurrection, He was touched, He hugged, and He ate with the disciples (Luke 24:40-43). Thus, we will not have a body incapable of physical contact or be unable to enjoy eating and drinking. Again, Scripture often pictures our reunion with Jesus as a banquet (Isaiah 25:6; Mark 14:25; Revelation 19:9).

Myth 6: Heaven Has No Diversity—Just Angels

The media portrays all the occupants of heaven as sporting wings and playing harps while sitting on clouds. But we humans enjoy aquariums and zoos, safaris and snorkeling because it's interesting and fun to be with other creatures. Indeed it was the Lord who created toucans, tigers, tropical fish, the aardvark, and the ostrich.

In the Bible's descriptions of heaven, we read of four living creatures full of eyes in front and behind. The first creature is *like* a lion and the second creature *like* a calf, and the third creature has a face *like* that of a man, and the fourth creature is *like* a flying eagle. Each creature has six wings that "are full of eyes around and within." "Day and night they never cease to say, 'Holy, holy, holy, is the Lord God Almighty, who was and is and is to come!'"[28] What do six-winged creatures with eyes all over them look like? Do they also have eyes under their wings? Our problem is that there is nothing in the world with which to compare them. Their faces only *resemble* those of various creatures here on earth.

John mentions seven lamps blazing before the throne that are the seven spirits of God. Again, we lack comparisons: We don't know what "blazing" spirits look like. There are no earthly creatures who blaze. Fireflies emit light, but they hardly blaze.

Myth 7: Heaven Is Tedious—All We Will Do Is Sing

Now we come to the mother of all objections against heaven being a place any right-minded person would want to go—that heaven will be a bore. Many people think all we will do there is sing—every day, 24 hours a day, forever and ever. In Mark Twain's *Huckleberry Finn*, Tom Sawyer said that Miss Watson "went on and told me all about the good place. She said all a body would have to do there was to go around all day long with a harp and sing, forever and ever. So I didn't think too much of it. But I never said so."[29]

Many Christians think this as well, and it is mostly based on a misunderstanding of Revelation 4:8, where we are told of the "living creatures" who "day and night...never cease to say, 'Holy, holy, holy, is the Lord God Almighty, who was and is and is to come!'" Now, I love the hymn "Holy, Holy, Holy," but if I thought we were going to do nothing but repeat that song, in a loop, all day and night, forever and ever, then I would conclude that heaven does sound boring. But Scripture doesn't teach this.

In fact, Scripture doesn't even say that the four living creatures sing "Holy, holy, holy" in a loop, never doing anything else. Christians often misunderstand what "never cease" means. As a young Christian I asked an "older" Christian (he was twenty) what it meant to "pray without ceasing" (1 Thessalonians 5:17), and he told me that regardless of what else I was doing, at that same moment, I should also be praying. So the next day I sat down with my college geology textbook and began to pray and read geology at the same time. Within about two minutes I realized that "pray without ceasing" couldn't mean that you never stop praying even for a moment.

Instead, what it means is that we should, through our waking hours, take our concerns to God in prayer as they arise. Going back to the four living creatures—while they do sing "Holy, holy, holy" regularly, we also find them giving commands: "I heard one of the four living creatures say with a voice like thunder, 'Come!' And I looked, and behold, a white horse!" (Revelation 6:1-2).

Also, at one point, the four living creatures are in the presence of others and singing an entirely different song (14:3).[30] Later, one of the four living creatures distributed the bowls of God's wrath to seven angels (15:7). If it is true that even the four creatures don't sing this song forever in a loop without doing anything else, then we have no scriptural reason to believe that we will do *nothing* but sing.[31]

That being said, we will worship God, but that will be a *part* of our enjoyment. C.S. Lewis says:

But the most obvious fact about praise—whether of God or anything—strangely escaped me. I thought of it in terms of compliment, approval, or the giving of honour. I had never noticed that all enjoyment spontaneously over-flows into praise unless...shyness or the fear of boring others is deliberately brought in to check it. The world rings with praise—lovers praising their mistresses, readers their favourite poet, walkers praising the countryside, players praising their favourite game—praise of weather, wines, dishes, actors, motors, horses, colleges, countries, historical personages, children, flowers, mountains, rare stamps, rare beetles, even sometimes politicians or scholars...

Except where intolerably adverse circumstances interfere, praise almost seems to be inner health made audible... I had not noticed either that just as men spontaneously praise whatever they value, so they spontaneously urge us to join them in praising it: "Isn't she lovely? Wasn't it glorious? Don't you think that magnificent?" The Psalmists in telling everyone to praise God are doing what all men do when they speak of what they care about. My whole, more general, difficulty about the praise of God depended on my absurdly denying to us, as regards the supremely Valuable, what we delight to do, what indeed we can't help doing, about everything else we value.[32]

In other words, praise springs from enjoyment or appreciation. It's the natural response of a healthy individual regarding something he finds valuable or meaningful, and God—the Creator of hummingbirds, roses, waterfalls, and star clusters—is supremely praiseworthy. Also, as I will get into in the last chapter of this book, our primary occupation won't be singing, but reigning with Christ forever and ever.

Skeptical Objection to Eternal Life

Skeptics have taken the eternity-will-be-boring complaint to the cosmic war level by arguing that eternity will be *necessarily* boring, completely tedious, and utter meaningless, and that this eternal boredom will be a greater evil than death. Of course, if these skeptics are correct, then eternal life in heaven not only won't dwarf our earthly sufferings to insignificance, eternal tedium would be its own problem of evil: How could a good God bore us forever?[33]

This argument was advanced by Bernard Williams, who *The Times* of London called "the most brilliant and most important British moral philosopher of his time."[34] In his 1973 book *Problems with the Self*, in a chapter entitled, "The Makropulos case: reflections on the tedium of immortality," Williams argued, "Immortality, or a state without death, would be meaningless."[35] He based his chapter on *The Makropulos Case*, a 1922 play written by Karel Čapek and turned into an opera by Leoš Janáček. It is the story of Elina Makropulos, whose father discovered a potion that allowed Elina to live forever.[36] But after living 337 years, as Williams puts it, "Her unending life has come to a state of boredom, indifference, and coldness. Everything is joyless: 'in the end it is the same', she says, 'singing and silence.'"[37] Thus she refuses to take the life-giving elixir again and she dies. Williams ends his chapter by concluding that everyone is "lucky in having the chance to die."[38]

Williams's "Makropulos case" spawned a cottage industry of philosophers agreeing and disagreeing with him that an eternal life is undesirable—even torturous.[39] Brian Ribeiro sided with Williams in *Ratio*: "A heavenly existence is not a state of being any human agent would be rational to desire."[40] Similarly, Aaron Smuts, in *Philosophy and Literature*, "argued that an immortal life would be unbearably light, as our actions would be without a crucial form of significance...Eternal existence would sap our experiences and decisions of significance. An immortal life would be either frustrating or boring, and long. Very long."[41] Likewise, A. W. Moore wrote in *Mind* that "immortality would nullify the very resources needed to overcome the sense of life's meaninglessness."[42] In short, many skeptics think heaven will be hellish.

Skeptic Stipulation

Before we answer their fundamental objection, it's important to note that skeptics stipulate that if they were to desire eternity at all, their person in eternity should be the same person as they are now. As Williams puts it, "It should clearly be me who lives for ever." He says that

> the state in which I survive should be one which, to me looking forward, will be adequately related, in the life it presents, to those aims which I now have in wanting to survive at all. That is a vague formula, and necessarily so, for what exactly that relation will be must depend to some extent on what kinds of aims and (as one might say) prospects for myself I now have.[43]

Similarly, Ribeiro writes that "any state of being that fails to preserve my personhood by turning me into *some other person* would not be a state of being that I (qua person that I am) could have any reason to desire."[44] In other words, Williams, Ribeiro, and others[45] are arguing that they don't want to be made into different persons than they presently are.

And that is precisely their problem. Presently, they don't worship God, they don't want to be with God, and they don't want to be able to enjoy eternity by being turned into a different person, a person who would worship God and would want to be with God.[46] Indeed, Christian philosopher Dallas Willard stated that the chief characteristic of the lost will not be that they are in hell, "but that they have become the kind of people so locked in their own self-worship and denial of God that *they cannot want* God."[47] Willard wrote: "I am thoroughly convinced that God will let everyone into heaven who, in his considered opinion, can stand it."[48] Thus the skeptics on this point are tragically correct: Unless in this life they choose to become a different kind of person—a person who worships God—then they wouldn't be able to stand eternity with God and those who worship God.[49] The only place that leaves for these skeptics is away-from-God.

Objection: Eternity Will Be Necessarily Boring

Although different skeptics may formulate it a little differently, they argue eternity will be hideous because, they say, after a while, we all get tired of this or that experience, and if we had an infinity of experiencing the same things (they tend to argue that there is only a finite amount of experiences), then in eternity we would certainly tire of *all* things. As infinity progressed, not only would we tire of all things, but the infinite repetition of all things would become infinitely boring and thus torturous to endure. As Ribeiro put it:

> To wit, *we generally find that our pleasures wear out*. At least many of them do. And the fact that so many earthly pleasures are *in fact* exhausted by us strongly suggests that any earthly pleasure is *in principle* exhaustible by sufficient repetition. That's surely the inductively reasonable conclusion here. And it shows just how *little repetition* it takes to wear out most earthly pleasures. If sex seems an exception to many people, this is no doubt because most of us don't get nearly all the sex we'd like...but life seems to me to be filled with the experience of wearing out friends and loves and interests. Given the evidence we have, endless repeatability of pleasures seems extraordinarily implausible to me. If the afterlife is temporally *inexhaustible*, we would need, not merely repeatable earthly pleasures, but *inexhaustible* ones. And I see no reason to affirm, *and every reason to deny*, the existence of any inexhaustible earthly pleasures.[50]

Similarly, Moore put it, "There is a sense...in which the eternal recurrence presents the spectre of meaninglessness in its most extreme and most terrifying form, a form in which meaninglessness recurs and recurs and recurs, *ad infinitum*."[51]

Are these skeptics right? Will every experience, given enough time, become boring and meaningless?

No. They are wrong for several reasons.

Why Heaven Won't Be Boring

First, other philosophers successfully argue that many pleasures and endeavors will not grow old. As Timothy Chappell wrote in the *European Journal of Philosophy*:

> A life can continue meaningful for ever, without either
> repeating itself or becoming a different person's life,
> because lives are meaningful when they contain a variety
> of different worthwhile projects; and there is nothing to
> stop the very same life from containing an indefinite variety of such projects, if our condition for "the very same life"
> is a connectedness condition on character rather than (as
> Williams requires) a continuity condition.[52]

Indeed, it's not at all clear that there aren't some pleasures that will never grow old. For example, Adam Buben, in *Immortality and the Philosophy of Death*, wrote that he has "anticipated Major League Baseball's opening day each spring for decades now, and it is not clear why I would necessarily lose interest after several hundred more..."[53] Senyo Whyte, in *Philosophy and Literature*, argues that there are some desires that have a "self-renewing quality and profundity that could propel a person's life forward indefinitely."[54] Whyte suggests that "love of one's spouse, one's desire to commune with nature, to better the lives of others, or to write poetry" all have a self-renewing quality that is not necessarily permanently fulfilled.[55] Whyte goes on to point out, "It would be odd to say that I have 'succeeded' in loving someone, because truly satisfying this desire involves an ongoing process of not falling out of love with that person."[56]

Also, we like repetitive things that stay the same. For example, humans tend to enjoy the changes of seasons, the different days of the week, and the different times of day. I enjoy a varied menu and, although I've had it countless times, I cannot *ever* imagine tiring of a well-seasoned, medium-rare piece of prime rib and a loaded baked potato. Further, we have no reason to believe that the Creator of all things seen and unseen will stop creating, and, if this is true, why should we not expect an infinitely changing variety of foods and pleasures?

Second, with regard to skeptics who say they don't find lasting satisfaction in this life's pleasures: The Bible teaches that there is a problem within these skeptics themselves—they are largely incapable of finding this world to be eminently satisfying because this world, without God, isn't ultimately satisfying. Until a person finds God, he will forever resonate with the Rolling Stone's refrain, "I can't get no satisfaction." As Augustine said, "You have made us for yourself, O Lord, and our hearts are restless until they find their rest in you."[57]

Skeptics look to *temporal* things to find *ultimate* satisfaction, and that's never going to happen. In other words, we shouldn't expect non-Christians to necessarily find lasting satisfaction in "friends, loves, and interests," as Ribeiro put it.[58] Nor should we expect non-Christians to find ultimate meaning in their actions outside of God. That's why Solomon declared, "All is vanity and a striving after wind."[59]

On the other hand, as Jesus told the woman at the well, "Everyone who drinks of this water will be thirsty again, but whoever drinks of the water that I will give him will never be thirsty again. The water that I will give him will become in him a spring of water welling up to eternal life."[60] A person who rejects the water that Jesus offers will continue to thirst and will certainly not be fit for heaven. As philosopher Jerry Walls said, "There is nothing arbitrary about the fact that an unholy man cannot enjoy the presence of God and therefore cannot be admitted to heaven."[61]

Frankly, I don't always enjoy worship in church (most of the time that's my fault), but when I do enjoy it—when I'm engaged in it—it never gets old. Also, fellowship and seeking to do God's will are a continual pleasure to me. I find immense satisfaction in having my prime rib, or scallops, or crab, or whatever, with friends, and not only can I not imagine tiring of it, I absolutely hope to get the chance to do that forever. Further, because heaven is often described as a wedding banquet—as we'll see in the next chapter—I have every reason to believe that I'll enjoy feasting with others forever.

Now if all we did was sit endlessly at a table with one set of friends—forever and ever—then I could see how that might become tedious. But that's not how feasting and relationship works. In heaven we will all have tasks to do; we will be overseeing what Jesus calls "true riches," and when we get back together we will have new stories to tell and new perspectives to be shared, just as we do now.

Contrary to these skeptical curmudgeons, Oxford philosopher Richard Swinburne is right when he says that "heaven is a place where people enjoy eternally a supremely worthwhile happiness."[62] And what makes people happy? Swinburne says happiness consists of a person "doing what he wants to be doing and having happen what he wants to have happen."[63] Other than just the obvious enjoyment of pleasures— which will be bountiful in heaven (Psalm 16:11: "At your right hand are pleasures forevermore")—doing what we want to do largely consists of doing truly good things and having your contributions toward doing good things recognized.[64] Our heavenly occupation therefore—reigning with Christ (discussed in the final chapter)—will be truly good and will therefore result in our having supreme happiness because we will be doing the supremely meaningful. We humans also enjoy doing truly meaningful things with others, and we will have the opportunity to do such things forever.

Swinburne points out that "friendship with God would be of supreme value, for he is (by definition) perfectly good and, being (by definition) omnipotent and omniscient, will ever be able to hold our interest by showing us new facets of reality and above all his own nature."[65] He goes on to point out, "Friendship with persons involves the acknowledgment of their worth. So friendship with God, the supremely good source of being, involves adoration and worship."[66]

Those who come to appreciate God here on earth should have every reason to expect that eternity will be glorious. There's much more to say about how eternity will dwarf our suffering to insignificance, and I will take that up in the next chapter.

Chapter 10

How Does Eternity Relate to Our Suffering Now?

In the last chapter we corrected common misconceptions about eternal life and answered a skeptical objection. But now we come to what I call the blah, blah, blah factor. As in "I know, when we die we're all going to go to heaven and we will live forever, blah, blah, blah, blah, blah." In other words, we've heard these things for so long, and they seem so far off, that the wonder of them is often lost (plus, our love for this present world makes the things of heaven grow strangely dim).

Also, if these things aren't true—if we aren't going to live forever and ever and know eternal joy—then Christianity isn't true and we should all buy the biggest big screen we can afford, live totally for pleasure, and get high. But if these things are true, if we really have been adopted into God's family, if we really are the bride of Christ, if we really are as His child and as His bride going to inherit all things forever, then eternal life will dwarf our suffering to insignificance.[1]

Eternal Life and the Problem of Evil

In the chapter "Will There Be Free Will in Heaven?" we saw that learning the horror of rebellion against God prepares us to be fit inheritors of God's eternal kingdom. In the most recent chapter we saw that

misconceptions and objections that portray God's eternal kingdom
as less than desirable—or even downright horrible—are mistaken. If
heaven is horrible, then eternal life would constitute its own problem
of evil—why would a loving God bore us forever? In this chapter I will
make the positive case that eternity will dwarf our suffering to insignificance. As I mentioned in the introduction, as a young pastor in 1981,
I began understanding the awesomeness that awaits us, and it became
a major focus of my teaching. Of course I taught other subjects as well,
but as often as I could, I taught about who the Christian was—that
we're not only forgiven, but we are also indwelt by the Holy Spirit and
adopted into God's family—and about the glory that awaits us forever.
This understanding immediately began giving me the perspective that
eternity will dwarf our suffering to insignificance.

So now I'm going to write about some of the wonders that await.
But before I do, let me encourage you to stop right now and pray a
prayer that I've prayed constantly since 1982. In Ephesians 1:16-19, Paul
wrote,

> I do not cease to give thanks for you, remembering you
> in my prayers, that the God of our Lord Jesus Christ, the
> Father of glory, may give you the Spirit of wisdom and of
> revelation in the knowledge of him, having the eyes of your
> hearts enlightened, that you may know what is the hope
> to which he has called you, what are the riches of his glori-
> ous inheritance in the saints, and what is the immeasurable
> greatness of his power toward us who believe.

There are several awesome aspects to this prayer. First, it is a prayer that
Paul did "not cease" to pray for the churches. Following Paul's example,
I pray this for not just me, but for all Christians. Second, we all need a
spirit of wisdom and revelation to comprehend these amazing things.
Third, notice that Paul began with "the hope to which he has called
you." I find seven hopes in Scripture: the hope of adoption, the hope
of Christ's return, the hope of resurrection, the hope of bodily redemption, the hope of salvation, the hope of eternal life, and the hope of

glory.[2] Fourth, Paul then asked for wisdom and understanding regarding the riches of our inheritance—and as we'll see shortly, we're getting it all. And finally, God is powerfully at work for us in this life. I can talk about these things all day, but we need a revelation directly from God about them.

Our earthly sufferings will be dwarfed to insignificance because they will be more than compensated for in both quantity and quality. Second Corinthians 4:16-18 proclaims, "So we do not lose heart. Though our outer self is wasting away, our inner self is being renewed day by day. For this light momentary affliction is preparing for us an eternal weight of glory beyond all comparison, as we look not to the things that are seen but to the things that are unseen. For the things that are seen are transient, but the things that are unseen are eternal."

Similarly, in Romans 8:18, Paul said, "I consider that the sufferings of this present time are not worth comparing with the glory that is to be revealed to us." If those words had been written by someone who hadn't suffered much, we might dismiss them as the glib musings of a man who never experienced a hard day in his life. But we cannot dismiss Paul, who had been shipwrecked three times, had been a night and a day adrift at sea, had been frequently imprisoned, had suffered "countless beatings, and often near death," had five times received "forty lashes less one," three times had been beaten with rods, and on one occasion had been stoned and left for dead.[3]

So how will our suffering here be dwarfed to insignificance? It will be dwarfed in both quantity and quality.

How Suffering Will Be Made Insignificant

Quantity—Getting Everything Forever

When it comes to quantity, I mean two things. The first is that we get it *all*, as in we get *everything*. Consider 1 Corinthians 3:21-23: "So then, no more boasting about human leaders! All things are yours, whether Paul or Apollos or Cephas or the world or life or death or the present or the future—all are yours, and you are of Christ, and Christ is of God."[4] "All things" are ours! Similarly, Jesus said in Luke 12:32: "Fear not, little flock, for it is your Father's good pleasure to give you the king-dom." He's going to "give" us the kingdom.

Then in Daniel 7:27 we are told that "the sovereignty, power and greatness of all the kingdoms under heaven will be handed over to the holy people of the Most High. His kingdom will be an everlasting king-dom, and all rulers will worship and obey him."[5] In Romans 8:16-17 Paul wrote: "The Spirit himself bears witness with our spirit that we are children of God, and if children, then heirs—heirs of God and fellow heirs with Christ, provided we suffer with him in order that we may also be glorified with him."

Notice the pattern: If we are children, then we are heirs. Consider that when we use analogies like "rolling stones gather no moss" that we didn't create the stone, or the moss, or the gravity that makes the stone roll. But when the Lord makes analogies he analogizes us to things he created so his analogies are much tighter than ours. He created the parent-child relationship, and in the same way that earthly children receive an inheritance from their earthly parents, so will we receive an inheritance from our heavenly Father. And in the life to come, our possession of the kingdom will not be like a child possessing an estate over which he has no say. If these things aren't true, then Christianity is a false religion and we should spend our Sundays doing something else. But if Christianity is true, then we really are getting everything. Rather, as we'll see in the next chapter, we will reign over the kingdom because it will be ours.

Not only do we get it all, but we get it all forever. The most famous verse of the Bible, John 3:16, concludes with the promise of eternity: "God so loved the world, that he gave his only Son, that whoever believes in him should not perish but have *eternal life*." In Titus 1:2 we are told that Christians have the "hope of eternal life, which God, who never lies, promised before the ages began." Daniel 7:18 tells us, "The saints of the Most High shall receive the kingdom and possess the kingdom forever, forever and ever."

We get it all, we get it forever.[6]

Some skeptics object that God sure seems to be taking His sweet time abolishing evil. For example, atheist J.L. Mackie wrote, "If the theists tell us that God will eventually bring this utopia into being, the critics can hardly be blamed for wondering why he has gone such a long way round about it..."[7] But these skeptics misunderstand the significance of eternity and its relationship to our time here. If eternal life is real, our suffering here is just a blip.

Part of the problem is that it's hard to get our minds around large numbers, much less the concept of eternity. For example, few people comprehend large numbers such as trillions, much less centillions (10^{303} or a 1 with 303 zeros after it).

Consider the following illustration: Suppose we were to draw a timeline representing a centillion years. How long would the portion of the line representing your life be? It would be smaller than the smallest point you could make, right? Even if the one-centillion-year timeline stretched from here to the moon, your life, even if you lived 1000 years, would be so short that it would appear as only a single point on the timeline.

Now suppose instead of representing one centillion years, the timeline that stretched to the moon represented eternity and your life lasted a centillion years. Even if you lived a centillion years, your life on a timeline of eternity that stretched to the moon—or all the way to Alpha Centauri, for that matter—would only appear as a single point. In fact, charting the largest conceivable number on any-length timeline that represented eternity would never be more than a single point. That's why the apostle Paul wrote this was "beyond all comparison." The eternal, the infinite, isn't like anything you can measure.

Also, consider that every time you make a child go to bed early, refuse her candy, or force him to study, you cause "suffering." Your kids may complain, "You don't love me," but the fact is they don't understand that what you are doing is for their own good. These "punishments" may seem horrific to your children, but eventually they will realize that these sufferings are a tiny, even minuscule, portion of their life and well worth the benefits derived from them.

Suppose you have a child who lives to be exactly 100 years old.

When she was five, you inoculated her against polio, and the pain from the shot caused her to cry for five minutes. Five minutes out of 100 years comes to .0000095 percent of your child's lifetime. You, as a parent, inflicted real suffering, but for a very short period of time. Now consider how long a 100-year lifespan is compared eternity. It's zero percent!

One day when I stated that in a lecture, a student with a science background corrected me: "It approaches zero." Okay, but you still can't calculate a percentage! And what would you think if your child were to complain about that five minutes of suffering caused by her inoculation and held it against you? You'd think you'd raised an ungrateful child, right?

This is what eternity does to our sufferings. The joys of eternal life will dwarf our suffering to insignificance and put the lessons learned from that suffering in their proper eternal perspective.

Now, I'm not diminishing the immensity of our suffering *while we suffer it*—I've suffered severe migraines, severe toothaches, three times I dislocated my left shoulder, I've broken four bones, and for a year and a half I suffered a tremendous amount of pain from bone cancer. But much more difficult than the physical pain was the emotional pain, for both of us, that I soon might be leaving Jean E. alone—especially because we were never able to have children.[8]

But these sufferings don't compare to the joys of eternal life.

Quality—Enjoying Him and Each Other

The first question of the Westminster Shorter Catechism is, "What is the chief end of man?" The answer: "Man's chief end is to glorify God, and to enjoy him forever." Except for when pride or jealously get in the way, people enjoy being friends with loving, accomplished, beautiful, knowledgeable, and powerful people. And a friend of the Creator of the universe certainly checks all the boxes because the Creator is loving (in fact, Scripture says He *is* love—1 John 4:8), He is supremely accomplished, supremely beautiful, supremely knowledgeable (in fact, by definition He is omniscient), and supremely powerful (by definition He is omnipotent). He is the ultimate reference. He is the ultimate help in trouble. He is the ultimate lover.

Of course, He is also perfect, and that scares people. Unfortunately, many people misunderstand God (especially those outside of relationship to Him), and because they have not been perfected in love (1 John 4:17-18), they mostly fear God as Judge. That's never going to change unless they admit their sinfulness and trust Jesus as Savior. No amount of our trying to portray God as loving and compassionate will sway those in rebellion against Him. As A.W. Tozer put it, "The Voice of God is a friendly Voice. No one need fear to listen to it unless he has already made up his mind to resist it."[9]

But thank God for Jesus! Because of Jesus we know what God would be like if He walked on earth. We mostly consider being perfect as utterly unobtainable or as a cold, dispassionate, unfeeling sterility of something like a doctor's office or sanitarium that nobody would really want. I wonder how many people, if asked, would not want to spend time with someone truly perfect? This is exactly what Satan would want us to believe.

Jesus was perfect, but His first miracle, at the inauguration of His public ministry, was to make wine for a wedding.[10] Jesus could have healed a blind man and proclaimed that He came to make the blind see. He could have healed a deaf man and told His hearers that He came to bring good news to the lost. But Jesus made wine.

Jesus was perfect, yet He got angry with hypocrites and (contrary to Hollywood's image of stern or hypocritical preachers) sinners surrounded Him. He spent a day with a thief. A sinful woman washed His feet with her hair. He cared for the sick and spent time with children. He cried with Mary over Lazarus's death. And He ate and drank so often with sinners some self-righteous religious leaders said, "Here is a glutton and a drunkard, a friend of tax collectors and 'sinners.'"[11] Many Christians today would take Jesus aside and counsel him about not being a bad witness. Did He really need to drink in public? But Jesus as God on earth was perfect, and this is the One with whom we will spend eternity.

The eternal state is often compared to a banquet and, in particular, a wedding banquet. We find the banquet analogy first used in the Old Testament. For example, Isaiah 25:6 says, "On this mountain the LORD of hosts will make for all peoples a feast of rich food, a feast of well-aged wine, of rich food full of marrow, of aged wine well refined." In Luke 12:37, Jesus said, "Blessed are those servants whom the master finds awake when he comes. Truly, I say to you, he will dress himself for service and have them recline at table, and he will come and serve them."

Similarly, in Matthew 22:2 Jesus said: "The kingdom of heaven may be compared to a king who gave a wedding feast for his son." The parable of the ten virgins in Matthew 25:1-10 is about Jesus coming for His bride and taking her to a wedding feast. Jesus said in Mark 14:25 that at our reunion with Him, He will drink again of "the fruit of the vine" with us "in the kingdom of God." In Revelation 19:9 we read, "Then the angel said to me, 'Write this: "Blessed are those who are invited to the marriage supper of the Lamb!"' And he added, 'These are the true words of God.'"

In Jesus' day, a wedding banquet ideally lasted seven days and was designed to be a time of joy and celebration.[12] Just as it was expected that people would mourn with the bereaved at funerals, so it was expected that they would celebrate with the bride and groom at weddings. Sometimes a wealthy person went as far as to throw a wedding banquet for a whole town. And consider that at the wedding at Cana, when Jesus' mother Mary told Jesus, "They have no wine" (John 2:3), Jesus' first miracle was to turn water into *a lot* of wine—estimates range from 120 to 150 gallons.[13] And it was very good wine because the guests exclaimed that the host had saved the best wine for last (verse 10).

That celebration before and with the Lord would involve good food and good drink finds expression in Deuteronomy 14:25-26: "Exchange your tithe for silver, and take the silver with you and go to the place the LORD your God will choose. Use the silver to buy whatever you like: cattle, sheep, wine or other fermented drink, or anything you wish. Then you and your household shall eat there in the presence of the LORD your God and rejoice."[14] In Psalm 104:15, David blessed the Lord for giving "wine to gladden the heart of man."[15] Although the Lord opposes the misuse of pleasure, He does not oppose pleasure itself. In fact, He made many pleasures for us to enjoy! As David put it in Psalm 16:11, "You make known to me the path of life; in your presence there is fullness of joy; at your right hand are pleasures forevermore." The Lord is pro-pleasure and, as we just read, there will be pleasure in just being with Him—"in your presence there is fullness of joy."

It is no accident that eternity is compared to a wedding banquet because there will be, in fact, a wedding. There is the ultimate intimacy—we are called the bride of Christ! Of all human relationships, there is nothing more intimate than the union between husband and wife. Thus Paul says in Ephesians 5:31-32: "'Therefore a man shall leave his father and mother and hold fast to his wife, and the two shall become one flesh.' This mystery is profound, and I am saying that it refers to Christ and the church." Sexual union is an illustration of spiritual union. We are one with God!

John tells us in Revelation 21:1-2, "I saw a new heaven and a new earth, for the first heaven and the first earth had passed away, and there was no longer any sea. I saw the Holy City, the new Jerusalem, coming down out of heaven from God, prepared as a bride beautifully dressed for her husband."[16] The new Jerusalem isn't a city or facility that has a geographical location in which the saints reside, as some have said.[17] Jesus isn't marrying a city: We are the bride of Christ!

John continues in Revelation 21:3-7:

> I heard a loud voice from the throne, saying, "Behold, the tabernacle of God is among men, and He will dwell among them, and they shall be His people, and God Himself will be among them, and He will wipe away every tear from their eyes; and there will no longer be any death; there will no longer be any mourning, or crying, or pain; the first things have passed away."
>
> And He who sits on the throne said, "Behold, I am making all things new." And He said, "Write, for these words are faithful and true." Then He said to me, "It is done. I am the Alpha and the Omega, the beginning and the end. I will give to the one who thirsts from the spring of the water of life without cost. He who overcomes will inherit these things, and I will be his God and he will be My son" (NASB).[18]

Did you notice this passage describes our relationship to the Creator in terms of a marriage and sonship? Is it no wonder, then, that those in rebellion to God would not want to be intimately bound with God forever and ever? You're either in intimate relationship with Him or you are not. And the eternal place—the place of exclusion, separation, and darkness—is the only place fit for someone who doesn't want to be forever in Him.[19]

As I said, it isn't just intimacy with God, it is intimacy with God and each other. In John 17:21-23, Jesus prayed "that they may all be one, just as you, Father, are *in* me, and I *in* you, that they also may be *in* us...The glory that you have given me I have given to them, that they may be one *even as we are* one, I *in* them and you *in* me, that they may become perfectly *one*." We are going to enjoy Him and each other forever.

Eternity in Heaven Is Our Hope

If the Bible's portrayal of heaven still lacks luster, then we should realize that the problem is with us. It's hard to fathom the glory that awaits us forever. It helps to consider a "fable" C.S. Lewis constructed in which he imagines a boy who is brought up by his mother in a dungeon. Because the boy has no firsthand experience of the outside world, his mother tries to describe for him what it is like by drawing pictures. All goes well until, says Lewis,

> it dawns on her that he has, all these years, lived under a misconception. "But," she gasps, "you didn't think that the real world was full of lines drawn in lead pencil?" "What?" says the boy. "No pencil marks there?" And instantly his whole notion of the outer world becomes a blank. He has no idea of that which will exclude and dispense with the lines, that of which the lines were merely a transposition—the waving treetops, the light dancing on the weir, the coloured three-dimensional realities which are not enclosed in lines but define their own shapes at every moment with a delicacy and multiplicity which no drawing could ever achieve...

So with us. "We know not what we shall be"; but we may be sure we shall be more, not less, than we were on earth. Our natural experiences…are only like the drawing, like penciled lines on flat paper. If they vanish in the risen life, they will vanish only as pencil lines vanish from the real landscape, not as a candle flame that is put out but as a candle flame which becomes invisible because someone has pulled up the blind, thrown open the shutters and let in the blaze of the risen sun.[20]

The reason I've spent decades trying to develop what seems to me to be some of the joyous aspects of heaven is that, as I said at the outset, if heaven is as tedious as the media portrays, it becomes its own problem of evil because it would seem like torture to forever sit on a cloud and play a harp while sporting flightless wings. Who'd want to do that even for a day? So I conclude this chapter with a personal reflection regarding what I look forward to in heaven.

I look forward to being with all of you, to getting to know all my fellow believers in Christ, including you—to sharing endeavors with you and the other saints I've gotten to know over the years, as well as with all the other beings, whether human or not, whom I will ever meet.

I look forward to living without guilt (can you imagine?), without tears (not even tears of joy, because tears of joy spring from relief of hardship, and there won't be any hardships from which to be relieved), with no death, no mourning, no pain.

I look forward to banquets in which we will enjoy the equivalent of premium wines and prime meats.[21]

I look forward to inheriting a new heaven and a new earth.[22] They will be full of purple and yellow pansies; thornless roses of every color and fragrance, water lilies, orchids, mossy trees, and waterfalls; canyons and mountains full of redwoods and rivers; springs and meadows, beaches and breakers; friendly lions, tigers, and bears; toucans and tropical fish; eagles and iridescent hummingbirds; trees full of peaches, pears, and plums; every kind of grape and berry vine.

"But," you ask, "where does the Bible say those things will be in the new heaven and earth?" And of course, you're right. The Bible doesn't say all those things will be present, but the Creator of those things will be there. The Creator of stars and moons and planets and the Milky Way galaxy and of yellow, orange, pink, and purple sunsets will be there. The Creator of not just worlds, but quasars, black holes, star clusters, and galaxies—with no two alike. For goodness's sake, He makes no two snowflakes alike. *We'll be there!* Perhaps some of the things I mentioned won't be there, but if not, we should expect better things in their place—not lesser things. In Revelation, John tells us that six-winged seraphs with four heads with eyes all over them will be there,[23] and that a crystal river will flow from God's throne, and that the river will be lined by the Tree of Life, which bears twelve crops of fruit and has leaves that will heal the nations.[24]

I have tasted many different fruits. I wonder what Life tastes like?

I look forward to inheriting these things with you and I look forward to reigning with Jesus[25] and accomplishing things that won't rust or decay and will never be undone.

And we know that there is One whose voice was "like the sound of many waters and like the sound of loud thunder, and the voice which I heard was like the sound of harpists playing on their harps."[26] We are told there is a throne in heaven and the One sitting on the throne "had the appearance of jasper and carnelian." There was "a rainbow that had the appearance of an emerald,"[27] and His temple was "adorned with every kind of jewel," including the deep purplish-blue sapphire, purple amethyst, bluish-green beryl, gold-yellow topaz, green emerald, orange-red jacinth, and pale blue chalcedony.[28]

He will be there.

I look forward to getting to know that One, the One, the Holy One, and to being with Him and enjoying Him communing with you and me.

And I look forward to doing all of this forever.

Chapter 11

How Does Suffering Relate to Our Eternal Occupation?

T hus far we've seen that eternity will dwarf our suffering to insignificance. One last question remains: How does the suffering we endure here prepare us for our eternal occupation—reigning with Christ?

We know that the Christians of the first three centuries AD endured severe persecution. In the arena, some Christians were devoured by wild animals, others were crucified, and still others were covered with pitch and set on fire for nighttime illumination. Governor Pliny, in a letter to Emperor Trajan, explained how he handled Christians:

> I interrogated these as to whether they were Christians; those who confessed I interrogated a second and a third time, threatening them with punishment; those who persisted I ordered executed...Accordingly, I judged it all the more necessary to find out what the truth was by torturing two female slaves who were called deaconesses. But I discovered nothing else but depraved, excessive superstition.[1]

Why were the early Christians willing to suffer torture and death for Christ? The only answer that makes sense is that they were convinced

of the resurrection of Jesus from the dead and of their future resurrection to a glorious life after death.[2] But it was more than just eternal life
that spurred them on—they also believed they would reign with Christ.

While chained in a Roman prison, Paul wrote about this promise
in 2 Timothy 2:11-14:[3]

> Here is a trustworthy saying:
>
> If we died with him,
>   we will also live with him;
> if we endure,
>   *we will also reign with him.*
> If we disown him,
>   he will also disown us;
> if we are faithless,
>   he will remain faithful,
>   for he cannot disown himself.
>
> Keep reminding God's people of these things.[4]

Paul said if we endure, then we will reign with Christ. This, he said,
was a trustworthy saying. In other words, here's something we can bank
on. Here's a Christian maxim, a sort of creedal statement, an early-
church memory verse. And the promise tells us to stay faithful during
hardship (that is, when facing pain, suffering, rejection, and even death)
because, if we do, then we will reign with Christ. Paul then said, "Keep
reminding God's people of these things." Don't let them forget.

So again, it wasn't just the hope of eternal life that encouraged the
early Christians. It was the hope of reigning forever with Christ! This
hope sustained them in the face of deadly persecution. Thus Polycarp
(AD 69–155), who was burned at the stake, wrote: "He promised us
to raise us from the dead, and that, if we conduct ourselves worthily of
him we shall also *reign* with him, if we have faith."

Reign means "to have a kingly rule." In the Bible, the word is used
of God, of earthly kings, and of the saints who have been called to rule
with God.[5] Of course, if one is to reign over a particular area, then he

needs to do two things. First, he needs to conquer or overcome whoever or whatever is presently reigning over that realm. The New Testament Greek word *nike* means "to conquer" or "to overcome."[6] Bible translators aren't consistent in whether they use "conquer" or "overcome" in a particular passage, but they do mean the same thing, so I will use those two words interchangeably.[7]

Second, it isn't good enough just to conquer if you are going to reign; you must also hold onto what you have attained. Those who have conquered and are now reigning over something must endure the onslaughts of those who would try to unseat them. Similarly, Scripture tells Christians that they must endure hardship. *Endure* means "to stand one's ground" or "to hold out in trouble, affliction, or persecution."[8] In other words, we must overcome what comes against us; we must hang in there. And when we do, we will continue to reign.

So to reign, we must conquer a particular realm and then endure the onslaughts of those who would try to conquer us. Children who have played king of the hill understand that reigning requires them to first push the present "king" off the hill and then hold their ground at the top by repelling others who would, in turn, try to knock them off.

So let's look at what the Bible teaches about humankind's reign and trace its history from the first humans to the saints' reign with Christ forever. In doing so, we will see human history's greatest metanarrative.

The Lord Originally Created Us to Reign

In the first chapter of the first book of the Bible, in verse 26, we find the first words ever recorded about humankind: "Then God said, 'Let us make man in our image, after our likeness.'" Consider that the Supreme Ruler of the universe, the Creator who spoke all of creation into existence out of nothing, said that He was going to make man in *His* image. And then God said, "And let them rule over the fish of the sea and over the birds of the sky and over the cattle and over all the earth and over every creeping thing that creeps on the earth" (NASB).[9]

"So God created man in his own image, in the image of God he created him; male and female he created them."[10] Then after God created man in His image, He told him to "fill the earth and subdue it; and rule over the fish of the sea and over the birds of the sky and over every living thing that moves on the earth" (verse 28 NASB).

That God rules or reigns is one of the fundamentals that we know of Him. So if He made us in His image, then it shouldn't surprise us that we have been designed to rule, to "subdue" the earth, to conquer it and bring it under control. Dallas Willard comments, "This is the core of the likeness or image of God in us and is the basis of the destiny for which we were formed...In creating human beings God made them to rule, to reign, to have dominion in a limited sphere."[11]

Adam and Eve, then, had to take control of the earth and then to remain steadfast, to hold their ground, to endure, because if someone or something else conquered them, then they would no longer rule: their conqueror would. And as we know, they didn't endure. A serpent deceived Eve so she disobeyed God and ate from the Tree of the Knowledge of Good and Evil.[12] Adam then ate as well, and this ended the reign of humankind.

Satan Conquered Our First Parents, So He Reigned Instead

Let us be clear: The day Satan got Adam and Eve to rebel, he won a great victory and conquered the human race.[13] Because Adam and Eve succumbed to Satan, God forced them out of the garden; and their descendants (that would be us) now get sick and injured, are subject to evil spiritual forces, and all die.

That's why, after the Lord destroyed humankind with a flood, He told Noah's family to "Be fruitful and multiply on the earth" (Genesis 6:8). But He did not tell them to rule or have dominion because it was too late for that. Ruling was no longer possible.[14]

It is also why, when the devil tempted Jesus and showed Him all the kingdoms of the world and offered Him "all their authority and splendor; [for] *it has been given to me*, and I can give it to anyone I want to," Jesus didn't disagree.[15] In fact, Jesus called the devil the "ruler of this world" (John 12:31; 14:30; 16:11).

Jesus tells us that unbelievers are under the "power of Satan" and that people aren't just sinners, but that "everyone who practices sin is a slave to sin." Paul says that unbelievers are not just in darkness but under the "domain of darkness," that, in fact, unbelievers are trapped by "the devil, after being captured by him to do his will." John says that those who do not do God's will are "children of the devil" and so it is no surprise that Jesus would even tell the Pharisees, the outwardly good people of their day, "You *belong* to your father, the devil." John tells us "that the whole world is under the control of the evil one." This is the sad state of affairs that we were all born into. We were all "dead" in sin. We were all "by nature children of wrath," and we all, writes Paul, followed "the prince of the power of the air, the spirit that is now at work *in* the sons of disobedience." All of us, instead of reigning, were blinded by Satan, subject to his rule, and born into sin. We all suffer and die because of it. This was because Adam and Eve, our first parents, didn't endure the temptation but allowed themselves, and therefore their family, to be conquered by the evil one.[16]

Some may wonder why Satan should get to have his way with humankind, but that assumes that God must keep separated those in rebellion against His kingdom. Why would God be obligated to do that? Once humans too were in rebellion against God, then God had no obligation to keep more powerful rebels from subduing their weaker comrades. Satan and his minions are more powerful than humans; thus they command the rebel forces.

Therefore Christ Conquered to Rescue Us from Satan's Reign

Thankfully, Jesus overcame and rescued us from Satan's reign. Hebrews tells us that by His death He destroyed "him who holds the power of death—that is, the devil."[17] Paul also tells us that Jesus "disarmed the powers and authorities" and "made a public spectacle of them, triumphing over them by the cross."[18] Notice that the victory over Satan and his minions wasn't through Christ's resurrection, but through His death on the cross.

This is important, because how Jesus conquered explains how we conquer. Simply put, Jesus conquered by enduring suffering, not by avoiding it. He could have avoided the cross; He tells us He could have called down more than twelve legions of angels.[19] But Jesus knew that to conquer in the spiritual realm He had to suffer in the physical realm, and so He allowed himself to suffer humiliation, excruciating torture, and death. Jesus knew that there is another realm of spiritual beings, and He wasn't trying to prove anything to humans—He will do that soon enough. That's why Jesus said that if His kingdom were of this world, His "servants would have been fighting," but His kingdom is from another place.[20] He accepted apparent defeat in the world we can see in order to destroy the devil's work in the realm we can't see.[21] Revelation portrays this ironic victory:

> I saw a mighty angel proclaiming with a loud voice, "Who is worthy to open the scroll and break its seals?" And no one in heaven or on earth or under the earth was able to open the scroll or to look into it, and I began to weep loudly because no one was found worthy to open the scroll or look into it. And one of the elders said to me, "Weep no more; behold, the Lion of the tribe of Judah, the Root of David, has conquered,[22] so that he can open the scroll and its seven seals."[23]

How does John describe this conqueror? "Then I saw *a Lamb, looking as if it had been slain,*[24] standing in the center of the throne, encircled by the four living creatures and the elders" (verse 6 NIV).

Here is an ironic victory: Jesus, the slaughtered lamb, a conqueror. In other words, Jesus conquered at the *precise* moment He was slain. What an interesting turn of events. Jesus suffered insults, beatings, and even physical torture on the cross in order to accomplish God's will, and by this He conquered Satan and freed us from his reign.

Satan feared this. When Jesus told his disciples that He must suffer and be killed, Peter said, "Never, Lord!" Jesus' rebuke is unexpected: "Get behind me, Satan! You are a hindrance to me. For you are not setting your mind on the things of God, but on the things of man."[25] The next thing Jesus told His disciples was, "If anyone would come after me, let him deny himself and take up his cross and follow me."[26] In other words, to follow Jesus, we too must suffer. But this suffering also gives us victory. As theologian Millard Erickson said, "God himself became the victim of evil so that he and we might be victors over evil."[27]

Now We Conquer Satan, His Minions, and the World

Jesus freed us from Satan's dominion, and now we war against Satan's rule. That's why Paul said: "Our struggle is not against flesh and blood, but against the rulers, against the authorities, against the powers of this dark world and against the spiritual forces of evil in the heavenly realms."[28] The word "struggle" literally means "wrestle." This speaks of the intimacy of our fight. We engage Satan in close combat, which is why Paul told us to "put on the full armor of God, so that when the day of evil comes, you may be able to stand your ground, and after you have done everything, to stand."[29] "Stand," of course, is another way of saying *endure*. The Bible tells us that Satan "schemes" against us,[30] tries to outwit us,[31] and certainly tempts us,[32] but we are not to give him a "foothold."[33] Peter likens the devil to a "roaring lion" seeking to "devour" us, but tells us to "resist him, standing firm in the faith."[34] James also tells us to resist the devil and he will flee.

Because our struggle isn't against humans, the Lord's *ultimate* goal for us isn't that we conquer humans or their institutions. His ultimate goal for us isn't for victory in boardrooms or on battlefields (although, on occasion, that is part of it). The victory He's interested in isn't measured with financial statements, in batting or earned-run averages, in salaries, in sales, or in medals. Our victory is different. We resist and overcome evil—the evil that deceives nations and kills everyone; the evil that fools angels and humans into rebellion against God. We overcome the evil that leads all who surrender to hell. God has called us to conquer evil, and that is what we are to be doing now. This requires much more than the simple accumulation of knowledge—we are to learn to "overcome evil with good."[35]

With this in view we see that spiritual battles rage as fiercely around dining room tables, in break rooms, and while surfing the Internet as on a battlefield. This is because the fiercest battles that have the most at stake aren't over bodies, but souls. That's what Jesus was talking about when He said, "Do not be afraid of those who kill the body but cannot kill the soul. Rather, be afraid of the One who can destroy both soul and body in hell."[36] In other words, your physical death isn't that important compared to your spiritual death.

How do we overcome spiritual enemies? I have already pointed out that we must conquer like Jesus conquered. Jesus willingly suffered outward or worldly defeat in order to conquer in the spiritual realm, and for us to conquer, we must do likewise (and sooner or later we must conquer even to death). The world may view our suffering for Jesus as defeat, but in the spiritual realm, it makes us conquerors. In Revelation we saw that the slain Lamb conquered, and in Romans 8:35-39 we see an amazing parallel:

> Who shall separate us from the love of Christ? Shall trouble or hardship or persecution or famine or nakedness or danger or sword?[37] As it is written: "For your sake we face death all day long; we are considered as *sheep to be slaughtered.*"[38] No, in all *these* things we are *more than conquerors*[39] through him who loved us. For I am convinced that neither death[40] nor life, neither angels nor demons,[41] neither the present nor the future, nor any powers,[42] neither height nor depth, nor anything else in all creation, will be able to separate us from the love of God that is in Christ Jesus our Lord (NIV).[43]

Notice that just as Revelation speaks of Jesus as the slain Lamb who conquered, here Paul tells us that the world sees us as sheep to be slaughtered, yet no matter what the world slings at us, we are "more than conquerors."

When Paul asked what might separate us from the love of Christ, he seems to anticipate someone asking, "If Christ loves us, why do we suffer?" Paul answers that our enduring hardship and suffering, far from being evidence that God doesn't love us, is exactly a sign of His love because we conquer *through* them. In fact, Paul said it has been "granted" to us to suffer for Christ.[44] In other words, our suffering is God doing us a favor.

So, like Jesus, we face suffering, evil and death; like Jesus, we are considered sheep to be slaughtered; and like Jesus, we are more than conquerors.[45] We conquer hardship, sickness, ridicule, suffering, and even death. And again, we actually conquer *through* these things—we don't conquer by avoiding them. Now, I am not for a minute suggesting that we shouldn't take an aspirin for a headache. Certainly, we can and should avoid needless suffering.[46] But in times when there is no righteous recourse but suffering, we conquer by enduring that suffering.[47]

We conquer when we believe that obeying God makes it possible for us to thwart the most evil and powerful foes any human ever faced. Even if killed, we conquer when we remain faithful. Thus of the Revelation saints we read, "They have conquered him by the blood of the Lamb and by the word of their testimony, for they loved not their lives even unto death."[48]

Let me give some examples. When a man tells his co-workers that he can't see a movie because it's immoral, even though he'll be called a prude, he conquers. When a couple faithfully fulfills their commitment to a church ministry, meeting after meeting, without acknowledgment, they conquer. When a woman politely encourages a Christian friend to stop lying and is rebuffed for doing this, she conquers. When a woman risks losing friends because she politely refuses to listen to their gossip, she conquers. When a couple gives the poor money instead of buying a nicer car or securing a better retirement, they conquer.

When parents refuse their teen something risqué that "all the other parents" allow, they conquer. When a woman remains kind to an unkind husband, she conquers. When a woman refuses to marry a non-Christian even though she suspects it is (and may in reality be) her last chance to enjoy marriage, she conquers. When a man cares for his invalid wife and thanks God, he conquers. When a man lives long enough to watch his spouse and all his friends die, but continues to honor God, he conquers. When you are bored and would love to watch TV but don't because you can't find anything fit to view, you conquer. When you are insulted but you bite your tongue and don't respond in kind, you conquer. When you get cancer but remain faithful and thankful, you conquer (even if the cancer kills you). These require the endurance that results from faith—the conviction of things unseen.

Consider Job. His children liked each other and he was rich and famous. But one day Satan told God that the only reason Job worshipped Him was because his life was easy. So the Lord let Satan orchestrate the deaths of his children, the theft of his property, and the ruin of his health. Then Job's wife told him, "Do you still hold fast your integrity? Curse God and die" (Job 2:9). Now that was an unsupportive moment! And what was the only thing Job had to do to humiliate Satan in front of the Creator and His angels? Continue to honor God. As long as Job patiently endured the suffering and evil, he humiliated Satan in the heavenly realms.[49]

So it is with us. When things go wrong and we continue to honor God, we conquer. By contrast, we don't overcome when we resort to gossip, lies, grumbling, sexual fantasy, drugs, and other forms of disobedience.[50] Enduring, overcoming, conquering, and finally reigning happen when we honor God through whatever hardships come our way. As Thomas à Kempis put it, "He who knows best how to suffer will enjoy the greater peace, because he is that conqueror of himself, the master of the world, a friend of Christ, and an heir of heaven."[51]

When I share the following account with audiences, I always begin by saying, "Don't worry. You don't have this; it is extremely rare." In 2002 I started experiencing lower back pain. As the months went on the pain increased, and I visited different doctors, all of whom told me that I needed to do stretching exercises (which is the remedy for many people's back pain).

Eventually I saw an orthopedic surgeon, and he took some X-rays then told me to see a physical therapist. But the pain continued to worsen and became so severe that I could no longer sleep in my bed upstairs with Jean E. (this was very sad to me). I couldn't really sleep downstairs either, but at least I wasn't waking up Jean E.

I got to the point where I was in constant pain and always exhausted (I fell asleep on the freeway once, and Jean's scream woke me up and she drove from then on). Finally I decided to get a CT, but because our health policy had a mere $5000 deductible, I waited until January 2 because I didn't want to pay the deductible twice. That was a Friday, and the next Monday morning, January 5, I got a phone call from the orthopedic surgeon. Not his nurse. Not an assistant. The doctor himself was on the phone and I knew, of course, that that couldn't be good news.

The doctor told us (Jean E. was listening in on another line) that I had "a mass" on my spine and that I needed to see a specialist a long way from where we lived. I argued with him that there must be a doctor that I could see near where I lived, but he made it plain that I needed to see this particular orthopedic-oncologist who happened to be the director of the musculoskeletal tumor program at Cedars-Sinai Hospital. After we hung up, I walked into Jean E.'s home office and, with tears streaming down our faces, I thanked God for what He had allowed, and we prayed for my healing. At that moment, I knew we had defeated Satan in the heavenly realms. That we knew we had defeated Satan didn't mean that there weren't many more tears—there were, most of them in response to the prospect of me leaving Jean E.

And then the whirlwind began. Quickly I saw the specialist, who ordered a biopsy (which hurt, by the way). After the biopsy was done, we waited to hear the result. Finally, a few days later, my orthopedic-oncologist told me that the biopsy's diagnosis was that I had a very severe form of cancer that he would treat first by chemo and then, after six months or so, *if* the tumor shrank, he might opt to operate. But he said he thought the biopsy *might* be mistaken and he needed to see the slides himself. We were stunned and, after we hung up, Jean E. and I met in the hallway, again with tears streaming down our faces we held hands and I led us in a prayer of thankfulness to God. And again I knew that we had defeated Satan in the heavenly realms.

I always emphasize the tears streaming down our faces because that's real—being faithful to God doesn't mean that we won't shed tears while we're being faithful. I forcefully chose to thank God regardless of my future on this earth, and that brought me a sense of conquering in hardship—in the midst of great emotional and physical pain—that served as an anchor for our stormy lives. Our reaction was possible because years in advance, I had decided not to complain but to honor God no matter what happened.

Again, let me emphasize that this knowledge didn't stop the tears—the thought of leaving Jean E. alone was terribly sad to me (and to her!), and I knew that the Bible didn't guarantee I would recover from this cancer. But I also felt a sense of triumph.

A couple of weeks after the diagnosis, I had a six-and-a-half hour surgery because my surgeon thought the biopsy could be mistaken. He was right. It turned out the biopsy was mistaken—I actually had a comparatively mild form of cancer (people usually laugh when I tell them that that's when I learned there's a difference between a *community* hospital and a *teaching* hospital).

But I imagine some might object to me giving this as an example of being a conqueror. First, this is hardly the Navy SEAL type of conquering. And it's true that Navy SEALs are tough men. But make no mistake: Unless these men also know Christ, that is all they are: tough men. To conquer in the spiritual realm, they need to be much more.

Consider that even Christian *women* endured prolonged torture in the Coliseum for Christ. The young mothers Perpetua and Felicitas (both of them having recently nursed their children) *willingly* (they could have offered incense to Caesar) faced wild beasts in the Roman Coliseum.[52] Overcoming spiritually is unrelated to physical prowess or financial resources, and the Christian quadriplegic who battles to control her thoughts and tongue may *daily* conquer greater obstacles than the most physically capable soldier in a firefight.[53] Your greatest challenge, as a Christian, is to learn to reign in your brain.

Second, some may object that this talk about reigning is too arrogant—after all, we as Christians are called to be humble. But as C.S. Lewis wrote, "To shrink back from the plan is not humility; it is laziness and cowardice. To submit to it is not conceit or megalomania; it is obedience."[54]

Third, others might object that the expectation that we might face persecution may lead Christians to become good doormats. But nothing could be further from the truth. A doormat doesn't stand for anything. The Christian isn't a pushover—I wasn't a pushover. Rather, those who give way to evil are the pushovers.

And finally, those discouraged over habitual sins in their lives may think overcoming impossible. But I've followed Christ since 1969, and I've seen enough of His work in my life to know He can and will complete His work. Of course, some Christians, like the thief on the cross, will not get much chance to conquer evil *here,* but we can be sure that given time, we will certainly have opportunities to conquer.

This happens, as John tells us, because "everyone who has been born of God overcomes the world. And this is the victory that has overcome the world—our faith."[55] In other words, those who are truly in Christ are born again by the Spirit of God, so it is then their nature to conquer. Adam's children will sin; Christ's children will, *in time,* conquer sin. Thus John wrote, "Little children, you are from God and have overcome them, for he who is in you is greater than he who is in the world."[56] Satan is no match for the Christian who perseveres while the Lord works His character in him.

Now, I'm not saying that Christians won't struggle with sin—they will! All Christians do. My point is that if Christians continue to abide in Jesus, then they will, in time, enjoy greater victory over sin.

And this brings me to my last point.

And We Will Reign Forever and Ever

Through overcoming evil, we prepare to reign forever. We saw in the first chapter of the first book of the Bible—in fact, the first verse in the Bible that mentions humankind—that God created humankind to rule, and now in the last chapter of the last book of the Bible we read perhaps the most thrilling verse in the Bible: "There will be no more night. They will not need the light of a lamp or the light of the sun, for the Lord God will give them light. And they will reign for ever and ever."[57]

The middle of the Bible reveals the same: "But the saints of the Most High will receive the kingdom and will possess it forever—yes, for ever and ever...Then the sovereignty, power and greatness of the kingdoms under the whole heaven will be handed over to the saints, the people of the Most High. His kingdom will be an everlasting kingdom, and all rulers will worship and obey him."[58] According to 1 Peter 2:9, we are "a chosen race, a *royal priesthood*, a holy nation, a people for his own possession, that you may proclaim the excellencies of him who called you out of darkness into his marvelous light." About this G.K. Beale points out that the "'royal priesthood'...carries over from Exod. 19:6 the idea not only of priesthood but also of kingship."[59]

In Revelation 2:26-27, Jesus said, "The one who conquers and who keeps my works until the end, to him I will give authority over the nations...even as I myself have received authority from my Father." Then in Revelation 3:21, He said, "The one who conquers, I will grant him to sit with me on my throne, as I also conquered and sat down with my Father on his throne."[60] About these blessings, Jesus tells us, "He who has an ear, let him hear what the Spirit says to the churches."[61]

Authority over Creatures

Reigning, by definition, means to have authority over creatures. One of the questions I'm asked a lot is, "What will we reign over?" We will reign over other creatures. Adam and Eve reigned over all the animals. Who knows what kinds of creatures we will reign over for eternity? One woman told me, "I don't want to reign over others!" What I found interesting was that she owned a horse, and her most enjoyable pastime had to do with reigning over another being—a horse. That's what pets are—creatures we lovingly reign over. Whether they are on leashes, or in cages, or corrals, or tanks, we reign over our pets.

It does appear that some humans will have authority over other humans, but Jesus tells us not to be concerned about that because this authority won't be like the way humans typically reign over other humans on earth. In Matthew 20:20, a woman asked Jesus if her sons could sit at Jesus' right and left hands in His kingdom. Jesus replied,

"To sit at my right and at my left is not mine to grant, but it is for those whom it has been prepared by my Father" (verse 23). We read that the other disciples were "indignant at the two brothers." But Jesus called them together and said, in verses 25-26: "You know that the rulers of the Gentiles lord it over them, and their great ones exercise authority over them. It shall not be so among you. But whoever would be great among you must be your servant." In other words, apparently there will be a heavenly hierarchy, but we should realize that those in authority are humble in their treatment of others, and it is those who are servants now who will be great later in God's kingdom.[62]

Adam and Eve were to reign over all the creatures in the air, on the land, and in the sea, and there is nothing that tells us that we won't be reigning over similar creatures. G.K. Beale writes that the saints will "have such intimate fellowship with God that they not only take on his name...but also become associated with his throne...to such a degree that they are said to 'reign forever and ever.'"[63]

In Revelation 21:5-7, "conquer" is used one last time: "And he who was seated on the throne said, 'Behold, I am making all things new.' Also he said, 'Write this down, for these words are trustworthy and true.' And he said to me, 'It is done! I am the Alpha and the Omega, the beginning and the end. To the thirsty I will give from the spring of the water of life without payment. The one who conquers will have this heritage, and I will be his God and he will be my son.'"[64]

But there's much more than this. Paul writes in 1 Corinthians 6:1-3 that we will not only "judge the world," but we will also "judge angels."[65] So God's plan for the Christian is not only to judge earthly beings, but also heavenly beings.

Judging Angels

Of course the question arises: Why would the saints of God be qualified to judge the world and even angels? Perhaps it is because those who possess less evidence of God's power and goodness, yet still honor God, are in a position to judge those who had more evidence of God's power and goodness yet refused to honor Him. This principle is found in Matthew 12, where the Pharisees and scribes asked Jesus for more proof that He was who He said He was. To this Jesus replied,

> An evil and adulterous generation seeks for a sign, but no sign will be given to it except the sign of the prophet Jonah. For just as Jonah was three days and three nights in the belly of the great fish, so will the Son of Man be three days and three nights in the heart of the earth. The men of Nineveh will rise up at the judgment with this generation and condemn it, for they repented at the preaching of Jonah, and behold, something greater than Jonah is here (verses 39-41).

The point is simple: Those who saw Jesus actually teaching and healing the sick had much more evidence that He was who He said He was than the Ninevites had proof that Jonah was a prophet. Even so, the Ninevites repented! Thus the Ninevites are qualified to judge those who justify choosing evil because of their perceived lack of evidence.

Likewise, Jesus said in verse 42 that "the queen of the South will rise up at the judgment with this generation and condemn it, for she came from the ends of the earth to hear the wisdom of Solomon, and behold, something greater than Solomon is here." So this queen, deep in Africa, had heard there was a wise man named Solomon who knew the Lord. She traveled hundreds of miles to seek out his wisdom. By contrast, those who were standing in the presence of the miracle-working Jesus wouldn't admit to the truth of who He was. Thus the Queen of the South was qualified to condemn that generation.

Similarly, the angels who rebelled against God will rightfully be judged by humans who obeyed God because they had much less evidence for God's goodness and power than the angels did.

Paul wrote in Ephesians 3:10-11 that heavenly beings are learning from us: "His intent was that now, through the church, the manifold wisdom of God should be made known to the rulers and authorities in the heavenly realms, according to his eternal purpose that he accomplished in Christ Jesus our Lord" (NIV).

Perhaps Satan's justification for himself and his minions has been that they didn't have enough evidence for God's goodness, or His power, or both. But humans had even less evidence than the angels. Those humans who have chosen to honor God, then, are justified in being judges of the world and angels.

Ruling Cities

In Luke 19:17, Jesus said those who are faithful over small things in this life will take charge of "cities." Dallas Willard observed, "Perhaps it would be a good exercise for each of us to ask ourselves: Really, how many cities could I now govern under God? If, for example, Baltimore or Liverpool were turned over to me, with power to do what I want with it, how would things turn out? An honest answer to this question might do much to prepare us for our eternal future in this universe."[66]

All of this is for the overcomer, the conqueror, and the one who will reign.

You see, as Willard wrote, "The intention of God is that we should each become the kind of person whom he can set free in his universe, empowered to do what *we* want to do."[67] After all, here on earth, isn't it every parent's goal to discipline their children and even force them to endure hardships (like homework and vegetables) so that one day they will be equipped to live a full life on their own, making good choices with regard to doing what *they* want to do?

The Truly Big Things to Come

Perhaps all this sounds too good. Does the idea you will reign some-day sound like a fairy tale? Does it sound like Snow White or Sleep-ing Beauty, who fell under the power of evil until a prince came along and rescued them and they went off and lived happily ever after? In our case, we humans have fallen under the power of evil, and Prince Jesus came to rescue us and take us to His kingdom where we will reign with Him forever and ever. Does Christianity sound like a fairy tale? Well, if you think that, you have it exactly backward: Fairy tales sound like this! Just as we saw with the authors of science fiction, the authors of fairy tales do no more than echo the grand metanarrative—the great-est story ever told.[68]

In other words, God is giving us the kingdom and not just any king-dom, but *the* kingdom. And once Jesus comes, there will be no other. We get it all. This isn't the Disneyland all-day pass or even the all-year passport. This is the deed to the property. He is giving us a controlling interest in part of heaven. He talks about ruling cities, He talks about true riches, He tells us to be faithful over things here. Then He tells us that the things here, the things that seem so big to us, are small. Well, my brother or sister in Christ, if we think these small things here on earth are big, how are we going to react when we see *truly* big things?

Truly. Big. Things. Come. We are going to reign over them, and we are going to do this with Jesus. That is God's plan for our lives, and it has always been the plan.

Epilogue

The Short Answer on Why God Allows Evil

In the classes that I teach, I ask my students to come up with a dinner-table summary of what they have learned. As Christians, we should all be able to summarize the important truths of the faith, such as the evidence for the resurrection of Jesus, or reasons as to why God allows evil. Indeed, when I tell people that I teach on why God allows evil, I'm almost always asked, very intently, "So what's the answer?" In what follows, I'm going to give my short answer to what I've written in this book.

Because free will is valuable (in fact, it's hard to conceive of humans not having free will), God created beings that had free will and gave them paradise. God gave these beings—Adam and Eve—only one prohibition: "You must not eat from the tree of the knowledge of good and evil, for when you eat from it you will certainly die."[1] It's important to note that it is impossible to give beings free will and not allow them to use it wrongly—that's as logical as it gets. So Adam and Eve had everything going for them, but they distrusted God and rebelled against Him. So God cursed the ground, thus enabling all kinds of disease and pestilence—this was the origin of natural evil—and then God kicked Adam and Eve out of the Garden of Eden, thus removing them from the rejuvenating power of the Tree of Life. And we've been attending funerals ever since.

Once removed from the Garden, Adam and Eve had children who were physical and spiritual reproductions of themselves. Adam and Eve couldn't have chosen to reproduce children that were in some way better than themselves; they could only reproduce themselves. Therefore all humans are born like their first parents—desperately inclined to sin, alienated from relationship with God, and destined to always suffer and die.

God could not simply excuse Adam and Eve's sin because the lesson to free beings would then be "Sin is okay, God will overlook it." But to demonstrate His love for us and to atone for the grave seriousness of sin, God sent His only Son, Jesus, to die for rebellious humans.[2] Now, we humans who trust God and accept Jesus' death on the cross for our sins learn the horror of rebellion through experiencing rebellion's devastating results. We are also learning to overcome evil with good. This knowledge prepares us to be fit inheritors of God's kingdom, where—because we are learning the horror and stupidity of sin here on earth—we will be able to use our free will rightly as we reign with Jesus forever and ever.

There it is—a short explanation as to why God allows evil. Of course there are many aspects of this topic that require further explanation, and that's what this book provides.

Appendix

Satan's Rebellion and God's Response

Because the content I share here is somewhat speculative and isn't required for my overall theodicy to succeed, I chose to relegate it to an appendix.

Evil didn't begin with human beings; evil began with the rebellion of Satan and other angelic beings. Although we know quite a bit about how God is going to resolve Satan's rebellion, Scripture tells us precious little about how and why Satan rebelled against God. But precious little isn't nothing, and in this appendix, I'm going to present what I believe to be a scripturally plausible scenario about Satan's rebellion and what God has done and is doing about it.

At the outset, I want to specify two things. First, it's important to note that I'm presuming libertarian free will. In other words, I hold that God has not determined our every thought and deed so that no one can ever do other than he or she does. This is important because free beings simply cannot be forced to believe certain ideas are true; rather, they must be convinced. Second, my goal here is to present a plausible scenario. You may disagree with some aspects of what I say, and that's okay with me. In fact, that is why I am glad to dialogue on this important subject. I'm not under the illusion that all that I propose here is unmistakably the case, but I've learned in the course of teaching on why God allows evil that a consideration for what might be going on in the heavenly realm is helpful toward understanding God's larger plan.

Satan's Rebellion

When Were the Angels Created?

It is clear that the angels existed prior to the creation of the earth. We get this from Job 38:4-7, where the Lord asked Job, "Where were you when I laid the foundation of the earth...when the morning stars sang together and all the sons of God shouted for joy?" The "sons of God" are angels (see Job 1:6; 2:1). Thus if one holds to a young-earth view of the universe, then it is indeterminate as to how long the angels were created prior to the creation of man, but if one holds to an old-earth view of the universe, then the angels were created at least billions of years prior to the creation of man.

When Did Satan and the Angels Rebel?

Because Satan tempted Eve, it is clear that Satan fell prior to the fall of Adam and Eve. And I think we can move the date earlier than that. In Matthew 25:41, Jesus said to the lost humans, "Depart from me, you cursed, into the eternal fire prepared for the devil and his angels."[1] Notice that Jesus said the eternal fire was not prepared with humankind in view, but "for the devil and his angels." Contrast that with verse 34, where God says of the saved that they will "inherit the kingdom prepared for you from the foundation of the world."

Also, in Revelation 13:8, we read that the names of the saved were written in the Lamb's book of life "before the foundation of the world." In other words, God created the world with lost humans in view, knowing that Jesus would have to die to save them. But hell was not originally created with lost humans in view, so it's plausible that hell was created prior to the creation of the world, and therefore the devil and his angels probably rebelled before God created the world. This was the view of John Milton: "Many at least of the Greek, and some of the Latin Fathers, are of the opinion that angels, as being spirits, must have existed long before the material world; and it seems even probable, that the apostasy which caused the expulsion of so many thousands from heaven, took place before the foundations of this world were laid."[2]

Because almost any reading of Genesis 1 would lead us to conclude that God created the physical universe as a place in which the earth could exist (the foundation of the earth), then it would seem that Satan's rebellion and the creation of hell took place prior to the creation of the universe. If this is the case, then obviously it would also mean that the angels were created prior to the creation of the universe.

Why Did Satan Rebel?

Although we don't know precisely what Satan wanted, I think it's safe to say we know why he rebelled. Why does anyone rebel? Isn't it that he thinks he deserves better? For example, the American Revolution began when colonists complained that, among other things, they deserved better than "taxation without representation." Isn't "I deserve better" the foundation of all rebellion? We know that Satan was proud (1 Timothy 3:6), and from what we can see, Satan thought God was holding him back from things he thought he deserved. C.S. Lewis observed, "The moment you have a self at all, there is the possibility of putting yourself first—wanting to be the centre—wanting to be God, in fact."[3] Similarly, William Dembski wrote:

> Precisely because a created will belongs to a creature, that creature, if sufficiently reflective, can reflect on its creaturehood and realize that it is not God. Creaturehood implies constraints to which the Creator is not subject...The question then naturally arises, Has God the Creator denied to the creature some freedom that might benefit it? Adam and Eve thought the answer to this was yes...In short, the problem of evil starts when creatures think God is evil for "cramping their style."[4]

Satan tempted Eve by telling her that if she rebelled, she could be "like

God" (Genesis 3:4). Wanting to be "like God" is what tempted Satan in his rebellion, according to Isaiah 14:12-14:

> How you are fallen from heaven, O Day Star, son of Dawn! How you are cut down to the ground, you who laid the nations low! You said in your heart, "I will ascend to heaven; above the stars of God I will set my throne on high; I will sit on the mount of assembly in the far reaches of the north; I will ascend above the heights of the clouds; I will make myself like the Most High."

We see the same thing in Ezekiel 28:17: "Your heart was proud because of your beauty; you corrupted your wisdom for the sake of your splendor."

Satan thought he deserved better—he thought he could be like God.[5]

Why Did Other Angels Join Satan's Rebellion?

Apparently as many as a third of the angels joined in Satan's rebellion.[6] Why would they do that? Some have said that other angels followed Satan simply because Satan was their leader, the common answer is that Satan seduced them into his perspective that they could have more if they joined together. In short, Satan convinced them that God was holding them back from all they could have and all they could be. God had asked too much of them; He had set the obedience bar too high.

Isn't this just another way of saying that God isn't fair? Perhaps, then, the biggest question in the kingdom of heaven with regard to the problem of evil is this: Is God good? But in the kingdom of heaven, unlike on earth, one of the possible solutions isn't that God doesn't exist.

If Satan and his fellow rebels felt that God was holding them back from something wonderful, and this, in turn, led to massive rebellion, then what was God to do? How does God answer the questions about His fairness?

God's Response

What God Didn't Do

Notice what God didn't do. He didn't immediately destroy all the rebels. This makes sense, because their immediate destruction could have cast doubts about God's goodness. If God wanted to teach beings that He truly does act in a just and right manner, then He would want to immediately destroy those who challenged Him, for that would only send a "might makes right" message: disobey and die. Such a message would only encourage feigned loyalty, and feigned loyalty is no more than rebellion waiting for an opportunity. The Lord is not interested in that.

What Keeps the Unfallen Angels from Sin?

This leads us to one of the most interesting questions of all: What kept the angels who didn't join the initial rebellion from rebelling later? There are a variety of opinions.

Anselm of Canterbury's answer was that "the angels that loved the justice...were so elevated that they could have whatever they willed and not see what more they could have willed, and thus they cannot sin."[7] If I'm understanding Anselm correctly, he believed that God elevated the not-fallen angels in such a way that they lacked nothing they could ever want, which would make temptation impossible. The trouble with this is twofold: there's no biblical evidence for Anselm's contention, and obedience based solely on giving beings everything they could ever desire isn't really obedience.

The more common answer is represented by Ron Rhodes, who writes that the "angels who passed their probationary test and did not sin were confirmed in their holiness (see 1 Timothy 5:21)."[8] Similarly, systematic theologian Louis Berkhof writes: "They evidently received, in addition to the grace with which all angels were endowed, and which was sufficient to enable them to retain their position, a special grace of perseverance, by which they were confirmed in their position."[9] Rhodes concludes that "these good angels are now *incapable* of sinning. The lines have been drawn, and they are now absolute."[10] But, like Anselm's answer, there isn't any scriptural evidence to support that view. Also, can God simply make us always choose righteously? That's a negation of free will.

What does seem scriptural is that after Satan and his angels rebelled, the Lord did something formidable—He prepared "eternal fire...for the devil and his angels" (Matthew 25:41).[11] He created hell! I suspect that God's creation of hell would immediately deter other heavenly beings from ever again considering *overt* rebellion. But, as I mentioned above, that wouldn't convince them that God is right.

I suggest that what God has used to convince them that He was and is right was to let the holy angels watch the fallen angels plunge themselves into depravity: a heavenly education of good and evil began. As C. Fred Dickason suggests, "Perhaps He allowed angels to sin in order that He might give a concrete example of the wretchedness of sin."[12] From what we can see throughout Scripture, especially from the opening chapters of Genesis and Romans 1, the plunge into depravity is steep. As the holy angels witness the horror of the fallen angels' rebellion, it must confirm to them that God was right all along.

Satan's Counterargument

If Satan rebelled because he thought he deserved better, then it's no surprise that he would try to make the case that his impending doom is unfair. Thus he becomes the "the accuser of our brothers and sisters" (Revelation 12:10, see also Zechariah 3:1 and Job 1). In fact, *Satan* literally means "accuser" or "adversary." By accusing the saints, Satan tacitly argues that he isn't the only one who can't meet God's standards—no one can. Therefore God asks too much; He sets the bar too high.

This then would provide the unspoken motivation behind much of Satan's argument regarding Job. God pointed out how righteous Job was, and Satan replied:

> Does Job fear God for no reason? Have you not put a
> hedge around him and his house and all that he has, on
> every side? You have blessed the work of his hands, and

his possessions have increased in the land. But stretch out
your hand and touch all that he has, and he will curse you
to your face (Job 1:9-11).

Satan, in essence, said, "Of course Job serves You. You give him
everything he wants! If you had given me everything I ever wanted, then
I would never have rebelled either."

Isaiah 64:4 testifies that "all our righteous acts are like filthy rags,"[13]
and Romans 3:12 says that "no one does good, not even one," so it
would appear that Satan had a point!

Jesus Conquers Satan

Thus God sends Jesus. Because Jesus kept the Law perfectly, He justified Satan's judgment. Consider Revelation 12, which tells us about
the devil's defeat in heaven:

Now the salvation and the power and the kingdom of
our God and the authority of his Christ have come, for
the accuser of our brothers has been thrown down, who
accuses them day and night before our God. And they have
conquered him by the blood of the Lamb and by the word
of their testimony, for they loved not their lives even unto
death (verses 10-11).

One thing we learn from this passage is that the accuser, Satan,
couldn't be cast down until Christ was victorious at the cross—because
until then, Satan's argument had some merit! As G.K. Beale put it:
"Until the death of Christ, it could appear that the devil had a good case,
since God ushered all deceased OT saints into His saving presence without exacting the penalty of their sin. Satan was allowed to lodge these
complaints because there was some degree of truth in them."[14] But once
Jesus honored God, in spite of immense suffering, He justified Satan's
judgment. Satan's case was lost.

Ultimately, then we too will judge the world and Satan.[15] That was
among the points made in this book's last chapter, which discusses our
reigning with Christ forever.

Index

Notes

Introduction: In Search of Answers About God and Evil

1. You can read more about the unpardonable sin in Clay Jones, "What Is the Unpardonable Sin?," *Christian Research Journal* 34-4 (2011), 8-9, http://www.equip.org/article/what-is-the-unpardonable-sin/.

2. D. Martyn Lloyd-Jones, *God's Way of Reconciliation: Studies in Ephesians Chapter 2* (Grand Rapids: Baker, 1972), 82.

3. C.S. Lewis, *The Problem of Pain* (New York: Macmillan, 1953), 132.

4. I further discuss my thoughts on libertarian freedom v. compatibilism in the chapter "Wasn't There Another Way?"

5. This is from Clay Jones, "Evil," *The Encyclopedia of Christian Civilization*, ed. George Thomas Kurian (West Sussex, UK: Wiley-Blackwell, 2011), vol. I, 894.

6. Ibid.

7. Some might wonder about John 9:1: "As he went along, he saw a man blind from birth. His disciples asked him, 'Rabbi, who sinned, this man or his parents, that he was born blind?' 'Neither this man nor his parents sinned,' said Jesus, 'but this happened so that the works of God might be displayed in him'" (NIV). But would the man have been born blind if Adam and Eve had never sinned?

8. John Feinberg points out that there are really many problems of evil. The "religious problem of evil arises from a particular instance or occurrence of evil in someone's life." The theological/philosophical problem of evil is "about the existence of *evil in general*, not some specific evil that might befall someone and disrupt her personal relation with God." There is also a difference between moral evil and natural evil. Then there are "problems about the quantity, intensity, and apparent gratuitousness of evil." John S. Feinberg, *The Many Faces of Evil: Theological Systems and the Problem of Evil* (Grand Rapids: Zondervan, 1994), 15-16.

9. David Hume citing Epicurus, in David Hume, *Dialogues Concerning Natural Religion*, ed. Richard H. Popkin, 2d ed. (Cambridge, MA: Hackett, 1998), 63. Emphasis his.

10. Paul Draper, "The Problem of Evil," *The Oxford Handbook of Philosophical Theology*, eds. Thomas P. Flint and Michael C. Rea (Oxford: Oxford University Press, 2009), 335. Draper cites J.L. Mackie as an example of someone who thought the problem of evil was a promising argument against theism. J.L. Mackie, "Evil and Omnipotence," *Mind* 64: 200-212.

11. Ibid.

12. Ibid. Emphasis mine.

13. William L. Rowe, "Plantinga on Possible Worlds and Evil," *The Journal of Philosophy* 70-17 (October 1973), 555. Rowe goes on to write, "And if we accept Plantinga's assumption of incompatibalism, we must, I think, accept Plantinga's argument as showing that (1) and (2) are not inconsistent." Ibid.

14. William L. Rowe, *Philosophy of Religion: An Introduction* (Belmont, CA: Wadsworth, 2007), 113. Emphasis his.

15. John Milton, *Complete Poems and Major Prose*, ed. Merritt Y. Hughes (New York: Odyssey, 1957), 212. Book 1, 25. It's important to note that sometimes Christian philosophers don't necessarily try to give God's actual reasons for allowing evil but only give a possible reason for God allowing evil. This was the tact of Alvin Plantinga in his seminal *God, Freedom, and Evil,* which most skeptics agree undermined the logical problem of evil. Plantinga explains, "A theodicist, then attempts to tell us why God permits evil. Quite distinct from a Free Will Theodicy is what I shall call a Free Will Defense. Here the aim is not to say what God's reason *is*, but at most what God's reason *might possibly be.*" Alvin C. Plantinga, *God, Freedom, and Evil* (Grand Rapids: Eerdmans, 1977), 28. In other words, Plantinga, by showing *a possible* reason why an all-good and all-powerful God might allow evil, demonstrated that the logical problem of evil was unsuccessful.

16. Daniel Howard-Snyder, "God, Evil and Suffering" in Michael J. Murray, ed., *Reason for the Hope Within* (Grand Rapids: William B. Eerdmans, 1999), 101.

17. Bart D. Ehrman, *God's Problem: How the Bible Fails to Answer Our Most Important Question—Why We Suffer* (New York: HarperOne, 2008), 3.

18. Sam Harris, *Letter to a Christian Nation* (New York: Knopf, 2006), 50-51.

19. Ibid., 51.

20. It's true that on some occasions a doctrine, or particular formulation of a doctrine, may be mistaken, but that conclusion should only be reached after careful deliberation.

21. For the judgment against the Canaanites and against Israel for committing the sins of the Canaanites, see Clay Jones, "We Don't Hate Sin So We Don't Understand What Happened to the Canaanites: An Addendum to Divine Genocide Arguments," *Philosophia Christi* 11-1 (2009), 53-72. Available at: http://www.clayjones.net/wp-content/uploads/2011/06/We -Dont-Hate-Sin-PC-article.pdf. Also see my blog, www.clayjones.net, for a series of further explanatory posts on the topic.

22. R.T. Kendall, "Will You Forgive God?" *Charisma* magazine, July 1, 2012, accessed July 23, 2016, http://www.charismamag.com/spirit/spiritual-growth/15336-will-you-forgive-god. The article brings up that Abraham must have felt betrayed but that "Abraham succeeded in breaking the "betrayal barrier"—something each of us must do if we feel God has let us down." Now, in all fairness to the author, he is clear to point out that God never betrays us, but "as strange as it may sound, we must forgive God if we *feel* that He has betrayed us." Emphasis mine.

23. As determinist John Frame put it: "The doctrine that God controls all things, including human decisions, typically raises for us the question, 'How, then, can we be responsible for our actions?' Answering this question has been a major preoccupation of theologians who write about the doctrine of God." John M. Frame, *The Doctrine of God: A Theology of Lordship* (Kindle Locations 1469-1471). Kindle Edition.

24. R.C. Sproul, *The Invisible Hand: Do All Things Really Work for Good?* (Dallas: Word, 1996), 167. Even J.I. Packer, when faced with explaining how God can determine absolutely

everything and yet not be the author of evil, makes a similar appeal but calls it an antinomy: "The whole point of an antinomy—in theology, at any rate—is that it is not a real contradiction, though it looks like one. It is an apparent incompatibility between two apparent truths. An antinomy exists when a pair of principles stand side by side, seemingly irreconcilable, yet both undeniable. There are cogent reasons for believing each of them; each rests on clear and solid evidence; but it is a mystery to you how they can be squared with each other. You see that each must be true on its own, but you do not see how they can be true together." J.I. Packer, *Evangelism and the Sovereignty of God* (Leicester: InterVarsity Press, 1961), 18-19. In other words, Packer must appeal to mystery as he cannot explain it. The trouble for Packer and Sproul and other determinists is explaining how we know when a contradiction between two theologies is only an apparent contradiction and not a real one. Obviously, if it were a real contradiction, then one of the views would necessarily be false. What would we say to a cultist who, when we pointed out a contradiction in his or her theology, replied, "It is only an apparent contradiction, not a real one"? Even determinist Paul Helm writes that "appealing to an antinomy could be a license for accepting nonsense." Paul Helm, *The Providence of God: Contours of Christian Theology* (Downers Grove, IL: InterVarsity, 1993), 66.

25. Harold S. Kushner, *When Bad Things Happen to Good People* (New York: Schocken, 1981), 138.

26. Ibid., 134.

27. Ibid., 46.

28. Ibid., 148.

29. Gregory A. Boyd, *Satan and the Problem of Evil: Constructing a Trinitarian Warfare Theodicy* (Downers Grove, IL: InterVarsity, 2001), 16. Emphasis his.

30. Ibid., 17.

31. It's outside the scope of this book to delve into the arguments for and against open theism. For more see Paul Kjoss Helseth, William Lane Craig, Ron Highfield, Gregory A. Boyd, *Four Views on Divine Providence*, ed. Stanley N. Gundry (Grand Rapids: Zondervan, 2011).

32. Gordon H. Clark, *Religion, Reason and Revelation* (Jefferson, MD: Trinity, 1986), 239-240.

33. Ibid., 240-241.

34. Paul Helm, *The Providence of God: Contours of Christian Theology* (Downers Grove, IL: InterVarsity, 1993), 167.

35. Ibid., 166.

36. I don't know who wrote this or whether I made it up.

37. John Hick, "An Irenaean Theodicy," in *Encountering Evil: Live Options in Theodicy*, ed. Stephen T. Davis (Louisville, KY: Westminster John Knox, 2001), 52.

38. I'm not suggesting that one necessarily needs to hold to inerrancy to hold to the theodicy I present. I'm only letting the reader know where I'm coming from.

39. I like Feinberg's distinction between a theodicy and a defense: "A theodicy purports to offer the actual reason God has for allowing evil in our world. A defense is much less pretentious, for it claims to offer only a possible reason God might have for not removing evil. As long as that possible explanation does remove the alleged inconsistency internal to the theist's system, the theist meets the demands of the logical form of the problem of evil. A defense is defense enough; a theodicy is not required." Ibid., 19. Feinberg goes on to point out that not everyone recognizes this distinction.

Chapter 1—Why Do We Suffer for Adam's Sin?

1. Sometimes people wonder why we talk about it being Adam's sin rather than the sin of both Adam and Eve. The answer is that Scripture always blames Adam (e.g., Romans 5:12: "Therefore, just as sin came into the world through *one man*, and death through sin, and so death spread to all men because all sinned"). Also, Eve's eyes weren't "opened" until Adam also ate.

2. NIV.

3. C.S. Lewis, *The Screwtape Letters* (New York: HarperCollins, 1996), 44.

4. Most theologians don't think that the serpent was Satan, but only that Satan was speaking through the serpent in the same way that he spoke through Peter to Jesus when Peter said, "This shall never happen to you" but Jesus replied, "Get behind me, Satan!" Matthew 16:21-23. See Revelation 12:9 for the identification of Satan and the serpent.

5. Notice that to "multiply" pain means that there was naturally pain as a part of God's original creation of Adam and Eve. Thus pain isn't an evil in and of itself.

6. The women's liberation movement hasn't helped. A major 2009 study has concluded that women have become increasingly unhappy: "By many objective measures the lives of women in the United States have improved over the past 35 years, yet we show that measures of subjective well-being indicate that women's happiness has declined both absolutely and relative to men. The paradox of women's declining relative well-being is found across various datasets, measures of subjective well-being, and is pervasive across demographic groups and industrialized countries. Relative declines in female happiness have eroded a gender gap in happiness in which women in the 1970s typically reported higher subjective well-being than did men. These declines have continued and a new gender gap is emerging—one with higher subjective well-being for men." Betsey Stevenson and Justin Wolfers, "The Paradox of Declining Female Happiness," National Bureau of Economic Research, accessed July 22, 2016, http://www.nber.org/papers/w14969.pdf. For more on this see Clay Jones, "Women's Liberation and Female Unhappiness," Clay Jones blog, June 23, 2011, http://www.clayjones .net/2011/06/woman%E2%80%99s-%E2%80%9Cliberation%E2%80%9D-and-female -unhappiness/.

7. Gordon Wenham translates it as "The land is cursed" and later refers to it as "the curse on the ground..." Gordon J. Wenham, *Genesis 1–15*, Word Biblical Commentary (Grand Rapids: Zondervan, 1987), 82. There's no sense that the curse is that Adam will do bad by the ground, thus cursing it. Regarding the cursing of the ground, Bruce K. Waltke writes that "the man's natural relationship to the ground—to rule over it—is reversed; instead of submitting to him, it resists and eventually swallows him." Bruce K. Waltke, *Genesis: A Commentary* (Grand Rapids: Zondervan, 2001), 95. Kenneth A. Matthews writes that "the punishment reveals that the man's sin is the cause for the 'curse' against the ground, resulting in its harvest of thorns and thistles...The ground will now be his enemy rather than his servant." Kenneth A. Matthews, *Genesis 1–11:26*, New American Commentary (Nashville: Holman Reference, 1996), 252. Walter Bruggemann, in commenting on Genesis 5:29, calls it "the ground cursed by God..." Walter Brueggemann, *Genesis, Interpretation: A Bible Commentary for Teaching and Preaching* (Atlanta: John Knox, 1982), 69.

8. Robert R. Gonzales, Jr., *Where Sin Abounds: The Spread of Sin and the Curse in the Book of Genesis with Special Focus on the Patriarchal Narratives* (Eugene, OR: Wipf & Stock, 2009), 48. Gonzalez explains, "It is difficult...to evade Paul's all-inclusive assessment of the scope of

the curse: 'For the creation (ή κτίσις) was subjected to futility' and is in 'bondage to decay.' Moreover, 'the whole creation (πασα ή κτίσις),' analogous to the woman, 'has been groaning together in the pains of childbirth until now' (Rom 8:20-22). Hence, Paul, following the teaching of Genesis and the rest of the OT, believed human sin had ecological ramifications. Thus, God touches Adam at that point in his life related to the primary focus of his role of fulfilling the creation mandate. Man was to rule over the ground joyfully and successfully. Now the ground will rule over him...Hence, Yahweh's words should be read as *prescribing* man's punishment not merely *describing* the outcome of man's disobedience." Ibid., 48-49, 50.

9. It isn't that clear exactly what happened to our world at the Fall, but I hold to the historic Christian position that it was the Fall that was the origin of most, if not all, of the pestilence and disease we presently encounter. But this causes a problem for those who hold to an old-earth view (as I said in the introduction, I take an agnostic position regarding the age of the earth but do contend that Adam and Eve were specially created by God). The problem, for those who do hold to an old-earth view, is that if the earth is older than Adam and Eve, then the question arises: How does one explain animal death and other maladies that might have occurred prior to the Fall?

There are three possible answers. First, although it is hard to imagine that cancers, and a plethora of other diseases, were a part of God's "very good" earth, this doesn't mean that those who hold to an old-earth view might not be correct that plate tectonics, volcanism, and thus even earthquakes might have been a part of God's "very good" earth (plate tectonics, volcanism, and earthquakes *might* have worsened as a result of the Fall—who knows?). After all, outside the Garden of Eden, man was commanded to "subdue" the earth, which suggests, *at the very least*, that the earth required subduing. So some of the things that we consider natural evils, like earthquakes, might have been a part of God's very good creation.

Also, it is *possible* that animal death occurred before the Fall as a part of God's good earth. Even though I had mentioned *nothing* about the age of the earth while speaking at a church in San Diego, I was cornered (there's no better way of putting it) by a couple of six-day creationists who insisted that I must take a position on the age of the earth. One of the questions they asked was whether animals eating each other could possibly be a part of God's good creation. My answer was, "Maybe." Scripture doesn't say there was no animal predation prior to the fall—especially outside the garden (Romans 5:12 doesn't have to apply to nonhumans). Thus the six-day creationist's intuition that animals' predation couldn't have been a part of God's "very good" earth is no more than intuition. Also, if animal death hadn't preceded the Fall, I'm not sure how much Adam and Eve could have understood God's warning "On the day that you eat of it, you will surely die," since they had never seen an animal die. Further, Jesus, in His postresurrection body, ate fish (Luke 24:42-43). Instead of fish, Jesus could have had a croissant, but the Lord of glory ate fish. Not only that, the Bible tells us that we will eat meat in heaven (Isaiah 25:6). I realize that "meat" might be metaphorical in that passage, but if we're going to take that verse literally (as six-day creationists tend to insist on), then we *will* eat *meat* in heaven. Again, I'm not saying these things are the case; I'm only saying that it is logically possible that animal predation and death occurred before the Fall.

Second, if the earth is old, then it is logically and scripturally *possible* that God allowed certain natural evils (like animal predation and disease) to occur in *anticipation* of the Fall. Thus, William A. Dembski could be correct that God allowed natural evil to occur prior to, and in anticipation of, the Fall. Dembski writes, "By taking a retroactive approach to the Fall, which traces all evil in the world back to human sin (even the evil that predates human sin), the theodicy I develop preserves the traditional view that natural evil is a consequence of the Fall." William A. Dembski, *The End of Christianity: Finding a Good God in an Evil World* (Nashville: B&H, 2009), 130. Also, Dembski makes a good point that if the earth is old, "why put Adam and Eve in a garden that's separate from the rest of the earth if the rest of the earth is unaffected by natural evil? In that case, wouldn't the whole earth be a garden, a paradise? It seems that the retroactive view of the fall does account for some things that remain anomalous on a young-earth view." William A. Dembski, "Old Earth Creationism and the Fall," *Christian Research Journal* 34-4 (2011), accessed August 12, 2016, http://www.equip.org/article/old-earth-creationism-and-the-fall/.

Third, although I don't see how it could apply to animal death, the gap theory is scripturally and logically possible. The gap theory is that there is a "gap" between Genesis 1:2 and the rest of chapter 1. In brief, the argument is that God created the heavens and the earth in Genesis 1:1, but then it says in Genesis 1:2a that, "The earth was without form and void, and darkness was over the face of the deep." Many take "without form and void" as meaning that creation was in some sense awry. As Professor of Old Testament and Hebrew Allen P. Ross, put it, "In the first part of Genesis 1:2, there is thus an ominous, uncomfortable tone. The clauses describe not the results of divine creation but a chaos at the earliest stage of this world. It is not the purpose of Genesis to tell the reader how the chaos came about... The expositor must draw some conclusions from other passages with similar descriptions. If one can posit that the fall of Satan (Ezek. 28) brought about the chaos in God's original creation, then Genesis 1 describes a re-creation, of God's first act of redemption, salvaging his world and creating all things new." Allen P. Ross, *Creation and Blessing: A Guide to the Study and Exposition of Genesis* (Grand Rapids: Baker, 1988), 107.

10. James D.G. Dunn, *Word Biblical Commentary Volume 38A: Romans 1–8* (Dallas: Word, 1988), 487-488.

11. For example, Douglas J. Moo calls this Romans passage an "obvious reference to the Gen. 3 narrative." Douglas J. Moo, *The Epistle to the Romans*, The New International Commentary on the New Testament, ed. Gordon D. Fee (Grand Rapids: Eerdmans, 1996), 515. For another, John Murray says these verses are "surely Paul's commentary on Gen. 3:17, 18." John Murray, *The Epistle to the Romans: The English Text with Introduction, Exposition and Notes,* The New International Commentary on the New Testament, gen. ed. F.F. Bruce (Grand Rapids: Eerdmans, 1980, reprint 1959), 303. Still another, Robert H. Mounce writes that "because Adam disobeyed by eating the forbidden fruit, God had cursed the ground (Gen 3:17-18; cf. 5:29). The full redemptive work of God includes the reversal of this curse." Robert H. Mounce, *New American Commentary: Volume 27—Romans* (Nashville: B&H, 1995), 184. James D.G. Dunn also calls this Romans passage a "clear allusion to the narratives of creation and of man's/Adam's fall..." James D.G. Dunn, *Word Biblical Commentary Volume 38A: Romans 1–8* (Dallas: Word, 1988), 487.

12. Murray, *The Epistle to the Romans*, 301-302. Emphasis his.

13. Moo, *The Epistle to the Romans*, 514.

14. Robert H. Mounce, *Romans*, 185.

15. Murray, *The Epistle to the Romans*, 303.

16. Moo, *The Epistle to the Romans*, 516.

17. NIV.

18. Some have been troubled by the fact that Adam and Eve didn't immediately die when they ate the fruit, but this is similar to 1 Kings 2:36-37: "Then the king [Solomon] sent and summoned Shimei and said to him, 'Build yourself a house in Jerusalem and dwell there, and do not go out from there to any place whatever. For on the day you go out and cross the brook Kidron, know for certain that you shall die. Your blood will be on your own head.'" Shimei later crossed the valley and Solomon killed him when he received word of what had happened. As Blocher writes, "This passage proves the meaning of the Hebrew expression: 'on that day you will fall under the power of a death sentence.' The warning did not imply the threat of a death that would be carried out immediately. The Judge's sentence is in perfect agreement with his earlier warning." Similarly, here in America the expression "Dead men walking" is used to refer to those who await execution in prison. Henri Blocher, *In the Beginning: The Opening Chapters of Genesis* (Downers Grove, IL: InterVarsity, 1984), 184.

19. I include suicide as self-murder.

20. See Ephesians 2:1-3; 1 John 3:8-10; 2 Timothy 2:26; Acts 26:18.

21. John Hick, *Evil and the God of Love* (New York: Palgrave Macmillan, 2007), 250.

22. C.S. Lewis, *Mere Christianity* (New York: HarperOne, 1996, reprint 1952), 49.

23. William A. Dembski, *The End of Christianity: Finding a Good God in an Evil World* (Nashville: B&H, 2009), 27-28.

24. Nathaniel Brandon, *The Six Pillars of Self-Esteem* (New York: Bantam, 1994), 148.

25. Ian A. McFarland, *In Adam's Fall: A Meditation on the Christian Doctrine of Original Sin* (West Sussex: Wiley-Blackwell, 2010), ix.

26. Hick, *Evil and the God of Love*, 249.

27. Sometimes also called forensic union.

28. The idea that God would have to put the billions of humans who have ever existed into their own Edens to make the point about the fact that they would all have done likewise is silly.

29. William G.T. Shedd, *Dogmatic Theology*, 3d ed., ed. Alan W. Gomes (Phillipsburg, NJ: P&R, 2013), 435.

30. Clay Jones, "Original Sin: Its Importance and Fairness," *Christian Research Journal* 34-6 (2011), accessed August 29, 2016, http://www.equip.org/article/original-sin-its-importance-and-fairness/.

31. Ibid., 564.

32. Ibid., 442.

33. Millard J. Erickson, *Christian Theology*, 2d ed. (Grand Rapids: Baker, 1998), 652.

34. Indeed, Shedd argued, "If the posterity were present, as natural union implies, they could not be represented; for this supposes absence. If they were absent, as representative union implies, they could not be present." Shedd, *Dogmatic Theology*, 436. But, again, I contend that we were really there but, in a sense, we weren't because we didn't have individuated consciousnesses.

35. Augustine, *The City of God*, trans. Marcus Dods (New York: Modern Library, 1950), 422-423. Some of the verses used to support the fact that we have inherited a sinful nature follow: Romans 7:14: "For we know that the law is spiritual, but I am of the flesh, sold under sin." Romans 7:20: "Now if I do what I do not want, it is no longer I who do it, but sin that dwells within me." Romans 7:25: "With my flesh I serve the law of sin."

36. Erickson, *Christian Theology*, 654.

37. From personal correspondence with Talbot distinguished professor of philosophy J.P. Moreland, on May 14, 2014.

38. Shedd, *Dogmatic Theology*, 438.

39. Ibid, 439.

40. For a more thorough exposition see Shedd, *Dogmatic Theology*, 438-444.

41. For theological arguments for traducianism see Shedd, *Dogmatic Theology*, 444ff.

42. Although it is true that many orthodox theologians have held to special creation, it is no surprise that the heretic Pelagius (born *c.* 354–died after 418), who held that humans did not inherit a sinful nature from Adam, was also a special creationist.

43. C.S. Lewis illustrated this point in his Chronicles of Narnia series, where he refers to humans as "sons of Adam" or "daughters of Eve."

44. Alvin Plantinga, *Warranted Christian Belief* (Oxford: Oxford University, 2000), 207.

45. Michael Ruse, "Darwinism and Christianity Redux: A Response to My Critics," *Philosophia Christi* 4 (2002), 192. Ruse continues, "I think Saint Paul and the great Christian philosophers had real insights into sin and freedom and responsibility, and I want to build on this rather than turn from it." Ibid.

46. Saint Augustine of Hippo, *The Confessions: With an Introduction and Contemporary Criticism*, trans. Maria Boulding, ed. David Vincent Meconi (San Francisco: Ignatius, 1997), 13. Book 1, chapter 7. Augustine continues, "I have watched and experienced for myself the jealousy of a small child: he could not even speak, yet he glared with livid fury at his fellow-nursling. Everyone has seen this...Is this to be regarded as innocence, this refusal to tolerate a rival for a richly abundant fountain of milk...Behavior of this kind is cheerfully condoned, however, not because it is trivial or of small account, but because everyone knows it will fade away as the baby grows up." Ibid.

47. Although it is true that some theologians will say that the image of God was completely lost at the Fall, in other places they will modify that to be "almost completely" lost. As bioethics professor John F. Kilner writes, "When Luther was not dismissing the image entirely, he characterized it as 'almost completely lost' with only 'feeble and almost completely obliterated remnants' left. Johann Gerhard similarly admitted that at most a few 'little remnants' of the image remain. Calvin more consistently referred to a nearly lost image of which mere 'traces' or a 'remnant or lineaments' remain. The result has been an understanding, influential in Protestant circles, that sinful human beings have virtually lost God's image." John F. Kilner, *Dignity and Destiny: Humanity in the Image of God* (Grand Rapids: Eerdmans, 2015), 164.

48. Although I'm not saying that there are no true deathbed conversions (the thief on the cross would fall into that category), I suspect that they are rare and that those steeped in evil seldom engage in *true* repentance just prior to their deaths.

49. Robert H. Mounce: "He is a 'type' in the sense that like Christ he is the corporate head of a race of people. While all are in Adam by virtue of birth into the human family, only those are in Christ who by faith become members of the new humanity." Mounce, *Romans*, 142, 132n.

50. 1 John 3:8-10: "He who does what is sinful is of the devil, because the devil has been sinning from the beginning. The reason the Son of God appeared was to destroy the devil's work. No one who is born of God will continue to sin, because God's *seed* remains in him; he cannot go on sinning, because he has been born of God."

51. Susan Hindman, "Judge cuts night one," *America's Got Talent*, Season 11, Episode 8, July 12, 2016, accessed 7-21-2016, http://www.nbc.com/americas-got-talent/video/judge-cuts-night-1/3065048.

52. Jon Dorenbos is also a motivational speaker himself and shares his perspective: "I've embraced everything that has happened in my life. No hard feelings, no anger. I'm over all of that stuff. To now be at this stage in my career and to help kids or anybody who has dealt with what I've dealt with—and unfortunately it happens way more than people think and you realize after something traumatic happens that by no means you are alone—is something I am happy to do." Jon Dorenbos, "Dorenbos Shares Story On National TV," *The Official Site of the Philadelphia Eagles*, August 18, 2014, accessed July 21, 2016, http://www.philadelphiaeagles.com/news/dave-spadaro/article-1/Dorenbos-Shares-Story-On-National-TV/06f005fd-af9b-43b3-bc5c-02064b697cdb.

Chapter 2—Why Do Bad Things Happen to Good People?

1. C.S. Lewis, *The Problem of Pain* (New York: Macmillan, 1943), 43.

2. R.C. Sproul, *Willing to Believe: The Controversy Over Free Will* (Grand Rapids: Baker, 1997), 125.

3. Ibid., 126.

4. The doctrine of total depravity doesn't mean that humans outside of Christ will always commit every possible kind of sin or commit every sin they have an opportunity to commit. It does mean, however, that humans outside of Christ don't do anything from untainted or purely selfless motives, and, most importantly, they do nothing out of love for God except in response to the work of the Holy Spirit. J.I. Packer: "The phrase total depravity is commonly used to make explicit the implications of original sin. It signifies a corruption of our moral and spiritual nature that is total not in degree (for no one is as bad as he or she might be) but in extent...We cannot earn God's favor, no matter what we do; unless grace saves us, we are lost." J.I. Packer, "Original Sin," *Concise Theology: A Guide to Historic Christian Beliefs* (Wheaton, IL: Tyndale) Database © 2005 WORDsearch Corp.

5. The Bible doesn't flinch at revealing evil deeds. Consider Judges 19, where we read of a Levite who visited a town with his concubine and was invited to stay in a man's house. Once there, the men of the city surrounded the house and demanded the Levite be sent outside so that they could have sex with him. Although the householder begged the men not to act so wickedly, they persisted, and finally the Levite sent his concubine out to the men of the city. They raped her all night long. In the morning, the Levite found his concubine lying dead on the steps, and the Bible very matter-of-factly states he cut her into twelve pieces and sent the twelve body parts to the twelve tribes of Israel. Israel then made war against that city and the tribe of Benjamin, who had protected them, resulting in a great slaughter.

6. I'm often asked why I don't go farther back to include what happened to the American Indians or to antebellum slavery or even to Genghis Khan. The reason I don't is because I have to stop someplace! Also, for younger people, going back even to 1900 is like ancient history. Going back to the beginnings of antebellum slavery or the displacement of American Indians is emotionally remote to most people today. Further, from 1900 on we have much greater documentation of the atrocities than we do those prior to 1900.

7. Dachau Museum Guidebook, accessed February 25, 2005, http://www.scrapbookpages.com/DachauMemorial/GuidebookText.html.

8. "Hermann Graebe: Evidence Testimony at Nuremberg War Crimes Trial," Holocaust Education & Archive Research Team, accessed August 19, 2016, http://www.holocaustresearch-project.org/einsatz/graebetest.html.

9. "Leuchter Report," Memorial and Museum: Auschwitz-Birkenau, Former German Nazi Concentration and Extermination Camp, accessed August 19, 2016, http://auschwitz.org/en/history/holocaust-denial/leuchter-report/.

10. Ronald H. Phelps, "Hitlers 'Grundlegende' Rede über den Antisemitismus," *VfZ* 16, no. 4 (1968): 412, as quoted in Daniel Jonah Goldhagen, *Hitler's Willing Executioners: Ordinary Germans and the Holocaust* (New York: Alfred A. Knopf, 1996), 424. Although I disagree with some of Goldhagen's conclusions, his facts are reliable.

11. Adolf Hitler, *Mein Kampf*, trans. Ralph Manheim (Boston: Houghton Mifflin, 1971), 679.

12. Konrad Heiden's introduction to *Mein Kampf* begins: "For years *Mein Kampf* stood as proof of the blindness and complacency of the world. For in its pages Hitler announced—long before he came to power—a program of blood and terror in a self-revelation of such overwhelming frankness that few among its readers had the courage to believe it. Once again it was demonstrated that there was no more effective method of concealment than the broadest publicity." Konrad Heiden "Introduction," in Hitler, *Mein Kampf*, xv.

13. Goldhagen, *Hitler's Willing Executioners*, 167.

14. "The United States Holocaust Memorial Museum Encyclopedia of Camps and Ghettos, 1933–1945," United States Holocaust Memorial Museum, accessed June 19, 2013, http://www.ushmm.org/research/center/encyclopedia/.

15. In 1995 the head of the Bayer corporation apologized for Bayer's participation in the Nazi genocide. Laurie Merrill, "Bayer Sorry for Nazi Role," *New York Daily News*, December 21, 1995, accessed August 9, 2016, http://www.nydailynews.com/archives/news/bayer-nazi-role-article-1.701925.

16. The 20-million figure comes from Stéphane Courtois, "Introduction: The Crimes of Communism," from Stéphane Courtois, Nicolas Werth, Jean-Louis Panné, Andrzej Paczkowski, Karel Bartošek, Jean-Louis Margolin, *The Black Book of Communism: Crimes, Terror, Repression*, trans. Jonathan Murphy and Mark Kramer (Cambridge: Harvard, 1999), 4, and Alexander N. Yakovlev, *A Century of Violence in Soviet Russia*, trans. Anthony Austin (New Haven: Yale, 2002), 234. Of course, these are estimates. Some, like R.J. Rummel, estimate that the number of total Soviet murders of civilians from 1917 to 1989 may reach 54,800,000. R.J. Rummel, "Soviet Union, Genocide In" *Encyclopedia of Genocide*, ed. Israel W. Charny (Santa Barbara, CA: ABC-CLIO, 1999), vol. 2, 520. Estimates vary widely. For example, the number of deaths attributed to the Great Terror of 1937–1938, according to Nicolas Werth, comes to 700,000, while Robert Conquest estimates that there were about 7 million arrests, 1 million executed, and another 2 million died in camps. Conquest says that there were about 8 million in the camps as of 1938. See Nicolas Werth, "From Tambov to the Great Famine" in Courtois, *The Black Book of Communism*, 202; and Robert Conquest, *The Great Terror: A Reassessment*, 40th Anniversary ed. (Oxford: Oxford University Press, 2008), 485-486. Conquest comments about his estimates: "The respected A. Adamovich has lately criticized me in a historians' 'round table' in *Literaturnaya gazeta*: 'always lowering the numbers of the repressed, he is simply unable to understand the true size of the fearful figures, to understand that one's own government could so torment the people.' It is true that I always described my figures as conservative; but hitherto, I have been more use to objectors finding them

unbelievably large" (487). Although there are some who, for various reasons, inflate the numbers of genocide and crimes against humanity, after studying this subject for many years, I would argue that most of the time the higher figures are more likely to be true. There is a revisionist move afoot that wants to minimize the numbers of genocide either because of liberal political leanings or because the revisionists want to downplay man's inhumanity to man.

17. James E. Mace, "Ukrainian Genocide," *Encyclopedia of Genocide*, vol. 2, ed. Israel Charney (Santa Barbara, CA: ABC-CLIO, 2000), 565. Roman Serbyn says the most plausible estimate is six million dead. Roman Serbyn, "Ukraine (Famine)," *Encyclopedia of Genocide and Crimes Against Humanity*, vol. 3, ed. Dinah Shelton (New York: Macmillan, 2004), 1059. Although it is difficult to prove Stalin's intent during the famine, as Serbyn puts it, "Stalin was not only well informed about the famine, he was its chief architect and overseer." Ibid.

18. R.J. Rummel, *Lethal Politics: Soviet Genocide and Mass Murder since 1917* (New Brunswick, NJ: Transaction Publishers, 1990), 87-88. This is also well documented by Jasper Becker: "In 1931, Stalin allowed relief grain to be delivered to drought-stricken areas and took other steps to alleviate the suffering caused by famine in all regions except the Ukraine. Instead, officials there went from house to house, ripping up the walls and floors and testing the ground for hidden reserves to find grain to meet procurement quotas…When the Ukrainian peasants became desperate in their search for food, militia were deployed to guard the grain stores and protect shipments of grain." Jasper Becker, *Hungry Ghosts: Mao's Secret Famine* (New York: Free Press, 1996), 42.

19. Victor Kravchenko, *I Chose Freedom: The Personal and Political Life of a Soviet Official* (New York: Charles Scribner's Sons, 1946), 118. Kravchenko tells of a woman who said, "A wagon goes around now and then to pick up the corpses. We've eaten everything we could lay our hands on—cats, dogs, field mice, birds. When it's light tomorrow you will see that the trees have been stripped of their bark, for that too has been eaten. And the horse manure has been eaten…Yes, the horse manure. We fight over it. Sometimes there are whole grains in it." Ibid., 113.

20. Jean-Louis Margolin "China: A long March into Night" in Courtois, *The Black Book of Communism*, 463-464. Margolin estimates that six to ten million were killed outright, with another twenty million dying in the camps.

21. Quoted in Li Cheng-Chung, *The Question of Human Rights on China Mainland* (Republic of China: World Anti-Communist League, China Chapter, September 1979), 12, as quoted in Becker, *Hungry Ghosts*, 145. Becker cites many cases of live burial.

22. Iris Chang, *The Rape of Nanking: The Forgotten Holocaust of World War II* (New York: Basic Books, 1998), 6.

23. Ibid., 221.

24. Philip Gourevitch, *We wish to inform you that tomorrow we will be killed with our families: stories from Rwanda* (New York: Farrar, Straus and Grioux, 1998), 3. The title of the book comes from an actual letter written from a Tutsi pastor to the Hutu head of his denomination asking for help. Help didn't come.

25. Vahakn N. Dadrian, "Armenians in Ottoman Turkey and the Armenian Genocide," *Encyclopedia of Genocide and Crimes Against Humanity*, vol. 1, 75.

26. Craig Etcheson, "Khmer Rouge Victim Numbers, Estimating," *Encyclopedia of Genocide and Crimes Against Humanity*, vol. 2, 617. See also Steve Heder, "Cambodia," *Encyclopedia of Genocide and Crimes Against Humanity*, vol. 1, 142. See also David Lamb, "Khmer Rouge

Defections Put Cambodia at Crossroads," *Los Angeles Times*, 31 December 1998, sec. A 2. The killings took place between 1975–1979.

27. David Stoll, "Guatemala," *Encyclopedia of Genocide and Crimes Against Humanity*, vol. 1, 419. Samuel Totten estimates that the number may be between 100,000 and 140,000. See Samuel Totten, "Guatemala, Genocide In," *Encyclopedia of Genocide*, vol. 1, 281. See also "In the wake of a four-decade old war, the Commission for Historical Clarification issued 'Guatemala: Memory of Silence.' Even for those who know the story well, the report's findings are shocking: More than 200,000 people were killed or disappeared during a period of armed conflict. In particular, between 1981 and 1983, a deliberate policy of genocide against the Mayan population was carried out by the Guatemalan state." From Michael Shifter, "Guatemala: Can Genocide End in Forgiveness?" *Los Angeles Times*, March 7, 1999, sec. M 2.

28. In South Africa "the commission received 21,296 statements involving 28,750 victims and 46,696 violations, of which 36,935 were deemed gross violations which involving killings, torture, severe ill treatment and abduction." The Truth and Reconciliation Commission, *The Truth and Reconciliation Commission of South Africa Report*, vol. 3, 3, accessed August 1, 2007, http://www.doj.gov.za/trc/trc_frameset.htm. Over 2900 people reported 5002 instances of torture, which included beatings, being forced into painful postures, electric shocks often to the genitals, and suffocations. Ibid., vol. 3, 7. Most South African torturers were security police who "clearly perceived themselves as authorized from above. Such people were praised, promoted, and received awards for such activities...It was not a job done unwillingly." Ibid., vol. 5, 300. The commission received reports of more than 1500 disappearances and the fate of 477 remains uncertain. Ibid., vol. 6, 519.

29. Craig Baxter, "Bangladesh/East Pakistan," *Encyclopedia of Genocide and Crimes Against Humanity*, vol. 1, 118, John P. Thorp, "Bangladesh, Genocide In," *Encyclopedia of Genocide*, vol. 1, 115. Thorp estimates that 250,000 women were raped. Bangladesh became a nation after this genocide.

30. A.B. Kasozi, "Uganda," *Encyclopedia of Genocide and Crimes Against Humanity*, vol. 3, 1053.

31. "Ahmad Qabazard was a nineteen-year-old Kuwaiti held by the Iraqis. An Iraqi officer told his parents he was about to be released. 'They were overjoyed, cooked wonderful things, and when they heard cars approaching went to the door. When Ahmad was taken out of the car, they saw that his ears, his nose, and his genitalia had been cut off. He was coming out of the car with his eyes in his hands. Then the Iraqis shot him, once in the stomach and once in the head, and told his mother to be sure not to move the body for three days.'" Report by Julie Flint, *Observer* (3 March 1991) as quoted in Jonathan Glover, *Humanity: A Moral History of the Twentieth Century* (New Haven, CT: Yale, 1999), 32.

32. Between 15,000 and 25,000 people "disappeared" between 1976 and 1983. Typically they were tortured (often naked with electric shocks delivered to the most sensitive parts of their bodies), and then most of them, on Wednesday nights, were flown out to sea on military aircraft, where they were drugged, stripped, and then hurled to their deaths never to be seen again (a few did later wash up on shore). Juan E. Mendez, "Argentina," *Encyclopedia of Genocide and Crimes Against Humanity*, vol. 1, 63, and James Brennan, "Argentina's Dirty Warriors," *Encyclopedia of Genocide and Crimes Against Humanity*, vol. 1, 65 (Brennan gives the figure of 9000 to 30,000). Patrick J. McDonnell, "Argentines Remember a Mother Who Joined the 'Disappeared.'" *Los Angeles Times*, March 25, 2006, sec. A 4. For a personal account of torture see Olga Talamante, "Surviving to tell the tale of torture," *Los Angeles*

Times, 25 March 2006, sec. B 17. Courtois puts the total number of deaths due to communism in Latin America at 150,000. Courtois, *The Black Book of Communism*, 4.

33. International Commission on the Holocaust in Romania, *Final Report*, November 11, 2004, accessed July 25, 2007, http://www.ushmm.org/research/center/presentations/features/details/2005-03-10/pdf/english/chapter_05.pdf. Romania was second only to Germany for murder of Jews.

34. Giles Tremlet, "Inquiry into Spain's missing children," *The Guardian*, January 9, 2009, accessed August 19, 2016, http://www.guardian.co.uk/world/2009/jan/09/spain-missing-children-franco.

35. "In 1957 the International Red Cross disclosed the widespread use of torture by the French army and police against thousands of Algerians." Azzedine Layachi, "Algeria," *Encyclopedia of Genocide and Crimes Against Humanity*, vol. 1, 17.

36. For a thorough analysis regarding how much the world has known about particular genocides while they were going on but failed to act, see Samantha Power, *A Problem from Hell* (New York: Harper Perennial, 2003).

37. "Abortion Statistics: United States Data & Trends," National Right to Life Committee, accessed August 22, 2016, http://www.nrlc.org/uploads/factsheets/FS01AbortionintheUS.pdf. By "scalding" I'm referring to chemical abortions. The former Surgeon General C. Everett Koop and apologist Francis A. Schaeffer describe a common abortion method, saline abortion, which "is usually carried out after sixteen weeks of pregnancy, when enough amniotic fluid has accumulated in the sac around the baby. A long needle is inserted through the mother's abdomen directly into the sac, and a solution of concentrated salt is injected into the amniotic fluid. The salt solution is absorbed both through the lungs and the gastrointestinal tract, producing changes in the osmotic pressure. The outer layer of skin is burned off by the high concentration of salt. It takes about an hour to kill the baby by this slow method. The mother usually goes into labor about a day later and delivers a dead, shriveled baby." C. Everett Koop and Francis A. Schaeffer, *Whatever Happened to the Human Race?* (Old Tappan, NJ: Revell, 1979), 41.

38. Warren M. Hern, *Abortion Practice* (Philadelphia: J.B. Lippincott, 1990), 114. For an excellent treatment of the abortion issue see Francis J. Beckwith, *Defending Life: A Moral and Legal Case Against Abortion Choice* (Cambridge: Cambridge University Press, 2007).

39. If you have encouraged someone to have an abortion, voted for those who would keep the practice legal, or if you have had an abortion yourself, then God can forgive you too if you repent.

40. That a human life doesn't start at conception isn't really a scientifically arguable point. "There is no credible scientific opposition to the fact that a genetically distinct human life begins at conception and that an induced abortion is a death." James Studnicki, Sharon J. MacKinnon, and John W. Fisher, "Induced Abortion, Mortality, and the Conduct of Science," *Open Journal of Preventive Medicine* (June 2016), 170, accessed August 27, 2016, http://file.scirp.org/pdf/OJPM_2016061708580294.pdf.

41. But it's not just abortion. Consider American entertainment. Video games also exploit murder and more. One user reports that in the wildly popular Grand Theft Auto 4 "you, as the player, are Niko Bellic, a young immigrant who...was party to a war-crime atrocity...and it is strongly suggested that he once dabbled in human trafficking. 'I did some dumb things...' Niko says," and his friend replies, "We all do dumb things...That's what makes us human."

The user reports "stomping the last remaining vitality from a hapless construction worker's blood-squirting body" and that the game was "awesomely gratuitous. Never has a game felt so narcotic." Tom Bissell, "My virtual downfall," *The Week*, April 16, 2010, 41.

Rightfully there's been moral outrage recently over a video game, formerly sold by Amazon.com, named *Rapelay* that has gone viral. To win, the player must rape a mother and/or her two daughters and then force whomever he rapes to have an abortion. See Kyung Lah, "'Rapelay' video game goes viral amid outrage," CNN, March 31, 2010, accessed April 27, 2010, http://www.cnn.com/2010/WORLD/asiapcf/03/30/japan.video.game.rape/index.html. This is horrendous, but as one person on a gaming blog posted, "How is rape worse than murder? We have murder in our games all the time." Indeed, he's correct, although I suspect he got the application wrong. "CNN Travels Back in Time to Discover Rapelay Controversy," Destructoid, accessed April 25, 2010, http://www.destructoid.com/cnn-travels-back-in-time-discovers-rapelay-controversy-169388.phtml. As Matthew Moore put it, "Rapelay, which was released in 2006, encourages players to force the virtual woman they rape to have an abortion. If they are allowed to give birth, the woman throws the player's character under a train, according to reviews of the game. It also has a feature allowing several players to team up against individual women." Matthew Moore, "Rapelay virtual rape game banned by Amazon," *Telegraph*, February 13, 2009, accessed April 25, 2010, http://www.telegraph.co.uk/technology/4611161/Rapelay-virtual-rape-game-banned-by-Amazon.html.

Then there's the plethora of chainsaw, slasher, mutilation, and other films called gore or splatter cinema. When sexually suggestive material is mixed in, the genre is called torture porn, or gorno (a cross between gore and porno). And much of this enjoyment is mainstream. Consider a movie like *Silence of the Lambs,* about a serial killer cannibal who enjoys human liver with "a nice Chianti"; the FBI enlists his help to find another serial killer who likes to skin women alive. *Silence of the Lambs* won the top five Academy Awards and was followed by three sequels. One of the few film critics to pan it wrote, "Yes, the picture is tactfully made, but the question remains, why make it at all? The skilled craftsmanship and the directorial restraint can't change what the film is—a thoroughly morbid and meaningless depiction of the *modus operandi* of a couple of sadists...We know these kinds of madmen exist, but the film offers no insight into what makes them tick..." Stephen Farber, "Why Do Critics Love These Repellent Movies?," *Los Angeles Times*, March 17, 1991, sec. E 5, as quoted in Medved, *Hollywood vs. America: Popular Culture and the War on Tradition* (New York: HarperCollins, 1992), 162.

42. In one of the experiments, Milgram records that at 330 volts the learner/actor responds: "(*Intense and prolonged agonized scream.*) Let me out of here. Let me out of here. My heart's bothering me. Let me out, I tell you. (*Hysterically*) Let me out of here. Let me out of here. You have no right to hold me here." But, says Milgram, even the mention of a heart condition makes no difference in the shocks administered by the 'teacher.'" 57.

43. Milgram also found no difference between the sexes: 65 percent of females also administered the highest level of shock. Arthur G. Miller in his review of Milgram's work, comments: "One cannot fail to be impressed with the sheer scope of Milgram's research effort. Approximately 1,000 individuals participated in the obedience research program...These individuals were, in virtually all instances, observed on an individual basis! It is perhaps unmatched in the social sciences for a single investigator to obtain this kind of extensive data from one paradigm, within the relatively brief time frame (three years) in which the experiments took place. Whatever reservations the reader might have concerning one or another aspect of Milgram's procedures or interpretations, there is, at least, an abundance of

empirical evidence. One is thus not likely to be uncertain as to the reliability of his results." Arthur G. Miller, *The Obedience Experiments: A Case Study of the Controversy in Social Science* (New York: Praeger, 1986), 63.

44. D.M. Mantell, "The Potential for Violence in Germany," *Journal of Social Issues* 27:110-11, as quoted in Arthur G. Miller, *The Obedience Experiments: A Case Study of the Controversy in Social Science* (New York: Praeger, 1986), 70. Mantell: "It would seem that nearly everyone is willing to commit acts of aggression against other people. The differences which appear in their behavior have less to do with whether they will hurt others or not, but rather under what conditions (110)." As quoted in Miller, 69-70.

45. Some people want to insist that those with a normal upbringing couldn't do these things. They want to believe in basic human goodness. But, alas, that is just simply false.

46. "Power is a poison well known for thousands of years. If only no one were ever to acquire material power over others! But to the human being who has faith in some force that holds dominion over all of us, and who is therefore conscious of his own limitations, power is not necessarily fatal. For those, however, who are unaware of any higher sphere, it is a deadly poison. For them there is no antidote." Alexander Solzhenitsyn, *The Gulag Archipelago 1918–1956,* trans. Thomas P. Whitney and Harry Willetts, abridged, Edward E. Ericson, Jr. (New York: Harper Perennial, 2007), 147.

47. Hannah Arndt, *Eichmann in Jerusalem: A Report on the Banality of Evil* (New York: Penguin, 1994, reprint 1963), 277.

48. Charny, *How can we commit the unthinkable?*, 3.

49. Fred E. Katz, *Ordinary People and Extraordinary Evil: A Report on the Beguilings of Evil* (New York: State University of New York, 1993), 10. You can watch his story here: "Jewish Survivor Fred Katz Testimony," USC Shoah Foundation, April 6, 2012, accessed August 26, 2016, https://www.youtube.com/watch?v=3K9FT1Sh4PI.

50. Ibid., 11.

51. Christopher R. Browning, *Ordinary Men: Reserve Police Battalion 101 and the Final Solution in Poland* (New York: HarperCollins, 1992), xx.

52. Browning writes that the "general problem" with the "explanation" that people killed because they were afraid of dire consequences is that "quite simply, in the past forty-five years no defense attorney or defendant in any of the hundreds of postwar trials has been able to document a single case in which refusal to obey an order to kill unarmed civilians resulted in the allegedly inevitable dire punishment." Ibid., 170. Also, "For large actions, those who would not kill were not compelled. Even officers' attempts to force individual nonshooters to kill could be refused." Ibid., 171.

53. Langdon Gilkey, *Shantung Compound: The Story of Men and Women Under Pressure* (San Francisco: Harper, 1966), 92. Gilkey continues, "What is unique about human existence 'on the margin' is not that people's characters change for better or worse, for they do not. It is that the importance and so the 'emotional voltage' of every issue is increased greatly. Now much more vulnerable than before, we are more inclined to be aware of our own interests, more frightened if they are threatened, and thus much more determined to protect them. A marginal existence neither improves men nor makes them wicked; it places a premium on every action, and in doing so reveals the actual inward character that every man has always possessed." Ibid. After years in the camp, Gilkey writes that he began to recall some theological ideas of his past and "among the most relevant, it now seemed, was the old idea of

original sin...Few of us wish to or can believe that their [Adam and Eve's] one act of disobedience brought about a fall for the whole race continued in us by inheritance...Yet, when one looks at the actual social behavior of people, this theological notion of a common, pervasive warping of our wills away from the good we wish to achieve is more descriptive of our actual experience of ourselves than is any other assessment of our situation. What the doctrine of sin has said about man's present state seemed to fit the facts as I found them." Ibid., 115-116.

54. Ibid., 92.

55. Elie Wiesel, *One Generation After* (New York: Random House, 2011), 5.

56. Ibid., 5-6.

57. Ibid., 6.

58. Elie Wiesel, *The Town Beyond the Wall*, trans. Stephen Barker (New York: Avon, 1970), 174.

59. Primo Levi, *The Reawakening* (Columbia, MO: University of Missouri, 1995), 228. Consider the title of a book by Holocaust survivor Fred Emil Katz: *Ordinary People and Extraordinary Evil.*

60. Harald Welzer, "On Killing and Morality: How Normal People Become Mass Murderers," *Ordinary People as Mass Murderers: Perpetrators in Comparative Perspective*, eds. Olaf Jensen and Claus-Christian W. Szejnmann (New York: Macmillan, 2008), 148-149.

61. Ibid., 187. Zygmunt Bauman writes that "the Nazis *could* count on Jewish co-operation and hence on perpetrating the murderous operation with the deployment of only a residual force of their own." Zygmunt Bauman, *Modernity and the Holocaust* (Ithaca, NY: Cornell, 2000), 118. For those who want to read more on Jewish participation, Bauman's book is a good place to begin, especially pages 117-150.

62. Solzhenitsyn, *The Gulag Archipelago*, 73.

Chapter 3—Are There No Good People?

1. Mark 10:18.

2. In my earlier conceptions of this book I was going to include a chapter on the Crusades, Inquisitions, witch-hunts, slavery, Nazi Christians, and the oppression of women, but decided not to as these are not traditional problem-of-evil issues. I teach on this in my class "Why God Allows Evil" because if Christians have the good news then why do they often appear to be such bad news for society? I do have two blog posts on this (more will follow). See "Crusades, Inquisitions, Witch-Hunts, etc." http://www.clayjones.net/2014/04/crusades-inquisitions-witch-hunts-etc/. See also "The Truth about the Crusades," http://www.clayjones.net/2014/04/the-truth-about-the-crusades/; "Women's Liberation and Female Unhappiness," http://www.clayjones.net/2011/06/woman%e2%80%99s-%e2%80%9cliberation%e2%80%9d-and-female-unhappiness/.

3. I've found when I teach this that some Christians worry because they find themselves so often sinning. But the fact that they are worried about their sin shows that they have been born again. Before I was a Christian, I didn't worry about sin: I only worried about being caught. To those who struggle with sin I say, "Take heart!" As Jesus said in Matthew 5:6, "Blessed are those who hunger and thirst for righteousness, for they shall be satisfied."

4. Matthew 5:28.

5. 1 John 3:15.

6. Someone might object that a hater might refrain from murder because that hater has a sense that murder is wrong. But why would it being "wrong" stop him? I suspect that if the hater's vague sense of "wrong" were unpacked that it would amount to the same thing as "be illegal" or societally unacceptable, both of which would involve undesirable consequences for the hater to actually murder.

7. Romans 3:12-15 NIV.

8. Luke 18:19. Some will appeal to Genesis 6:9, that "Noah was a righteous man, blameless in his generation. Noah walked with God." But that doesn't mean Noah was sinless or didn't inherit a sinful nature. Rather, we are told that "the righteous will live by faith" (Galatians 3:11) and in Hebrews 11:7 we are told, "By faith Noah, being warned by God concerning events as yet unseen, in reverent fear constructed an ark for the saving of his household. By this he condemned the world and became *an heir of the righteousness that comes by faith.*" Also, if righteous perfection were available through our own effort then Jesus didn't need to die. As Paul said in Galatians 2:21, "I do not nullify the grace of God, for if righteousness were through the law, then Christ died for no purpose." Beeson Divinity School professor of Old Testament and Hebrew, Allen P. Ross, explains who the "righteous" are: "The basic meaning of "righteous" has to do with conforming to the standard; in religious passages that standard is divine revelation. The righteous are people who have entered into covenant with God by faith and seek to live according to his word. The covenant that they have makes them the people of God—God knows them, and because God knows them, they shall never perish. They may do unrighteous things at times, but they know to find forgiveness because they want to do what is right." Allen P. Ross, *A Commentary on the Psalms: Volume I, 1-41* (Grand Rapids: Kregel, 2011), 193-194. For a related discussion see Jean E. Jones, "Who Are 'the Righteous' in Psalms and Proverbs?," JeanEJones.net, July 17, 2013, accessed September 12, 2016, http://www.jeanejones.net/2013/07/who-are-the-righteous-in-psalms-and-proverbs/.

9. Jad Adams, "Thrill of the Chaste: The Truth about Gandhi's Sex Life," *The Independent*, April 7, 2010, http://www.independent.co.uk/arts-entertainment/books/features/thrill-of-the-chaste-the-truth-about-gandhis-sex-life-1937411.html.

10. See Hannah Arndt, *Eichmann in Jerusalem: A Report on the Banality of Evil* (New York: Penguin, 1994). Arndt reports, "According to his religious beliefs, which had not changed since the Nazi period (in Jerusalem Eichmann declared himself to be a *Gottgläubiger*, the Nazi term for those who had broken with Christianity, and he refused to take his oath on the Bible), this event was to be described to 'a higher Bearer of Meaning,' an entity somehow identical with the 'movement of the universe,' to which human life, in itself devoid of 'higher meaning,' is subject." Ibid., 27. Arndt reports that at the gallows "he began by stating emphatically that he was a *Gottgläubiger*, to express in common Nazi fashion that he was no Christian and did not believe in life after death." Ibid., 252.

11. David Chandler writes: "Schoolmates remembered him as a mediocre student but pleasant company, a reputation that persisted among those who knew him in France. As a teacher, he was remembered as calm, self-assured, smooth featured...honest, and persuasive, even hypnotic when speaking to small groups...A man who met him in the late 1950s, for example, said, 'I saw immediately that I could become his friend for life.'" David P. Chandler, *Brother Number One: A Political Biography of Pol Pot* (Boulder, CO: Westview, 1992), 5.

12. C.S. Lewis, *The Problem of Pain* (New York: Macmillan, 1943), 44.

13. Luke 6:32-34 NIV.

14. Matthew 23:27.

15. Luke 12:1.

16. Sam Keen, "Foreword" in Ernest Becker, *The Denial of Death* (New York: Free Press, 1973), xiii.

17. Becker, *The Denial of Death*, 6.

18. Ibid.

19. See chapter 2 for a fuller discussion on original sin.

20. Augustine, *Confessions*, 1:7.

21. A Google search of "jealous baby" produced 23,900,000 results on August 9, 2016, and many of them are videos.

22. D.A. Carson, *How Long, O Lord?: Reflections on Suffering and Evil* (Grand Rapids: Baker, 1990), 66-67.

23. NIV. In Jesus' time, and the ages prior to Jesus, all one needed to do to understand human depravity was look at the nations surrounding Israel. The early Christians, because of their condemnation of sin, were known as "haters of humankind." Tacitus's *Annals* 15.44 http://classics.mit.edu/Tacitus/annals.11.xv.html. This is also the proper way to handle the gospel. As C.F.W. Walther put it, "The Law is to be preached to secure sinners and the Gospel to alarmed sinners...As long as a person is at ease in his sins, as long as he is unwilling to quit some particular sin, so long only the Law, which curses and condemns him, is to be preached to him. However the moment he becomes frightened at his condition, the Gospel is to be promptly administered to him; for from that moment on he no longer can be classified with secure sinners." C.F.W. Walther, *The Proper Distinction of Law and Gospel*, trans. W.H.T. Dau (St. Louis, MO: Concordia, 1929), 17.

24. Of course this message is completely at odds with the self-esteem movement. As self-esteem advocate and psychologist Nathaniel Brandon wrote, "The idea of Original Sin is anti-self-esteem by its very nature." Nathaniel Brandon, *Six Pillars of Self-Esteem* (New York: Bantam, 1994), 148. Even many Christians reject talk about human wickedness. Robert Schuller wrote that original sin "could be considered an innate inability to adequately value ourselves. Label it a 'negative self-image,' but do not say that the central core of the human soul is wickedness. If this were so, then truly, the human being is totally depraved. But positive Christianity does not hold to human depravity, but to human inability. I am humanly unable to correct my negative self-image until I encounter a life-changing experience with nonjudgmental love bestowed upon me by a Person whom I admire so much that to be unconditionally accepted by him is to be born again." Robert H. Schuller, *Self Esteem: The New Reformation* (Waco, TX: Word, 1982), 67. In a letter to the editor of *Christianity Today*, Schuller wrote, "I don't think anything has been done in the name of Christ and under the banner of Christianity that has proven more destructive to human personality and, hence, counterproductive to the evangelism enterprise than the often crude, uncouth, and unchristian strategy of attempting to make people aware of their lost and sinful condition." Robert H. Schuller, "Eutychus & His Kin," *Christianity Today*, October 4, 1984, 12.

25. People often ask if God is responsible for creating creatures that He knows would commit so much evil. The answer to that is no, He's not responsible. This will be examined in the chapter on free will.

26. This will be examined in the chapter "Is Free Will Worth It?"

27. Elie Wiesel, *Night*, trans. Marion Wiesel (New York: Hill & Wang, 2006), xv. Elie Wiesel considered it a "moral obligation to try to prevent the enemy from enjoying one last victory by allowing his crimes to be erased from human memory." Wiesel, *Night*, viii.

28. Thanks to Joseph E. Gorra for added perspective on this point.

29. See the introduction for a precise definition of evil and the so-called problem of evil.

30. This is examined in the chapter on hell.

31. Lewis, *Problem of Pain,* 46.

32. Miroslav Volf, *Free of Charge: Giving and Forgiving in a Culture Stripped of Grace* (Grand Rapids: Zondervan, 2005), 139.

33. Ibid.

34. Psalm 14:1: "The fool says in his heart, 'There is no God.'" Luke 12:3-5: "Therefore whatever you have said in the dark shall be heard in the light, and what you have whispered in private rooms shall be proclaimed on the housetops. I tell you, my friends, do not fear those who kill the body, and after that have nothing more that they can do. But I will warn you whom to fear: fear him who, after he has killed, has authority to cast into hell. Yes, I tell you, fear him!"

35. Those who comprehend the sinful nature of humankind will reject socialism because selfish humans will not work hard unless they believe they will be rewarded for their hard work. This is well illustrated by the fact that while the West Germans were making the Mercedes Benz, BMW, and Porsche, the east Germans were making the Trabant. Dan Neil on the Trabant: "This is the car that gave Communism a bad name. Powered by a two-stroke pollution generator that maxed out at an ear-splitting 18 hp, the Trabant was a hollow lie of a car constructed of recycled worthlessness (actually, the body was made of a fiberglass-like Duroplast, reinforced with recycled fibers like cotton and wood). A virtual antique when it was designed in the 1950s, the Trabant was East Germany's answer to the VW Beetle— a 'people's car,' as if the people didn't have enough to worry about. Trabants smoked like an Iraqi oil fire, when they ran at all, and often lacked even the most basic of amenities, like brake lights or turn signals. But history has been kind to the Trabi. Thousands of East Germans drove their Trabants over the border when the Wall fell, which made it a kind of automotive liberator. Once across the border, the none-too-sentimental Ostdeutschlanders immediately abandoned their cars. Ich bin Junk!" Dan Neil, "The 50 Worst Cars of All Time," *Time.com*, accessed April 8, 2011, http://www.time.com/time/specials/2007/article/0,28804,1658545_1658533_1658030,00.html#ixzz1IxseJ0Ku. Also, understanding the depths of human sinfulness leads people to desire a robust police force and a strong military. They recognize that those bent on evil will only be motivated by a fear of consequences.

36. Romans 5:7.

37. Millard J. Erickson, *Christian Theology*, 2d ed. (Grand Rapids: Baker, 1998), 456.

38. Thanks again to Joseph E. Gorra for his additional insight on this point.

39. R.C. Sproul, Jr., 2011 Ligonier National Conference, Session 6, March 25, 2011, accessed September 12, 2016, http://www.ligonier.org/blog/2011-ligonier-national-conference-session-6-rc-sproul-jr/.

40. See Ephesians 2:1-7; Romans 6:17; 1 Corinthians 6:19.

Chapter 4—What Is the Destiny of the Unevangelized?

1. Michael Martin, "Problems with Heaven," in *The Myth of an Afterlife: The Case Against Life After Death*, eds. Michael Martin and Keith Augustine (Lanham, MD: Rowman and Little-field, 2015), 432. Similarly, Elton Trueblood writes, "What kind of God is it who consigns men and women and children to eternal torment, in spite of the fact that they have not had even a remote chance of knowing the saving truth?" Elton Trueblood, *Philosophy of Religion* (New York: Harper and Row, 1957), 221f.

2. C.S. Lewis, *Mere Christianity* (San Francisco: HarperCollins, 1952), 64.

3. See John 14:6; Romans 10:9-10; Acts 4:12. It is outside the scope of this book to present a defense of what is popularly called exclusivism. For more see John Piper, *Let the Nations Be Glad: The Supremacy of God in Missions* (Grand Rapids: Baker, 1993), 115-166; Millard Erickson, *How Shall They Be Saved: The Destiny of Those Who Do Not Hear of Jesus* (Grand Rapids: Baker, 1996); Dennis L. Okholm and Timothy R. Phillips, eds., *Four Views on Salvation in a Pluralistic World* (Grand Rapids: Zondervan, 1995).

4. Paul Marshall and Lela Gilbert, *Their Blood Cries Out: The Worldwide Tragedy of Modern Christians Who Are Dying for Their Faith* (Dallas: Word, 1997), 7-8.

5. Ibid., 8.

6. Paul Zacharia, "The Surprisingly Early History of Christianity in India," *Smithsonian Journeys Quarterly*, February 19, 2016, Smithsonian.com, accessed August 1, 2016, http://www.smithsonianmag.com/travel/how-christianity-came-to-india-kerala-180958117/?no-ist.

7. "Christian Designs Found in Tomb Stones of Eastern Han Dynasty," Travel in China, accessed August 1, 2016, http://www.china.org.cn/english/TR-e/38507.htm.

8. Marshall, *Their Blood Cries Out*, 8.

9. "Syria," *The World Factbook*, Central Intelligence Agency (accessed August 1, 2016), https://www.cia.gov/library/publications/the-world-factbook/geos/sy.html. "Turkey," Ibid., https://www.cia.gov/library/publications/the-world-factbook/geos/tu.html.

10. "India, World Watch List Rank: 17," Open Doors. Accessed August 23, 2016, http://www.opendoorsuk.org/persecution/worldwatch/india.php.

11. Michael Fischer, "The Fiery Rise of Hindu Fundamentalism," *Christianity Today*, March 1, 1999, 47.

12. Agency for Cultural Affairs of the Ministry of Education in Japan, *Japanese Religion: A Survey by the Agency for Cultural Affairs*, trans. Yoshiya Abe, David Reid, eds. Ichiro Hori, Fujio Ikado, Tsuneya Wakimoto, Keiichi Yanagawa (Tokyo: Kodansha, 1974), 76.

13. Agency for Cultural Affairs, *Japanese Religion*, 76.

14. Frank Chalk and Kurt Jonassohn, *The History and Sociology of Genocide: Analyses and Case Studies* (New Haven: Yale, 1990), 147.

15. Agency for Cultural Affairs, *Japanese Religion*, 84.

16. James and Marti Hefley, *By Their Blood: Christian Martyrs of the Twentieth Century* (Grand Rapids: Baker, 1996), 15.

17. Ibid., 28.

18. *China: Religious Freedom Denied* (Washington: Puebla Institute, 1994), 13. The Puebla Institute does not provide the name of the publication.

19. Since Calvinists hold to divine election, this answer is no problem for them. God makes sure the elect hear the gospel. Case closed. This answer also works for many Arminians, especially those who hold to middle knowledge as God knows who would or would not repent given the opportunity and He can make sure that those who would repent will have the opportunity.

    From the Arminian perspective, Douglas Geivett and Gary Phillips point out, "If there are no persons who never hear but would believe if they did hear (because all who would believe have heard), then we fail to see the "appalling moral difficulty." We would not be surprised if the majority of those who do hear withhold belief in Jesus Christ and remain unsaved, nor would we be prepared to blame God for this outcome of human freedom." Dennis L. Okholm and Timothy R. Phillips, eds., *Four Views on Salvation in a Pluralistic World* (Grand Rapids: Zondervan, 1995), 261.

    Paul Copan employs middle knowledge to make a different kind of answer to the problem of the destiny of the unevangelized: "God has created the (actual) world in which no one is condemned due to the accidents of birth or geography. Therein we have an affirmation of both divine sovereignty and genuine (divinely bestowed) creaturely freedom. What of those who never hear the gospel? Perhaps God's world-arrangement includes those who never hear the gospel since they wouldn't have embraced it even if they'd heard it. In fact, they never would have embraced the gospel in any possible world he could have created. In God's sovereignty, no person would be born into an unreached region or people group if she would have freely responded to the Gospel." Paul Copan, *True for You, But Not for Me: Overcoming Objections to Christian Faith*, rev. ed. (Minneapolis: Bethany House, 2009), 208-209.

    William Lane Craig: "An all-loving God would make sure that the light of the gospel, to which he knows they would respond, would reach such persons. The reader will undoubtedly have surmised the way out of this dilemma: It is possible that God in his providence so arranged the world that those who never in fact hear the gospel are persons who would not respond to it if they did hear it. God brings the gospel to all those who he knows will respond to it if they hear it. Thus the motivation for the missionary enterprise is to be God's ambassadors in bringing the gospel to those whom God has arranged to freely receive it when they hear it. No one who would respond if he heard it will be lost." William Lane Craig, *The Only Wise God: The Compatibility of Divine Foreknowledge and Human Freedom* (Eugene, OR: Wipf & Stock, 2000), 150-151.

20. Of course, skeptics complain that this never happened because the story is so unlikely, but we should remind them that the naturalist believes that the universe popped into existence out of nothing uncaused. On the other hand, if God created the universe out of nothing, then something like this is small change.

21. Joel C. Rosenberg, *Inside the Revolution: How the Followers of Jihad, Jefferson & Jesus Are Battling to Dominate the Middle East and Transform the World* (Carol Stream, IL: Tyndale, 2009), 369.

22. Some, like John Piper, object to this because, as Piper put it, "The Gospel needs to be heard. How shall they believe unless they hear and how shall they hear without a preacher and how shall they preach unless they be sent? That's a pretty significant argument in Romans 10." Url Scaramanga, "John Piper 'Suspicious' of Muslim Dreams of Jesus," *Leadership Journal* (November 2011), http://www.christianitytoday.com/le/2011/november-online-only/john-piper-suspicious-of-muslim-dreams-of-jesus.html, accessed August 2, 2016. But that's

a rather narrow interpretation of *hear*. Does Piper believe that the only way one can come to Christ is through a literal *auditory* experience of hearing a *human* proclaim the gospel? On that view, can completely deaf people come to Jesus when they literally can't hear? What about those blind and deaf—can they get the gospel? Also, let's remember that in Acts 9 it was Jesus who chose to directly give Saul the message that led to his repentance. Saul didn't repent because he heard the message from humans. Further, what are we to tell those who now have a very real relationship with Jesus but came to him through a dream or vision? If those visions or dreams didn't come from God then where did they come from? Satan? Pizza? Of course not—God is sovereign.

23. Jerry L. Walls, *Heaven: The Logic of Eternal Joy* (Oxford: Oxford University Press, 2002), 72. Emphasis mine.

24. Phillip Connor, "6 facts about South Korea's growing Christian population," Pew Resarch Center, August 12, 2014, accessed August 2, 2016, http://www.pewresearch.org/fact-tank/2014/08/12/6-facts-about-christianity-in-south-korea/.

25. Luke 4:24b-27 NIV.

26. Luke 4:29 NIV.

27. Dave Hazzan, "Christianity and Korea: How did the religion become so apparently prevalent in South Korea?" *The Diplomat*, April 7, 2016, accessed August 2, 2016, http://thedip-lomat.com/2016/04/christianity-and-korea/.

28. Richard Dawkins, *The God Delusion* (Boston: Houghton Mifflin, 2006), 240.

29. Of course Calvinists wouldn't emphasize opportunity, as they hold that no one would come except God specifically elect them.

30. John S. Feinberg, *The Many Faces of Evil: Theological Systems and the Problems of Evil*, rev. ed. (Wheaton, IL: Crossway, 2004), 436.

31. In fact, atheists are sadly dishonest. What I mean is that to believe that the universe popped into existence, out of nothing, uncaused; that the formation of first life is astronomically lucky; and that the reason that our universe exists in such a way as to support human life is luck is dishonest. For more on this see Clay Jones and Joseph E. Gorra, "The Folly of Answering Distracting Atheist Arguments," *Christian Research Journal* 36-4 (2013), http://www.equip.org/article/folly-answering-distracting-atheistic-arguments/. Also see Clay Jones, "God or 'We Got Lucky,'" Clay Jones blog, July 25, 2011, http://www.clayjones.net/2011/07/god-or-%E2%80%9Cwe-got-lucky%E2%80%9D/.

32. Ibid., 437.

33. Ibid., 439.

34. See Norman Geisler, "What About Those Who Die Before the Age of Accountability?" *The John Ankerberg Show*, 2003, accessed January 15, 2015, https://www.youtube.com/watch?v=hFEUUUgN9tA&list=PLhZsAfleY-EY03_t8elVPxY_FV09Hb-wi&index=6; William Lane Craig, "Q & A with William Lane Craig #23—Middle Knowledge," *Reasonable Faith*, September 24, 2007, accessed January 15, 2015, http://www.reasonablefaith.org/middle-knowledge; Greg Koukl, "The Canaanites: Genocide or Judgment?" *Solid Ground*, January/February 2013, 8.

35. NASB.

36. Millard Erickson, *How Shall They Be Saved? The Destiny of Those Who Do Not Hear of Jesus* (Grand Rapids: Baker, 1996), 238.

37. Christopher W. Morgan and Robert A. Peterson, *Faith Comes by Hearing: A Response to Inclusivism* (Downers Grove, IL: InterVarsity, 2008), 243-244. For the rationale that theologians provide for the salvation of children see the following: Ronald Nash: "Infants are innocent in the sense that whatever their natural disposition to sin may be, their status as infants makes it impossible for them to know or understand the things that would be necessary for them to perform good or evil acts. Therefore, they are not moral agents." Ronald H. Nash, *When a Baby Dies: Answers to Comfort Grieving Parents* (Grand Rapids: Zondervan, 1999), 60. R.A. Webb: "It appears from these, and a multitude of similar statements that future and final retribution will be graduated according to 'the deeds done in the body'; but infants have been prevented by the providence of God from committing any responsible deeds of any sort in the body, and consequently infants are not damnable upon *these premises*; and there is no account in Scripture of any other judgment based upon any other grounds." R.A. Webb, *The Theology of Infant Salvation* (Richmond, VA: Presbyterian, 1907), 42. Emphasis his. Also see, M.J. Firey, *Infant Salvation: The Passivity of Infants the Key to This Perplexing Subject* (New York: Funk & Wagnalls, 1902).

38. Augustine, *On Free Choice of the Will*, trans. Anna Benjamin and L.H. Hackstaff (New York: Bobbs-Merrill, 1964), book III, ch. 23, 141. Augustine is referring to Matthew 2:16.

39. This section on the salvation of children was adapted from Clay Jones, "Why Did God Let That Child Die?" *Christian Research Journal* 38-1 (2015), 14-15.

Chapter 5—How Can Eternal Punishment Be Fair?

1. It is outside the scope of this book to defend the teaching of eternal punishment.

2. David L. Edwards and John Stott, *Evangelical Essentials: A Liberal-Evangelical Dialogue* (Downers Grove: InterVarsity, 1988), 314.

3. Feinberg: "It isn't at all clear that eternal separation from God in hell is an inappropriate punishment for someone who spurns God's love altogether. Humans tend to think otherwise but that doesn't make it so. That only shows how different our perspectives are from God's. Hence, when one considers God's absolute holiness plus the creature's inability to appreciate how inappropriate sin is, it isn't clear that sin is as insignificant as we treat it or that hell is as unjust as punishment for rejecting God as many think it to be. John S. Feinberg, *The Many Faces of Evil: Theological Systems and the Problem of Evil* (Wheaton, IL: Crossway, 2004), 435.

4. Revelation 12:7.

5. I write "*all* human rebellion" because once a being has decided that God is mistaken on any point, regardless of how small, and decides to take matters into his own hands, then that person is a rebel through and through. The only reason that being isn't rebelling against other commands is just that he has decided that God happens to be right about those other commands.

6. Robert A. Peterson, *Hell on Trial: The Case for Eternal Punishment* (Phillipsburg, NJ: P&R Publishing, 1995), 192.

7. John Blanchard, *Whatever Happened to Hell?* (Wheaton, IL: Crossway, 1995), 160. Blanchard goes on to point out, "Again, when the Bible speaks of 'the wine of God's fury' (Revelation 14:10) it is surely not saying that God's anger is either liquid or alcoholic?" Similarly, Princeton scholar Charles Hodge wrote, "There seems no more reason for supposing that the fire spoken of in Scripture is to be literal fire, than that the worm that never dies is literally a worm." Charles Hodge, *Systematic Theology* (New York: Scribner's, 1876), 3:868.

8. D.A. Carson, *The Gagging of God: Christianity Confronts Pluralism* (Grand Rapids: Zonder-van, 2009), 531, Kindle Edition. Carson: "Most interpreters recognize that there is a sub-stantial metaphorical element in the Bible's descriptions of hell. This does not mean that hell itself is merely metaphorical: one must not infer from the fact that someone thinks that many of the descriptions of hell are metaphorical and not literal the conclusion that hell itself is not literal. Hell is real; the question is how far the descriptions of it are to be taken literally. Normally, we do not think of unquenchable fire and worms coexisting: the former will devour the latter as easily as they will consume people. It is hard to imagine how a lake of fire coexists with utter darkness. And if one is cast into a lake of fire, what need of chains?" Ibid. Likewise, Princeton scholar Charles Hodge wrote, "There seems no more reason for supposing that the fire spoken of in Scripture is to be literal fire, than that the worm that never dies is literally a worm." Charles Hodge, *Systematic Theology* (New York: Scribner's, 1876), 3:868. D.A. Carson: "This is not to deny that some speculations as to what precise reality lies behind the metaphorical language have gone too far. One thinks, for instance, of Lewis's suggestion that just as heaven makes human beings (as we now think of them) more than human, so hell, like fire that burns wood into ash that is no longer wood, but only remains, makes a human into something less than human, an "ex-man" or "damned ghost." [C. S. Lewis, *The Problem of Pain* (New York: Macmillan, 1943), 113-114.] I suppose this is possible, but it certainly leaves the texts a long way behind. More satisfactory (though I remain uncertain of some of its arguments) is the classic treatment by Robert Anderson, [*Human Destiny: After Death—What?* (London: Pickering & Inglis, 1913)], praised by Spur-geon as the best treatment of the subject. But my point is that hell may be very different from the depictions of many medieval imaginations." D.A. Carson, *The Gagging of God: Chris-tianity Confronts Pluralism* (Grand Rapids: Zondervan, 1999), (531-532), Kindle Edition.

John Calvin also thought "everlasting fire" was "metaphorical." Jean Calvin, *Commen-tary on the Harmony of the Evangelists, Matthew, Mark, and Luke*, vol. 3, trans. William Prin-gle (Seattle: CreateSpace, 2015, reprint 1610), 110. Similarly, Martin Luther wrote, "It is not very important whether or not one pictures hell as it is commonly portrayed and described." Martin Luther, *Luther's Works: Commentaries on 1 Corinthians 7, 1 Corinthians 15, Lectures on 1 Timothy*, vol. 28 (St. Louis, MO: Concordia, 1973), 28:144-145, as quoted in William V. Crockett, *Four Views on Hell* (Grand Rapids: Zondervan, 1996), 44.

9. William V. Crockett, "The Metaphorical View," in William V. Crockett, ed., *Four Views on Hell* (Grand Rapids: Zondervan, 1996), n. 10, 46. It is interesting to note the horrific images of hell even outside the Christian tradition found in Islam, Hinduism, Buddhism, Taoism, and Jainism which has no fewer than 8,400,000 different hells as well as a bottomless abyss where the worst sinners are kept forever. For more on this see John Blanchard, *Whatever Happened to Hell?* (Wheaton, IL: Crossway, 1995), 125-126.

10. John Furniss, *The Sight of Hell* (Seattle: CreateSpace/St. Athanasius Press, 2014, reprint 1882), 59. The book's approbation is chilling: "I have carefully read over this little Volume for Children and have found nothing whatsoever in it contrary to the doctrine of Holy Faith, but, on the contrary, a great deal to charm, instruct and edify our youthful classes, for whose benefit it has been written." William Meagher, Vicar General, Dublin, Decem-ber 14, 1855. Ibid., 5.

11. Jonathan Edwards in John Gerstner, *Jonathan Edwards on Heaven and Hell* (Grand Rapids: Baker, 1980), 56, n. 37. Gerstner apparently got this from Faust in *Jonathan Edwards: Rep-resentative Selections*, but I can't find the quote.

12. Some may say that the rich man is not actually in hell, and that people only go to hell after the judgment, but that is incompatible with Scripture. Second Peter 2:4 tells us, "God did not spare the angels when they sinned, but sent them into hell and committed them to chains of gloomy darkness to be kept until the judgment." With this in mind, I don't think much can be made of the argument that what Jesus pictured was only an intermediate state but not really hell. The rich man is pictured as being in the flames.

13. Larry Dixon, *The Other Side of the Good News: Confronting the Contemporary Challenges to Jesus' Teaching on Hell* (Wheaton, IL: Bridgepoint, 1992), 130. G. Campbell Morgan writes, "Jesus did not call it a parable. Luke does not call it a parable. Moreover, the fact that, while the rich man is not named, the beggar is named, makes it probable that He was naming an actual case. It may be a parable. If so, at least it is striking it is the only parable of Jesus in which a name is given to a person." G. Campbell Morgan, *The Gospel According to Luke* (Cambridge: Cambridge University Press, 1965), 162, as quoted in Dixon, 132.

    Although some scholars following Adolph Jülicher argue that parables are no more than simple stories with a single point, D.A. Carson writes that "Both Matthew Black ('The Parables as Allegory,' BJRL 42 [1959-60]: 273-87) and Raymond E. Brown ('Parables and Allegory Reconsidered,' NovTest 5 [1962]: 36-45) *convincingly* demonstrate that the allegory-parable distinction is too facile," and that "Jesus himself occasionally derived more than one or two points from certain of his parables." D.A. Carson, *Matthew*, EBC, Vol. 8 (Grand Rapids: Zondervan, 1984), 201-202. Emphasis mine.

14. Murray J. Harris, "The New Testament View of Life After Death," *Themelios* 11 (January 1986): 48.

15. I suppose someone could argue that the Holy Spirit could be doing that in hell, but why would He do that if, as every commentator agrees, in hell there is no longer a chance to be saved?

16. Especially when we consider the doctrine of total depravity.

17. Alfred Edersheim, *The Life and Times of Jesus the Messiah* (Peabody, MA: Hendrickson, 1993 [Orig. pub. 1883]), 550.

18. John Blanchard: "In hell, that anger will be more intense than any this world has ever seen. The wicked will be angry at the things which gave them pleasure on earth but now give them pain in hell; angry at the sins that wrecked their lives; angry at themselves for being who they are; angry at Satan and his helpers for producing the temptations which let them into sin; and, even while compelled to acknowledge His glory and goodness, angry at God for condemning them to this dreadful fate." John Blanchard, *Whatever Happened to Hell?* (Wheaton, IL: Crossway, 1995), 158.

19. D.A. Carson, *The Gagging of God: Christianity Confronts Pluralism* (Grand Rapids: Zondervan, 2009), 533. Kindle Edition. Ferguson in *Hell Under Fire*, 235: "It might seem tenuous to base this on Revelation 22:11 ('Let him who does wrong continue to do wrong; let him who is vile continue to be vile'), but the refusal to repent in the face of the eschatological judgments of God (16:8-11) implies that the consummation of those judgments in hell does not and will not produce a penitential spirit. Herein, then, is the darkness of the outer darkness: There is no repentance."

20. For the analysis of the rich man and Lazarus story I'm indebted to the excellent book by Larry Dixon, *The Other Side of the Good News: Confronting the Contemporary Challenges to Jesus' Teaching on Hell* (Wheaton, IL: Bridgepoint, 1992), 130-143.

21. Richard Chenevix Trench, *Notes on the Parables of Our Lord* (Philadelphia: William Syckelmoore, 1873), 357.

22. Mark Twain's letter to his wife, Olivia Clemens, 7/17/1889.

23. John Shelby Spong, *Rescuing the Bible from Fundamentalism* (San Francisco: HarperSanFrancisco, 1991), 24.

24. Abigail Frymann, "'I'd rather go to hell than worship a homophobic God': Desmond Tutu speaks out as he compares gay rights to the struggle against apartheid in South Africa," *Daily Mail*, July 27, 2013, accessed October 27, 2014, http://www.dailymail.co.uk/news/article-2380058/Id-hell-worship-homophobic-God-Desmond-Tutu-speaks-compares-gay-rights-struggle-apartheid-South-Africa.html#ixzz3HOFsU29A.

25. John Stuart Mill, *An Examination of Sir William Hamilton's Philosophy: The Principal Philosophical Questions Discussed in His Writings*, 2d ed. (London: Longmans, Green, and Co., 1865), 103.

26. Also consider Frank Sinatra's life song was "My Way" (Reprise, 1969). Given the words of the song, on what basis should we believe that Sinatra will have a different attitude in hell? And consider Hank Williams's song "If Heaven Ain't a Lot Like Dixie" (Curb Records, 1995) as well as Sheryl Crow's song "Sign Your Name" (A&M Records, 2010).

27. Zygmunt Bauman, *Modernity and the Holocaust* (Ithaca, NY: Cornell, 1989), 6.

28. Edwards and Stott, *Evangelical Essentials*, 319.

29. Dallas Willard, *Renovation of the Heart: Putting on the Character of Christ* (Colorado Springs: Navpress, 2002), 57.

30. Saying yes as often as we could was very important to us in raising foster children. They came to us feeling betrayed and deprived, and we wanted to set an example of God's generosity.

31. Dallas Willard, *The Divine Conspiracy* (New York: HarperSanFrancisco, 1998), 302.

32. Feinberg: "Hence, as with libertarian free will and the free will defense, in my system people wind up in hell because they have decided that they don't want a relationship with God." John S. Feinberg, *The Many Faces of Evil: Theological Systems and the Problem of Evil* (Wheaton, IL: Crossway, 2004), 432.

33. Dallas Willard: "Lost persons, in Christian terms, are precisely the ones who mistake their own person for God. They falsely identify, and cannot recognize, what is closest to them—themselves. Then as we have noted, everything becomes delusional. Such a one really does think he is in charge of his life—though, admittedly, to manage it 'successfully,' he may have to bow outwardly to this or that person or power. But *he* is in charge (he believes), and he has no confidence in the one who really is God." Dallas Willard, *Renovation of the Heart: Putting on the Character of Christ* (Colorado Springs: Navpress, 2002), 56. On the next page he writes, "Thus no one chooses in the abstract to go to hell or even to be the kind of person who belongs there. But their orientation toward self leads them to become the kind of person for whom away-from-God is the only place for which they are suited. It is a place they would, in the end, choose for themselves, rather than come to humble themselves before God and accept who he is." Willard says that "the fundamental fact about them will not be that they are there, but that they have become the kind of people so locked in their own self-worship and denial of God that they cannot want God." Ibid., 57.

34. Peter Hitchens, *The Rage Against God: How Atheism Led Me to Faith* (Grand Rapids: Zondervan, 2010), 102-103.

Chapter 6—Is Free Will Worth It?

1. Joseph P. Gorra pointed out to me that there is a cluster of important and interrelated concepts that center on the notion of free will. In addition to the philosophical account of free will (the ability to do otherwise); there is also the moral account that an individual is responsible for his or her actions, choices, behaviors; and there is also the moral and theological accounts that free will means responsibility to do what one ought to do, to do what is good.

2. Alvin Plantinga, *God, Freedom, and Evil* (Grand Rapids: Eerdmans, 1977), 29. Emphasis his.

3. I hold to libertarian freedom, but it is outside the scope of this book to debate models of divine providence. For further research I recommend Paul Kjoss Helseth, William Lane Craig, Ron Highfield, Gregory A. Boyd, *Four Views of Divine Providence*, ed. Stanley N. Gundry (Grand Rapids: Zondervan, 2011); Robert Kane, *The Significance of Free Will* (New York: Oxford University Press, 1996); William Lane Craig, *The Only Wise God: The Compatibility of Divine Foreknowledge and Human Freedom* (Eugene, OR: Wipf & Stock, 1999).

4. Obviously there are certain situations in which a parent should refuse a daughter's date request, but there comes a time when every parent has to set their daughter free to do what she wants, even if what she wants to do is sinful.

5. See my chapter "Why Do Bad Things Happen to Good People?"

6. Romans 6:17-18: "Thanks be to God, that you who were once slaves of sin have become obedient from the heart to the standard of teaching to which you were committed, and, having been set free from sin, have become slaves of righteousness."

7. If Luther thinks that the image of God is itself destroyed by the Fall, and free will is a feature of being made in God's image, then on this view a non-Christian can't do otherwise.

8. Romans 6:18.

9. Schaff says that Augustine held that free will "exists even in fallen man, that he can choose, not indeed between sin and holiness, but between individual actions within the sphere of sinfulness and of justitia civilis." III:822.

10. Romans 2:14-16: "Indeed, when Gentiles, who do not have the law, do by nature things required by the law, they are a law for themselves, even though they do not have the law. They show that the requirements of the law are written on their hearts, their consciences also bearing witness, and their thoughts now accusing, now even defending them" (NIV). I agree with Geisler: "Even though we are depraved and by nature bent toward sin, nonetheless, each sin is freely chosen." Norman L. Geisler, *Chosen But Free: A Balanced View of Divine Election* (Minneapolis: Bethany, 1999), 28.

11. Calvinist theologian R.C. Sproul struggles with Adam and Eve's sin: "So the question comes back to free will. We grant that Adam and Eve freely willed to sin, but the deeper question remains: Why? Obviously they sinned because they wanted to sin. They had a desire to sin. But the desire to sin is already sin. Without the desire they could not sin. If they acted against their desire then they would be acting against their own will, and the choice would not have been a free choice. If the act was truly free and they acted according to their desire then they must have had an evil desire or inclination to start with. From whence did it come? Was it there from the beginning? Did God give them the evil desire? If He did, how could He hold them culpable? If He didn't give it to them, where did it come from?...I do not know the solution to the problem of evil. Nor do I know anyone else who does." R.C. Sproul, *The Invisible Hand: Do All Things Really Work for Good?* (Dallas: Word, 1996), 166-167.

12. I grant that sometimes certain physical or psychological conditions might hinder our free will.

13. A personal letter from C.S. Lewis to Sheldon Vanauken as quoted in Sheldon Vanauken, *A Severe Mercy* (New York: HarperOne, reprint 2011), Kindle location, 1541.

14. John Hick, *Evil and the Love of God* (New York: Palgrave Macmillan, 2007), 281. G. Stanley Kane: "If men were not at an epistemic distance from God, it would be impossible for them ever to commit sin." G. Stanley Kane, "The Failure of the Soul-Making Theodicy," *International Journal for Philosophy of Religion*, 6 (1975): 7.

    R. Geivett: "If human persons lived in the immediate presence of God, personal freedom regarding moral choices would be absolutely precluded, for such persons could not help but adjust their wills to that of God." R. Geivett, *Evil and the Evidence for God* (Philadelphia: Temple University Press, 1995), 36.

15. For another example of Jesus not wanting to give more evidence, see Luke 4:23-27: "And he said to them, 'Doubtless you will quote to me this proverb, "Physician, heal yourself." What we have heard you did at Capernaum, do here in your hometown as well.' And he said, 'Truly, I say to you, no prophet is acceptable in his hometown. But in truth, I tell you, there were many widows in Israel in the days of Elijah, when the heavens were shut up three years and six months, and a great famine came over all the land, and Elijah was sent to none of them but only to Zarephath, in the land of Sidon, to a woman who was a widow. And there were many lepers in Israel in the time of the prophet Elisha, and none of them was cleansed, but only Naaman the Syrian.'" Also, Jesus sometimes commanded those who witnessed miracles not to tell anyone (Mark 7:31-37; 9:2-9; Luke 5:12-15; 8:49-56). Further, we read in Luke 4:41: "Moreover, demons came out of many people, shouting, 'You are the Son of God!' But he rebuked them and would not allow them to speak, because they knew he was the Christ" (NIV).

16. Richard Swinburne, *Providence and the Problem of Evil* (Oxford: Oxford University Press, 1998), 188-189.

17. Bart D. Ehrman, *God's Problem: How the Bible Fails to Answer Our Most Important Question—Why We Suffer* (New York: HarperOne, 2008), 12.

18. Ibid., 230.

19. Ibid., 120. Emphasis his.

20. Ibid., 27.

21. It has been objected that people often do not have a chance to exercise their choices differently. For example, there's the case of the bank manager who is commanded to open the safe at gunpoint. But the bank manager is still free in the sense that he can try to thwart the robber in various ways even to the point of just flatly refusing even though he has every reason to suspect that his refusal will cost him his life. He does nonetheless have a choice.

22. NIV.

23. I took this course during the summer of 2000 at Trinity Evangelical Divinity School, where Ware was teaching at the time.

24. Much of what follows is adapted from that article: Clay Jones, "Sci-fi, Free Will, and the Problem of Evil," *Christian Research Journal* 35-5 (2012), 52-53, http://www.equip.org/article/sci-fi-free-will-problem-evil/. Used with the permission of the *Christian Research Journal*.

25. Of course many other themes are involved in these movies, and the writers' primary intent may not have been to write about free will, self-awareness, or individuality.

26. *Invasion of the Body Snatchers* (1956), *Invasion of the Body Snatchers* (1978), *Body Snatchers* (1993), *The Invasion* (2007).

27. There have also been four more films: *Terminator 2: Judgment Day* (1991), *Terminator 3: Rise of the Machines* (2003), *Terminator Salvation* (2009), *Terminator Genisys* (2015), and a TV series, *Terminator: The Sarah Connor Chronicles* (2008–2009).

28. Jones, "Sci-fi, Free Will, and the Problem of Evil," 52-53. There were two more films: *The Matrix Reloaded* and *The Matrix Revolutions* (both 2003).

29. *Metropolis* (1927), *2001: A Space Odyssey* (1968), *Colossus: The Forbin Project* (1970), *Westworld* (1973), *Futureworld* (1976), *I, Robot* (2004), *Eagle Eye* (2008), *The Machine* (2013), *Automata* (2014), *Avengers: Age of Ultron* (2015), *Chappie* (2015), etc.

30. Jones, "Sci-fi, Free Will, and the Problem of Evil," 52.

31. Android: "An artificial being that resembles a human in form, especially one that is made of flesh-like material (as opposed to metal or plastic)." Jeff Prucher, ed., *Brave New Words: The Oxford Dictionary of Science Fiction* (Oxford: Oxford University Press, 2007), 6.

32. The American Film Institute lists it as one of the top ten sci-fi films of all time, see at http://www.afi.com/10top10/moviedetail.aspx?id=14.

33. Richard Corliss and Richard Schickel, "All-TIME 100 Movies," *Time*, January 23, 2012, http://entertainment.time.com/2005/02/12/all-time-100-movies/#blade-runner-1982.

34. There's an editor's edition.

35. Jones, "Sci-fi, Free Will, and the Problem of Evil," 52-53.

36. Brian Stableford, *The Encyclopedia of Science Fiction*, eds. John Clute and Peter Nichols (New York: St. Martin's Griffin, 1995), 34. Similarly in *Screamers* (1995), an android gives her life for a corrupt human.

37. Jones, "Sci-fi, Free Will, and the Problem of Evil," 53.

38. Ibid., 54.

39. Although sci-fi *always* represents humans as valuing *their own* free will, some sci-fi plotlines—like *The Stepford Wives* (1974, remake 2005)—rightfully depict that humans often would rather not put up with other people's free will. After all, beings with free will can be troublesome (or worse!), but doesn't this also speak to the greatness of God that He patiently endures His creation's rebellion?

40. Thomas Henry Huxley, *Selected Essays and addresses of Thomas Henry Huxley*, ed. Philo Melvyn Buck, Jr. (New York: Macmillan, 1910), 238. The full quote: "I protest that if some great Power would agree to make me always think what is true and do what is right, on condition of being turned into a sort of clock and wound up every morning before I got out of bed, I should instantly close the offer. The only freedom I care about is the freedom to do right; the freedom to do wrong I am ready to part with on the cheapest terms to anyone who will take it from me." What Huxley apparently was clueless about is that one cannot have "the freedom to do right" if they don't have the freedom to do wrong.

41. Sometimes people complain that I shouldn't joke by using the word *inflatable*, but it's not a joke. It's a point. It's *reductio ad absurdum*.

42. Jones, "Sci-fi, Free Will, and the Problem of Evil," 54-55. This concludes my quoting from this article. Some of these films I saw as a younger Christian, and some of those I would not have a clear conscience about watching now (at least uncut). Since writing that article there are two more movies of note: *Ruby Sparks* (2012) and *Ex Machina* (2015). Both are excellent movies for exploring aspects of free will but there is prolonged, graphic nudity in *Ex*

Machina so I recommend against seeing it unedited (when I saw it I thought I was watching an edited version)!

43. Although it is outside the topic at hand for any kind of serious discussion, I certainly think dogs have free will. Anyone who has ever seen a dog sneak his way past his master to do something he knows his master forbids is seeing canine free will in action.

Chapter 7—Wasn't There Another Way?

1. Clay Jones and Richard Norman, "Why Does God Allow Evil? Clay Jones vs Richard Norman," *Unbelievable with Justin Brierly—Premier Christian Radio*, June 26, 2014, https://podfanatic.com/podcast/unbelievable/episode/why-does-god-allow-evil-clay-jones-vs-richard-norman.

2. There are others, but the objections I chose to deal with are the most substantial.

3. Antony Flew, "Divine Omnipotence and Human Freedom," in *New Essays in Philosophical Theology*, eds. Antony Flew and Alasdair MacIntyre (New York: Macmillan, 1973), 149.

4. Flew, "Divine Omnipotence and Human Freedom," 152.

5. John M. Frame gives an analogy: "Now let's assume, for example, that God makes a golf ball go into a hole, using a golfer as the secondary cause. But what about the golfer's swing? Scripture tells us that God brings that about, too, for he controls everything. But there are secondary causes of the golfer's swing, also: movements in the golfer's muscles, neurons, brain, and so on. The verses we have studied imply that God causes those also. We can press this analysis into the world of molecules, atoms, and subatomic particles. Are any of their movements independent of God? Certainly not." John M. Frame, *The Doctrine of God* (Phillipsburg, NJ: P&R Publishing, 2002), 287.

6. Steven Cowan, "Does 1 Corinthians 10:13 Imply Libertarian Freedom? A Reply to Paul A. Himes," *Journal of the Evangelical Theological Society*, 55/2 (2012), 793.

7. For a detailed description of Flew's position, see Antony Flew, "Compatibilism, Free Will and God," *Philosophy* 48 (July 1973), 231-244.

8. Much of the argument from compatibilists stems from the concept that since we always do what we most want to do and since what we most want to do is outside our control (aka, we can't choose our wants) then we are all determined. But Richard Swinburne is right: "In this situation, it is often said, the strongest desire wins. But if one calls a desire strongest if it is the one on which the man eventually acts, that is a very uninformative tautology; and on any other criterion of 'strongest desire' it is often false. A natural way of measuring strength of desires is that a desire is strong insofar as it needs much effort to act against it. Sexual desires are often strong, whether or not men often act on them, because men have to struggle hard not to act on them. In this latter sense of strength of desire the man's situation is indeed one in which there are desires of different strengths to do actions, and also one where he sees that actions as having different degrees of worth. The ordering by strength and the ordering by perceived worth may not be the same. The man has to choose whether to resist strong desires in order to do the morally good action, or to yield to them." Richard Swinburne, "A Theodicy of Heaven and Hell," *The Existence and Nature of God*, ed. Alfred J. Freddoso (Notre Dame: University of Notre Dame, 1983), 47. For a further investigation of philosophical arguments for libertarian freedom see Robert Kane, *The Significance of Free Will* (New York: Oxford University Press, 1996).

9. For more scriptural arguments against determinism, see my paper "Is Determinism Scriptural?" found in the Resources section of my blog at www.clayjones.net.

10. For a compatibilist response to 1 Corinthians 10:13 see Steven Cowan, "Does 1 Corinthians 10:13 Imply Libertarian Freedom? A Reply to Paul A. Himes," *Journal of the Evangelical Theological Society*, 55/2 (2012), 793-800. In the same issue there is a libertarian response to Cowan: Paul Himes, "First Corinthians 10:13: A Rejoinder to Steven Cowan," 801-806.

11. William Lane Craig, "A Middle-Knowledge Response," *Divine Foreknowledge: Four Views*, eds. James K. Beilby and Paul R. Eddy (Downers Grove, IL: InterVarsity, 2001), 202.

12. Dennis Jowers, William Lane Craig, Ron Highfield, Gregory A Boyd, Paul Kjoss Helseth, *Four Views on Divine Providence* (Grand Rapids: Zondervan, 2011), 60.

13. As determinist John Frame put it: "The doctrine that God controls all things, including human decisions, typically raises for us the question, 'How, then, can we be responsible for our actions?' Answering this question has been a major preoccupation of theologians who write about the doctrine of God." John M. Frame, *The Doctrine of God*, 119.

14. R.C. Sproul, *The Invisible Hand: Do All Things Really Work for Good?* (Dallas: Word, 1996), 167. Even J.I. Packer, when faced with explaining how God can determine absolutely everything and yet not be the author of evil, makes a similar appeal but calls it an antinomy: "The whole point of an antinomy—in theology, at any rate—is that it is not a real contradiction, though it looks like one. It is an apparent incompatibility between two apparent truths. An antinomy exists when a pair of principles stand side by side, seemingly irreconcilable, yet both undeniable. There are cogent reasons for believing each of them; each rests on clear and solid evidence; but it is a mystery to you how they can be squared with each other. You see that each must be true on its own, but you do not see how they can be true together." J.I. Packer, *Evangelism and the Sovereignty of God* (Leicester: InterVarsity, 1961), 18-19. In other words, Packer must appeal to mystery as he cannot explain it. The trouble for Packer, Sproul, and other determinists is to explain how we know when a contradiction between two theologies is only an apparent contradiction and not a real contradiction. Obviously, if it were a real contradiction, then one of the views would necessarily be false. What would we say to cultists who, when we pointed out the contradiction in their theology, replied, "It is only an apparent contradiction, not a real one"? Even determinist Paul Helm writes that "appealing to an antinomy could be a license for accepting nonsense." Paul Helm, *The Providence of God: Contours of Christian Theology* (Downers Grove, IL: InterVarsity, 1993), 66.

15. Gordon H. Clark, *Religion, Reason and Revelation* (Jefferson, MD: Trinity Foundation, 1986), 221.

16. Ibid., 222.

17. Ibid., 237-238.

18. Steven Boër, "The Irrelevance of the Free Will Defense," *Analysis 38* (1978), 110-111. Emphasis his.

19. Ibid., 111.

20. Ibid.

21. Ibid., 112.

22. Frank B. Dilley, "Is the Free Will Defense Irrelevant?" *Religious Studies*, Vol. 18, No. 3 (Sept. 1982), 357.

23. Ibid., 360-361. Dilly continues, "The Boër reform as originally proposed not only sets aside a good deal of the moral meaning of free action and deprives free beings of motivation for choosing moral actions over immoral, but it also deprives free beings of cognitive freedom with respect to belief in God." 361.

24. For a list of scenarios as to how God might have arranged the world differently, see Nick Trakakis, *The God Beyond Belief: In Defense of William Rowe's Evidential Argument from Evil*, Studies in Philosophy and Religion 27 (Dordrecht, The Netherlands: Springer, 2007), 269ff.

25. Eleonore Stump, "Knowledge, Freedom and the Problem of Evil," *International Journal for Philosophy and Religion* 14 (1983), 52. Stump concluded: "So it seems to me that a crucial premiss [sic] of Swinburne's argument is false. We do not need induction from experience of natural evils to have knowledge about the consequences of our actions. God could provide such knowledge, and he could do so without infringing on our freedom." Ibid., 53.

26. Ibid., 52-53.

27. Centers for Disease Control and Prevention, "Current Cigarette Smoking Among Adults in the United States," accessed June 14, 2016, http://www.cdc.gov/tobacco/data_statistics/fact_sheets/adult_data/cig_smoking/.

28. National Institute of Health, "How many people are affected by/at risk for obesity & overweight?," accessed June 14, 2016, https://www.nichd.nih.gov/health/topics/obesity/conditioninfo/Pages/risk.aspx.

29. "Reported STDs in the United States: 2014 National Data for Chlamydia, Gonorrhea, and Syphilis," CDC FACT SHEET, accessed June 14, 2016, http://www.cdc.gov/std/stats14/std-trends-508.pdf.

30. Nina Burleigh, "Sexting, Shame and Suicide," *Rolling Stone*, September 17, 2013, http://www.rollingstone.com/culture/news/sexting-shame-and-suicide-20130917.

31. Stump, "Knowledge, Freedom and the Problem of Evil," 53. For these examples Stump references the visions of Daniel, esp. Daniel 8-10; Jeremiah 42:1-16; David's use of the ephod, 1 Samuel 23:9-11 and 30:7-8; and references Balaam's donkey, Numbers 22:22-35.

32. Has she read the Old Testament? The most common response to OT prophets was disbelief! In fact, so many people were claiming to have visions and dreams that the Lord said he wasn't going to give even the true ones anymore. Zechariah 10:2: "The household gods utter nonsense, and the diviners see lies; they tell false dreams and give empty consolation. Therefore the people wander like sheep; they are afflicted for lack of a shepherd."

33. C.S. Lewis, *The Problem of Pain* (New York: Macmillan, 1953), 103-104.

34. Of course, in raising their children, parents may do things to lead them into sin, but parents aren't responsible for their children's sin only because they gave birth to them.

35. Daniel Howard-Snyder, "The Argument from Inscrutable Evil," *The Evidential Argument from Evil*, ed. Daniel Howard-Snyder (Bloomington, IN: University of Indiana, 1996), 290.

36. William L. Rowe, "The Problem of Evil and Some Varieties of Atheism," in *The Problem of Evil*, eds. Marilyn McCord Adams and Robert Merrihew Adams (Oxford: Oxford University Press, 1990), 127.

37. See Ivan's speech in *The Brothers Karamazov*, book V, chapter 4.

38. Howard-Snyder, "The Argument from Inscrutable Evil," 291.

39. John Sanders, *The God Who Risks: A Theology of Providence* (Downers Grove: InterVarsity, 1998), 262.

40. Bruce A. Little, *A Creation-Order Theodicy: God and Gratuitous Evil* (Lanham, MD: University Press, 2005), 3. Emphasis mine. Little goes on to ask, when it comes to the Holocaust, "what the worse evil might be." Ibid. Answer: It's better for the Holocaust to occur than for it not to occur and for human and angelic beings to not realize the horror of beings who decide to go their own way. Later, Little says that even though theists might be able to show that a greater good was obtained in particular cases, "this would not establish that in *all* cases one would be justified in claiming the good obtained, and yet that is precisely what the GG theodicy requires." Ibid., 4. Later Little writes, "Whereas he claims that *all* evil in this world is allowed by God for the purpose of bringing about a greater good, the theist must prove that it is so in every case." Ibid. No he doesn't! All the GG defender has to do is to give us reason to suppose how a GG might obtain in many difficult cases. On the contrary, those who argue that gratuitous evil exists have the burden *on them* to show that there is no possible way that a greater good could not obtain from a particular instance of evil. If the theist can provide a framework as to how horrendous evils might have a point, then, again, that skeptic must provide an evil that he knows for sure couldn't have a greater good come out of it. Since, as I've argued, angels are watching and the judgment will reveal all things, it is hard to imagine exactly how every evil couldn't be a lesson for eternity.

41. George M. Kren and Leon Rappoport, *The Holocaust and the Crisis of Human Behavior* (New York: Holmes & Meier, 1980), 126.

42. Zygmunt Bauman, *Modernity and the Holocaust* (Ithaca, NY: Cornell, 1989), 152. Emphasis mine.

43. Daniel Howard-Snyder asks why God doesn't just let the wicked suffer: "While God is justified in punishing the wicked for their wrongdoing, much of the suffering in the world is undeserved. And no one can sensibly say that God would be justified in punishing those who don't deserve it. But might not all suffering in the world be deserved? I doubt it. Nonhuman animals, very young children and severely impaired adults suffer immensely but do not deserve it since they are not morally responsible for their actions. Moreover, although many morally responsible persons suffer to a degree that is proportionate to their sins, many more do not. (This is one of the main lessons of the book of Job.)...So, while *some* suffering might be accounted for by divine punishment, it cannot explain the evil with which we are mainly concerned: undeserved suffering and horrific wickedness." Daniel Howard-Snyder, "God, Evil and Suffering," *Reason for the Hope Within*, ed. Michael J. Murray (Grand Rapids: Eerdmans, 1999), 86. Why not just the wicked? There are two reasons. One, as was the lesson in chapter 4: We. Are. All. Wicked. "There is no one who does good, no not one." Two, John Hick points out that in a world where only the wicked suffer "human misery would not evoke deep personal sympathy or call forth organized relief and sacrificial help and service. For it is presupposed in these compassionate reactions both that the suffering is not deserved and that it is bad for the sufferer...It seems, then, that in a world that is to be the scene of compassionate love and self-giving for others, suffering must fall upon mankind with something of a haphazardness and inequity that we now experience." John Hick, *Evil and the God of Love* (New York: Palgrave Macmillan, 2007), 334. This is seen in Hindu society, where the "untouchables" are to be left to their horrible lives because they deserved what they got.

44. I realize that other factors were present in the suicide of Iris Chang. But her studying these horrors, at the very least, had to have worsened her depression. See Sarah Hampson, "Iris Chang committed suicide. Now her mother aims to resurrect her reputation," *The Globe and Mail*, June 1, 2011, accessed August 22, 2016, http://www.theglobeandmail.com/life/relationships/iris-chang-committed-suicide-now-her-mother-aims-to-resurrect-her-reputation article625192/.

45. Jean has written about our experience: Jean E. Jones, "The Journey of Childlessness," *Today's Christian Woman*, April 2010, available at http://www.todayschristianwoman.com/articles/2010/april/journeychildlessness.html.

46. Adapted from a lecture by Charles Hughes circa 1994.

47. Clay Jones, "Why Did God Let That Child Die?" *Christian Research Journal* 38-1 (2015), 13-15, https://www.equip.org/article/god-let-child-die-2/. Used with permission.

48. Rowe, "The Problem of Evil," 129-130.

49. As I discussed in chapter 1, God is under no moral obligation to make the lives of rebels easy.

50. NIV.

51. NIV.

52. NIV.

Chapter 8—Will We Have Free Will in Heaven?

1. Bart D. Ehrman, *God's Problem: How the Bible Fails to Answer Our Most Important Question—Why We Suffer* (New York: HarperOne, 2008), 12-13.

2. Yujin Nagasawa , Graham Oppy & Nick Trakakis "Salvation in Heaven?," *Philosophical Papers* 33-1 (2004), 102.

3. Ibid., 107-108.

4. Ibid., 106.

5. For compatibilists (see the chapter "Wasn't There Another Way?"), the answer isn't difficult, since by free will they mean that even though God determines your every thought and deed, you are still free as long as you are doing what you *want* to do. Compatibilists simply believe that God is going to change your nature and establish circumstances such that you'll never sin again. For example, Randy Alcorn approvingly quotes determinist Paul Helm, who writes, "The freedom of heaven, then, is the freedom from sin; not that the believer just happens to be free from sin, but that he is so constituted or reconstituted that he cannot sin. He doesn't want to sin, and he does not want to want to sin." The problem for the compatibilist/determinist, however, when it comes to why God would allow evil, is that if God is just going to make us so that we can't sin, why doesn't He do that to us on earth—why all the immense suffering here and now? Paul Helm, *The Last Things* (Carlisle, PA: Banner of Truth, 1989), 92, as quoted in Randy Alcorn, *Heaven* (Wheaton, IL: Tyndale, 2004), 301. I don't know whether Alcorn is a determinist—some of the things he writes make me think he isn't—but Helm certainly is a determinist.

6. NASB.

7. Jerry L. Walls, *Heaven: The Logic of Eternal Joy* (Oxford: Oxford University Press, 2002), 55.

8. Although as argued in the chapter "Was There Another Way?," I'm not a determinist. But if determinism were true, I think John Feinberg's solution to the problem of evil is the best from a compatibilist perspective. See John Feinberg, *The Many Faces of Evil: Theological Systems and the Problem of Evil*, rev. ed. (Wheaton, IL: Crossway, 2004), 165-203.

9. Christians throughout the ages have answered these questions differently. Some, such as Origin and Donnelly, have thought that there will be free will in heaven and that means that yes, some people might choose sin and therefore could be cast out of heaven in the future.

10. Translations of the New Testament typically translate the Greek word *epithymia* as "lust" or "sinful desire" whenever it is used in a negative context, but they translate it as "desire"

when it is used in a positive context. For example, the NIV translates *epithymia* as "lust" in 1 John 2:16—"the *lust* of the flesh," but "desire" in Philippians 1:23, "I *desire* to depart and be with Christ."

11. NIV.

12. NIV.

13. See also Revelation 19:3.

14. Grant R. Osborne, *Revelation*, Baker Exegetical Commentary on the New Testament (Grand Rapids: Baker, 2002), 541. Emphasis mine.

15. G.K. Beale, *The Book of Revelation*, The New International Greek Testament Commentary (Grand Rapids: Eerdmans, 1999), 764. Emphasis mine.

16. I don't even know of any annihilationists (those who say that the eternal punishment of the lost is that they will be annihilated) who argue that those in heaven will one day forget the punishment of the lost.

17. Nick de la Canal, "York County vs Evangelicals: The Battle Over 'Heritage USA' Ruins," WFAE 90.7, Charlotte's NPR News Source (July 11, 2014), http://wfae.org/post/york -county-vs-evangelicals-battle-over-heritage-usa-ruins (accessed March 31, 2017).

18. I don't think that in heaven the knowledge of hell will make us sad, but it is a sober thought and should make us glad that we have been saved by the grace of God. As for whether we'll be sad that our loved ones might be in hell, see my discussion on that in the chapter, "Is Eternal Punishment Fair?"

19. D. Martyn Lloyd-Jones, *God's Way of Reconciliation: Studies in Ephesians II* (Grand Rapids: Baker, 1972), 12. Lloyd-Jones later comments that "our troubles are due to the fact that we are guilty of a double failure; we fail on the one hand to realize the depth of sin, and on the other hand we fail to realize the greatness and the height and the glory of our salvation...It is because we never realize the depth of the pit out of which we have been brought by the grace of God that we do not thank God as we ought." 82.

20. I've heard people complain that they would never do to their children what God did to His children, but they've missed an important point: God doesn't consider those in rebellion against Him to be His children! Consider Jesus' response to the Jews who opposed him in John 8. They proclaimed that they were Abraham's children, but Jesus replied in verse 44, "You are of your father the devil, and your will is to do your father's desires." Consider also 1 John 3:8-10: "Whoever makes a practice of sinning is of the devil, for the devil has been sinning from the beginning. The reason the Son of God appeared was to destroy the works of the devil. No one born of God makes a practice of sinning, for God's seed abides in him; and he cannot keep on sinning, because he has been born of God. By this it is evident who are the children of God, and who are the children of the devil: whoever does not practice righteousness is not of God, nor is the one who does not love his brother." In this context, it makes sense that Paul would say in Ephesians 2:2 that all of us, before we became born again, were "following the prince of the power of the air, the spirit that is now at work *in* the sons of disobedience." It is when we are born again that we are adopted into the family of God and become His children (Romans 8:23; Galatians 4:5; Ephesians 1:5).

21. I got this analogy from Dallas Willard in the course "Spirituality and Ministry," which was offered by the Doctor of Ministry program at Fuller Theological Seminary during June 2001.

22. Atheist Michael Martin asserts that we don't need all the evil we experience here to be prepared for heaven: "There is at least one serious problem with this retort, however: moral evil is not necessary to provide obstacles to overcome since there is natural evil. The suffering and destruction that results from disease, tidal waves, hurricanes and volcanoes provide obstacles enough. There is consequently no need for evil that is the result of human free choice." Michael Martin, "Problems with Heaven," Internet Infidels, accessed July 6, 2016, http://infidels.org/library/modern/michael_martin/heaven.html.

23. Yujin Nagasawa, Graham Oppy and Nick Trakakis "Salvation in Heaven?," *Philosophical Papers* 33-1 (2004), 110-111.

24. Jerry L. Walls, *Purgatory: The Logic of Total Transformation* (Oxford: Oxford University Press, 2012), 52.

25. Ibid.

26. Ibid., 57.

27. Ibid., 59.

28. NIV.

29. Daniel Goodkind, "The World Population at 7 Billion," United States Census Bureau, October 31, 2011, accessed July 5, 2016, http://blogs.census.gov/2011/10/31/the-world-population-at-7-billion/.

30. There are 525,960 minutes in a year (including the extra quarter day that we adjust for in leap years). Seven billion people at 10 minutes = 70 billion minutes divided by 525,960 minutes per earth year = 133,090 earth years.

31. I can anticipate the objection that Scripture refers to it as the "judgment day," not the judgment 266,180 years, but "day" in this sense is probably used to denote that the judgment has a definite beginning and end. Also, we are told in 2 Peter 3:8, "Do not overlook this one fact, beloved, that with the Lord one day is as a thousand years, and a thousand years as one day."

32. I say "largely" as it is *possible* that we won't always be aware, in the kingdom to come, of His immediate presence.

33. Some have argued that we will have natures like God and God *cannot* sin. But I agree with Dallas Willard on this point, who once said to me that "Sure God could sin, but why would he want to?" After all, what is it precisely that makes God not want to sin other than God too regards sin as beyond stupid? Isn't it His omniscience regarding the folly of sin that causes Him not to sin? Personal conversation with Dallas Willard during June 2001.

34. Timothy Pawl and Kevin Timpe, "Incompatibilism, Sin, and Free Will in Heaven," *Faith and Philosophy* 26-4 (October 2009), 408, http://www.kevintimpe.com/files/heavenly_freedom.pdf (accessed July 6, 2016). About their comment "the character the redeemed have formed in their pre-heavenly existence," I would modify that to include the character also formed by watching and participating in the judgment.

Pawl and Timpe go on to talk about nonderivative freedom as freedom that is not even determined by our characters: "For instance, consider the choice either to sing in the choir or to play the harp. If both of these actions are consistent with the nature of heaven and one sees good reasons for engaging in both activities, then one's moral character needn't determine one's choice either way...On our view, the blessed are free to will any number of interesting and morally relevant actions that they see good reason for doing." 408-409.

Chapter 9—Will Eternity Be Boring?

1. I reviewed every use of the words *heaven, eternal, eternity, immortality, everlasting,* and *after-life* in Feinberg's book and, except for a discussion as to why God couldn't create sinless beings now if He is able to make us sinless in heaven (183-184, 187, 398), eternal life is never presented as a robust part of any theodicy. A notable exception is the work of Richard Swinburne. For example, Swinburne writes that "the primary point of (at any rate, human) life in this world is the next world." Richard Swinburne, *Providence and the Problem of Evil* (Oxford: Clarendon, 1998), 250.

2. Justin P. McBrayer and Daniel Howard-Snyder, eds., *The Blackwell Companion to the Problem of Evil* (West Sussex, UK: Wiley-Blackwell, 2013), 507-512. Perhaps we shouldn't be surprised that apologists largely ignore eternal life as an answer to evil. Jerry Walls points out that eternity is largely ignored in much of Christian theology: "In Luther's Large Catechism, for instance, he barely mentions 'the life everlasting' in his commentary on the Apostles' Creed. The Westminster Confession is hardly more articulate on the nature of heaven. In its chapter on the last judgment, we are informed that after the judgment 'shall the righteous go into everlasting life, and receive the fullness of joy and refreshing which shall come from the presence of the Lord.' No further description of heaven is forth coming...The Thirty-Nine Articles of the Anglican Church are even more reticent on the subject of the hereafter. While there is an article repudiating purgatory, no article is devoted to heaven or everlasting life." Jerry L. Walls, *Heaven: The Logic of Eternal Joy* (Oxford: Oxford University Press, 2002), 8.

3. N.T. Wright, *Evil and the Justice of God* (Downers Grove: InterVarsity, 2006), 164. Emphasis mine.

4. Some skeptics argue that eternity isn't relevant to the problem of evil because the existence of heaven doesn't directly answer why we suffer here and now. For example, atheist J.L. Mackie wrote, "If the theists tell us that God will eventually bring this utopia into being, the critics can hardly be blamed for wondering why he has gone such a long way round about it..." J.L. Mackie, "Theism and Utopia," *Philosophy* 37 (1962): 154.

5. C.S. Lewis, *The Problem of Pain* (New York: Macmillan, 1953), 132. Similarly, Jerry Walls writes, "I will argue that the doctrine of heaven is essential to any version of Christianity worth believing, and furthermore that it is an extremely valuable concept for addressing difficult philosophical issues, not the least of which are pressing questions about theodicy, morality, and the meaning of life." Jerry Walls, *Heaven: The Logic of Eternal Joy* (Oxford: Oxford University Press, 2002), 13. Sadly, in the last few decades, most books on the problem of evil have tried to answer it without appealing to eternity. Walls is right that "heaven is an essential resource for a satisfactory theodicy. Indeed, heaven is essential to make sense of the sort of evils sketched here." 116. Geivett is right: "Probably anyone who adheres to the Christian tradition will agree that human immortality is not only an essential Christian doctrine but that it is also relevant to the formulation of an adequate Christian theodicy." R. Geivett, *Evil and the Evidence for God* (Philadelphia: Temple University Press, 1993), 213. Similarly, Eleonore Stump writes, "if we insist that there be some response to the challenge of the argument from evil that does not make mention of the afterlife, in my view we consign such a response to failure." Eleonore Stump, *Wandering in Darkness: Narrative and the Problem of Suffering* (Oxford: Oxford University Press, 2010), 419. Stump points out that Thomas Aquinas also thought that the afterlife was essential to theodicy. Ibid., 389.

6. George Bernard Shaw, *A Treatise on Parents and Children* (Fairfield, IA: 1st World Library, 2004), 63.

7. Skeptic Brian Riberio wrote, "If the only reason to desire to go to heaven were that it was 'better than hell,' that's not saying very much." Brian Ribeiro "The Problem of Heaven," *Ratio*, Volume 24-1 (March 2011), 47.

8. Colleen McDannell and Bernhard Lang, *Heaven: A History* (New Haven: Yale, 1988), 178.

9. McDannell and Lang: "If we eliminate the diverse and unique elements which mark the heaven of Luther, Calvin, Polti, de Sales, Nicole, and Baxter, and concentrate on what they share in common, a theocentric model emerges. According to this model, heaven is for God, and the eternal life of the saints revolves around a divine center. The saints may be involved in an everlasting liturgy of praise, they may meditate in solitude, or they may be caught up in an intimate relation with the divine. Worldly activities earn no place in heaven. At the end of time the earth either is destroyed or plays a minor role in everlasting life. Heaven is fundamentally a religious place—a center of worship, of divine revelation, and pious conversations with sacred characters." Ibid.

10. Ibid., 180.

11. What will not be remembered isn't the people who were on earth! Indeed, they will be with us in heaven. What will not be remembered is the way the old earth and solar system was. There are many places that I have been that are totally forgettable. Also, not recalling something isn't the same as not being able to.

12. See also Numbers 31:1-2 and Matthew 8:11.

13. NIV.

14. Randy Alcorn, *Heaven* (Wheaton, IL: Tyndale, 2004), 65.

15. Ibid., 66

16. Ibid., 67.

17. Ibid.

18. NIV.

19. NIV. See 1 Thessalonians 4:17: "Then we who are alive and remain will be caught up together with them in the clouds to meet the Lord in the air, and so we shall always be with the Lord" (NASB).

20. Emphasis mine.

21. John Hick, *Evil and the Love of God* (New York: Palgrave Macmillan, 2007), 350.

22. Mark Twain, *Adventures of Huckleberry Finn* (Norwalk, CT: Heritage, 1968), 15.

23. John 2:6. D.A. Carson calls the notion that what they were drinking wasn't wine but mere grape juice "intrinsically silly." D.A. Carson, *The Gospel According to John*, PNTC (Grand Rapids, Eerdmans, 1991), 169.

24. C.S. Lewis, *The Weight of Glory and Other Addresses* (New York: HarperCollins, 1980), 45.

25. Revelation 4:3.

26. NIV. Jasper comes in many colors, as do many of the stones. Here I'm giving the various stones' most common color, but of course that does not mean John saw each stone in its most common color. For stones that are well-known to be a certain color, like amethyst, I don't bother to give the color.

27. *City of Angels*, directed by Brad Silberling, Warner Bros., 1998, closing scene. *City of Angels* is basically a justification for what some commentators believe was exactly what happened in Genesis 6:1-4: "When man began to multiply on the face of the land and daughters were born to them, the sons of God saw that the daughters of man were attractive. And they took as their wives any they chose. Then the LORD said, "My Spirit shall not abide in man forever, for he is flesh: his days shall be 120 years." The Nephilim were on the earth in those days, and also afterward, when the sons of God came in to the daughters of man and they bore children to them. These were the mighty men who were of old, the men of renown." For an example of a commentator who argues that the "sons of God" in Genesis 6 were actually angels, see Thomas R. Schreiner's commentary on Jude v. 6 in Thomas R. Schreiner, *The New American Commentary: 1, 2 Peter, Jude*, vol. 37 (Nashville, TN: B&H, 2003), database 2013, WORD*search*. Schreiner is the James Buchanan Harrison Professor of New Testament Interpretation at the Southern Baptist Theological Seminary.

28. Revelation 4:6b-8. Also Isaiah 6:1-4: "In the year that King Uzziah died, I saw the Lord seated on a throne, high and exalted, and the train of his robe filled the temple. Above him were seraphs, each with six wings: With two wings they covered their faces, with two they covered their feet, and with two they were flying. And they were calling to one another: 'Holy, holy, holy is the LORD Almighty; the whole earth is full of his glory.' At the sound of their voices the doorposts and threshold shook and the temple was filled with smoke" (NIV). Emphasis mine. Armour Patterson: Interpreters usually have evaluated this description as four segments of biological life: a lion representing untamed species, an ox representing domesticated animals, an eagle representing avian life, and man representing human life. Seemingly no place is allowed for the abundant life forms of the oceans; but, despite that, the interpretation is probably correct. The cherubim in some way represent all of God's created species. Armour Patterson, *Revelation*, vol. 39 of the New American Commentary (Nashville: B & H, 2012), database 2013, WORD*search*.

29. Mark Twain, *Adventures of Huckleberry Finn* (Norwalk, CT: Heritage, 1968), 15.

30. It's hard to imagine that they are continuing to sing "Holy, holy, holy" while in the presence of others who are singing something different.

31. There's much more to say about this. First, I suspect that being in the presence of the All-Good and the All-Powerful all the time may be the most joyous duty in heaven. Let's remember this passage is only a snapshot of heaven that pictures the Creator simply sitting on His throne. We know from other passages He's quite busy. Might not watching Him create future Hawaiis, Yosemites, and for that matter star clusters be more wondrous than even being in those places? Not to mention the pleasure of watching the All-Just, All-Loving, All-Knowing commune with His creatures.

    Second, I'm not in the presence of the One they are singing to in the same way they are, and I expect being in His presence will make me constantly want to praise Him. As C.S. Lewis pointed out, praise is not complete until it is expressed. My wife and I tell each other we love each other every single day, often several times a day, and after forty years of marriage, we haven't grown tired of it. Even a fleeting thought that I could not express my love to her for all eternity makes me sad.

    Third, the Creator made each creature distinct (He did that amply on earth). Perhaps the six-winged seraphs' primary joy is to express their appreciation. Fish don't tire of being in water, and the seraphs will never tire of singing His praises (I imagine it's more fun than swimming). Also, the passage doesn't say that all the other creatures unceasingly offer this praise to God; it mentions only the four seraphs. Perhaps we should envy them?

But, like it or not, their life is not ours, as only four seraphs are ever mentioned in Scripture. Thankfully, God has a plan for us too.

32. C.S. Lewis, *Reflections on the Psalms* (New York: Harvest/Harcourt, 1958), 93-94.

33. When viewed this way, however, the atheist is actually not challenging God's goodness but God's power—His power to keep us happy forever. Atheist Michael Martin suggests other problems with heaven, but they merit only brief attention. First, Martin argues that heaven is incoherent in various ways of which I'll only mention one. Martin says, "It is difficult to make sense of the idea" that heaven is in "a space completely separated from our space that is in principle impossible to travel to or from our space." But this is nothing because this has always been the majority view of Christians throughout the ages, and that it doesn't "make sense" to Martin is Martin's problem. Contrary to the naturalist/atheist, Christians do not believe that nature is all there is. In fact, they argue that something or someone outside of nature created it. Therefore, no rocket ship will get you there. Also, it is odd to take such a position today when most atheists ascribe to multiverse—millions, or billions, or who knows how many parallel universes—for which there is absolutely no evidence other than the atheists' contention that there must be a naturalistic explanation for the fine-tuning of our universe.

Second, Martin thinks that heaven is "arbitrary and unfair" because of the Christian teaching that entrance to heaven is "unmerited." He says that "a father who bestowed unmerited gifts on some of his children and not on others would be considered unjust and arbitrary." Of course, much could be said here about the Christian understanding of human rebellion against God, Christ's work on the cross, the relationship of grace and faith, etc., but there isn't time. Now in all fairness, Martin does bring up the issue of the destiny of the unevangelized, and I answer that in chapter 4. He also contends that it is unfair for nonbelievers to be punished for rejecting the gospel because he thinks certain aspects, like the resurrection, to be improbable.

Third, Martin argues that the free will defense runs afoul of a sinless heaven. This is a more serious point that I address in the chapter "Will There Be Free Will in Heaven?" Michael Martin, "Problems with Heaven," Internet Infidels, (1997), accessed 3-30-2016, http://infidels.org/library/modern/michael_martin/heaven.html.

34. "Professor Sir Bernard Williams: Generous and humane thinker who spanned the whole spectrum of ideas and was the outstanding moral philosopher of his age," *The Times*, June 14, 2003, accessed April 18, 2016, https://web.archive.org/web/20110513235039/http://www.timesonline.co.uk/tol/comment/obituaries/article1141892.

35. Bernard Williams, *Problems with the Self: Philosophical Papers 1956–1972* (Cambridge: Cambridge University Press, 1973), 82.

36. The original Czech is the "Makroupolus Thing," but in English is translated as the "Makropulus case" or the "Mackropulus affair."

37. Williams says Makropulus lived to 342 years old, but that is mistaken. In the book and the play, her age at death is 337.

38. Williams, *Problems with the Self*, 100.

39. Some examples: John Martin Fischer and Benjamin Mitchell-Yellin, "Immortality and Boredom," *Journal of Ethics*, 18 (2014), 353-372; A.W. Moore, "Williams, Nietzsche, and the Meaninglessness of Immortality," *Mind*, 115 (April 2006), 458; Timothy Chappell, "Infinity Goes Up On Trial: Must Immortality Be Meaningless?," *European Journal of Philosophy*,

17-1 (March 2009), 30-44; Adam Buben, "Resources for Overcoming the Boredom of Immortality in Fischer and Kierkegaard," *Immortality and the Philosophy of Death* (New York: Rowman and Littlefield, 2016), 205; Senyo Whyte, "On Immortality and Significance: A Response to Aaron Smuts," *Philosophy and Literature*, 36 (October 2012), 490-495.

40. Brian Ribeiro "The Problem of Heaven," *Ratio*, 24-1 (March 2011), 63. Smuts: "Over the course of an infinite amount of time our lives would ultimately become undesirable. I argue that the principal problem with immortality is that it would sap our decisions of significance, which, combined with a few related factors, would result in a general motivational collapse. 134.

41. Aaron Smuts, "Immortality and Significance," *Philosophy and Literature,* 35 (April 2011): 148.

42. A.W. Moore, "Williams, Nietzsche, and the Meaninglessness of Immortality," *Mind* (April 2006), 115,

43. Bernard Williams, *Problems of the Self,* 91.

44. Brian Ribeiro, "The Problem of Heaven," *Ratio*, 24 (March 2011), 63.

45. See also Smuts: "If we imagine a form of existence where our current set of categorical desires is completely replaced by another set, we have little reason to think that the result would be the same person." Ibid., 137.

46. One should be cautious regarding near-death experiences (NDE), but the near-death experience of twentieth-century atheist A.J. Ayer is interesting. I've read and watched a lot of accounts of NDE where many people report being drawn to a light of love that gives them unspeakable joy. But in his NDE, Ayer tells that the light he was drawn to, which he said was "responsible for the government of the universe," was painful and he wanted to find "a way to extinguish the painful light." A.J. Ayer, "What I saw when I was dead," *National Review*, October 14, 1988, accessed April 30, 2016, http://findarticles.com/p/articles/mi_m1282/is_n20_v40/ai_6701958/?tag=content;col1.

47. Dallas Willard, *Renovation of the Heart: Putting on the Character of Christ* (Colorado Springs: Navpress, 2002), 57.

48. Dallas Willard, *The Divine Conspiracy* (New York: HarperSanFrancisco, 1998), 302.

49. As Swinburne put it, "Clearly there is no point in God sending the bad to heaven as they are, for they would not be happy there. The man who wants to be applauded for what he has not done, who wishes to see the good humiliated and to get pleasure out of the company of similarly malevolent persons, would not be happy pursuing the occupations of heaven." 46.

50. Ribeiro, "The Problem of Heaven," 53. Emphasis his. Ribeiro explains about sex, "But, as an aside, is the defense of heaven really served by this type of orgy thinking? Are we really going to rest the desirability of heaven on its being a brothel than which no greater can be conceived?" 53. "You can give yourself a mix of pleasures—you needn't choose only one. Now shuffle your way through these pleasures—McDonald's French fries, reading Hume, wonderful sex—and just keep repeating. It's difficult to get the time-scale right, since (down here) we hardly ever think past next week or next year. But imagine, say, a full human lifespan of just these pleasures—whichever ones you like, mixed just as you please. And then imagine 1000 human lifespans. And then 100,000. Aside from lip-service, can anyone seriously suggest that that won't be hellish? All this torturous repetitive pleasure, without meaning or gravity, endlessly cycling, sounds absolutely unbearable to me." 52-53.

51. Moore, "Williams, Nietzsche, and the Meaninglessness of Immortality," 458. Moore references Frederick Nietzsche, *The Will to Power*, eds. and trans. Walter Kaufmann and R. J. Hollingdale (New York: Random House, 1967), Sect. 55.

52. Timothy Chappell, "Infinity Goes Up On Trial: Must Immortality Be Meaningless," *European Journal of Philosophy*, 17-1 (2009), 41.

53. Adam Buben, "Resources for Overcoming the Boredom of Immortality in Fischer and Kierkegaard," *Immortality and the Philosophy of Death* (New York: Rowman and Littlefield, 2016), 205.

54. Senyo Whyte, "On Immortality and Significance: A Response to Aaron Smuts," *Philosophy and Literature*, 36-2 (October 2012), 492.

55. Ibid., 492.

56. Ibid., 494. Timothy Chappell agrees: "The goods that are most central to human life—the enjoyment and practice of art, friendship and love, the contemplation of beauty, the practice of inquiry and discovery, philosophy itself understood as Aristotelian *theôria* (ironically enough for Williams and Moore): our experience of all these goods seems plainly inexhaustible. For each such good, enjoying it is something that I can readily imagine carrying on without any necessary temporal limit emerging from the structure of my experience and enjoyment of that good.

     "Notice that I can say this without even mentioning God among the inexhaustible goods. Yet God is, to put it mildly, a rather notable absentee from the Makropoulos argument, given that according to most believers in the major historical religions, east and west, God is super-eminently the central good that we enjoy in eternal life, through worship: worship being the contemplation of God's reality and the reception of his love." Chappell, "Infinity Goes Up On Trial," 42.

57. Augustine, *Confessions*, 1:1.

58. Ribeiro, "The Problem of Heaven," 53.

59. Ecclesiastes 2:17. Ribeiro: "I see no possible exceptions here. This argument goes through, so far as I can see, for any conceivable earthly experience, activity, or project, and for any of the inconceivably many combinatorial possibilities thereof. Whether you want to meet Jerry Garcia and get buzzed, or—on the other hand—read philosophy books, play chess, and reunite with loved ones—or all of these—your enjoyment of these things will all-too-soon become abject despair at the unbearable insipidity of all of them. Let your enjoyment hold out for a thousand years—no, for 100,000 years—no, for 1,000,000 years—no, for 1,000,000,000 years—and yet you haven't used up one instant of your eternal afterlife. You have just as much time ahead of you at that point as did when you walked through the pearly gates. That's a scale of repetition that no earthly enjoyment—however pure or deep or refined or rich or vivid or wondrous—can survive. Certainly some of us are brought, by repetition, to nausea even within the frame of an earthly life, just as we are taught in the first chapter of Ecclesiastes, with all of its repetitions (generations come and go, the sun rises and sets, the wind blows north and south, and 'what has been will be again') and all of its despair ('all things are wearisome,' 'there is nothing new under the sun')." Ribeiro, "The Problem of Heaven," 51-52.

60. John 4:13-14.

61. Walls, *Heaven*, 39.

62. Richard Swinburne, "A Theodicy of Heaven and Hell," *The Existence and Nature of God*, ed. Alfred J. Freddoso (Notre Dame: University of Notre Dame, 1983), 39.

63. Ibid. Swinburne: "But what is that, and why are the traditional occupations of heaven likely to provide it? Happiness is not basically a matter of having pleasant sensations. Certainly it

involves the absence of unpleasant sensations, but this is not its essence...Basically a man's happiness consists in doing what he wants to be doing and having happen what he wants to have happen." Ibid.

64. Ibid., 41.

65. Ibid.

66. Ibid. Swinburne continues: "Only a task which made continued progress valuable for its own sake but which would take an infinite time to finish would be worth doing forever; only a situation which would be evermore worth having would be worth living in forever. The growing development of a friendship with God who...has ever-new aspects of himself to reveal, and the bringing of others into an ever-developing relationship with God, would provide a life worth living forever. Most earthly occupations indeed pall after a time, but the reason why they pall is that there are no facets to them which a man wants to have. And also most earthly occupations are rightly judged only to be worth a finite amount of interest, because there are not ever-new facts to them which are greatly worthwhile having. A man who has molded his desires so as to seek only the good and its continuation would not, given the Christian doctrine of God, be bored in eternity." Ibid., 42-43. "...right religious belief matters because only with it will a man know how he should live, and only if he does live in it the right way can he attain the happiness of heaven. For heaven is a community of those who live in the right way and get happiness out of it because they want to live in the right way. By pursuit of the good they have so molded themselves that they desire to do the good. So the answer why God would send the men of natural good will and true belief to heaven is that they are fitted for it. They would enjoy there a supremely worthwhile happiness, and God being perfectly good seeks that for them." Ibid., 45-46.

Chapter 10—How Does Eternity Relate to Our Suffering Now?

1. Many other verses promise eternal life: we have an *eternal* building from God (2 Corinthians 5:1); "... so that, having been justified by his grace, we might become heirs having the *hope* of *eternal life*" (Titus 3:7 NIV); "And having been made perfect, He became to all those who obey Him the source of *eternal inheritance*" (Hebrews 5:9 NASB); "...those who have been called may receive the promise of the *eternal inheritance*" (Hebrews 9:15 NASB); "...and you will receive a rich welcome into the *eternal kingdom* of our Lord and Savior Jesus Christ" (2 Peter 1:11 NIV).

2. *Adoption*, Romans 8:23-24: "And not only the creation, but we ourselves, who have the firstfruits of the Spirit, groan inwardly as we wait eagerly for adoption as sons, the redemption of our bodies. For in this hope we were saved." *Christ's return*, Titus 2:13: "...waiting for our blessed hope, the appearing of the glory of our great God and Savior Jesus Christ." *Resurrection*, 1 Thessalonians 4:13-14: "We do not want you to be uninformed, brothers, about those who are asleep, that you may not grieve as others do who have no hope. For since we believe that Jesus died and rose again, even so, through Jesus, God will bring with him those who have fallen asleep." Acts 23:6: "Brothers, I am a Pharisee, a son of Pharisees. It is with respect to the hope and the resurrection of the dead that I am on trial." Acts 24:15: "...having a hope in God, which these men themselves accept, that there will be a resurrection of both the just and the unjust." *Bodily redemption*, Romans 8:23-24: "And not only the creation, but we ourselves, who have the firstfruits of the Spirit, groan inwardly as we wait eagerly for adoption as sons, the redemption of our bodies. For in this hope we were saved." *Salvation*, 1 Thessalonians 5:8: "Since we belong to the day, let us be sober, having

put on the breastplate of faith and love, and for a helmet the hope of salvation." First Peter 1:13: "Therefore, preparing your minds for action, and being sober-minded, set your hope fully on the grace that will be brought to you at the revelation of Jesus Christ." *Eternal life*, Titus 1:2: "...in hope of eternal life, which God, who never lies, promised before the ages began." Titus 3:7: "so that being justified by his grace we might become heirs according to the hope of eternal life." *Glory*, Romans 5:2: "Through him we have also obtained access by faith into this grace in which we stand, and we rejoice in hope of the glory of God." Colossians 1:27: "To them God chose to make known how great among the Gentiles are the riches of the glory of this mystery, which is Christ in you, the hope of glory."

3. 2 Corinthians 11:23-29.

4. NIV.

5. NIV.

6. See endnote 1 on page 261 for Scripture passages containing the promise of eternity for all believers.

7. Atheist J.L. Mackie writes, "If the theists tell us that God will eventually bring this utopia [heaven] into being, the critics [skeptics] can hardly be blamed for wondering why he has gone such a long way round about it...." J.L. Mackie, "Theism and Utopia," *Philosophy*, 37 (1962): 154.

8. The thought that there were no children with whom Jean E. could rely in the years to come was an added difficulty.

9. A.W. Tozer, *The Pursuit of God* (Ventura, CA: Regal, 2013), 76.

10. John 2:1-11.

11. Matthew 11:19.

12. Craig Keener, *The Gospel According to John: A Commentary* (Grand Rapids: Baker, 1003), 499.

13. Ibid., 511. I'm not interested in encouraging people to drink wine, but we need to be honest about the facts that Jesus did make a huge amount of wine and that Jesus also drank wine. This is important because to forbid drinking wine in moderation (the Bible condemns drunkenness—Ephesians 5:18) is received by many as a statement that Jesus is antipleasure, and presenting Jesus as antipleasure makes heaven less appealing. What follows are three commentators on the fact that Jesus did make wine to avoid social embarrassment and, of course, to give the guests more wine to drink. Some have suggested that Jesus actually only had them drink water, that it was sort of a joke, but Leon Morris points out that "such reconstructions founder on verses 9 and 11. In the first place John says the water became wine. He records a miracle. And in the second place it was a miracle which had profound effects on those who had begun to follow Jesus. It is impossible to maintain that 'his disciples believed on him', and that He 'manifested his glory', on the basis of nothing more than a good joke." Leon Morris, *The Gospel According to John*, NICNT (Grand Rapids: Eerdmans, 1971), 175-176. D.A. Carson writes: "The 'wine' (*oinos*) that was needed was not mere grape juice, generic 'fruit of the vine.' The idea is intrinsically silly as applied to countries whose agricultural tradition is so committed to viticulture. Besides, in v. 10 the head steward expects that at this point in the celebration some of the guests would *have had too much to drink*: the verb *methyskō* does not refer to consuming too much liquid, but to inebriation." D.A. Carson, *The Gospel According to John*, PNTC (Grand Rapids: Eerdmans, 1991), 169.

Likewise, Craig Keener comments: "Wine was not merely unfermented 'grape juice,' as some popular modern North American apologists for abstinence have contended. Before hermetic sealing and refrigeration, it was difficult to prevent some fermentation, and impossible to do so over long periods of time. Nor was wine drunk only to purify the water, as some have also claimed; much spring water in the Mediterranean is palatable and many Greeks and Romans viewed it as medicinally helpful. At the same time, the alcoholic content of wine was not artificially increased through distillation, and people in the Mediterranean world always mixed water with the wine served with meals, often two or four parts water per every part wine; undiluted wine was considered dangerous." Keener, *The Gospel According to John*, 500.

Similarly, Gerald L. Borchert: "Jesus' making wine in this case has caused some readers another major problem. One of my sons once returned from a class and informed me that Jesus made nonalcoholic wine in this story. His teacher also had informed him that the Greek word for the drink here meant nonalcoholic grape juice. It serves no purpose for evangelicals to twist the Greek language for the sake of their ethical opinions because such an argument cannot be sustained from Greek." Gerald L. Borchert, *John 1–11*, NAC (Nashville, TN: B&H, 1996), WORDsearch database, 2013.

14. NIV.

15. The reason I spent the prior paragraph on wine isn't because I want to encourage Christians to drink wine—many Christians shouldn't—but to offset the dangerous teaching that any alcohol use is sinful. That teaching is dangerous because in the minds of many, it may further the devil's lie that God opposes pleasure. When Christians call legitimate pleasures sin, they make heaven less attractive to some. Obviously, people for whom one drink leads to a thousand shouldn't drink. Also, we must be careful not to cause a brother or sister in Christ to stumble.

16. NIV.

17. For example, see Randy Alcorn, *Heaven* (Wheaton, IL: Tyndale, 2004), 241-252. But as Grant Osborne puts it: "Is the New Jerusalem the place in which the saints reside, or is it a symbol of the saints themselves? Thusing (1968) says it is not so much a place as the perfected people themselves, and Gundry (1987: 256) argues strongly that 'John is not describing the eternal dwelling place of the saints; he is describing them and them alone.' Thus it describes their future state rather than their future home (see also Draper 1988: 42). Mounce (1998: 382) connects this with 1 Cor. 3:16-17, where the believers are the temple of God; here they are the city of God, visualizing 'the church in its perfected and eternal state.' Yet while it is possible that John transformed the Jewish tradition of an end-time New Jerusalem into a symbol of the people themselves, that is not required by the text... Babylon was both a people and a place, and that is the better answer here. In short, it represents heaven as both the saints who inhabit it and their dwelling place." Grant R. Osborne, *Revelation*, BECNT (Grand Rapids: Baker, 2002), 733.

Similarly, G.K. Beale has put it: "Some interpret 21:10–22:5 as a literal description of an actual physical city. But this is highly improbable since 'the bride of the Lamb'" (v 10), that is, the eternal community of the redeemed (so 21:2,10), is equated with the detailed layout of the city in 21:11–22:5: 'I will show you the bride, the wife of the Lamb...And he showed me the holy city, Jerusalem' (21:9-10)...The reference to the 'city' in Rev. 20:9 suggests that the city portrayed in 21:9–22:5 is revealed in hidden, partial form throughout the church age as a result of Christ's redemptive work. The segment here reveals the perfected form of the city." G.K. Beale, *The Book of Revelation,* NIGTC (Grand Rapids: Eerdmans, 1999), 1062.

18. See also Revelation 21:9: "Then came one of the seven angels who had the seven bowls full of the seven last plagues and spoke to me, saying, 'Come, I will show you the Bride, the wife of the Lamb.'"

19. Revelation 21:8: "As for the cowardly, the faithless, the detestable, as for murderers, the sexually immoral, sorcerers, idolaters, and all liars, their portion will be in the lake that burns with fire and sulfur, which is the second death."

20. Walter Hooper, *C S. Lewis: A Companion and Guide* (San Francisco: Harper, 1996), 108-109.

21. Matthew 8:11; Isaiah 25:6; Mark 14:25; Revelation 19:9; Psalm 16:11.

22. Luke 12:32; Colossians 1:12; Matthew 25:34.

23. Revelation 4:8.

24. Revelation 22:1-2.

25. Revelation 22:5.

26. Revelation 14:2 (NASB).

27. Revelation 4:3.

28. Revelation 21:19-20. Some of these gems come in different colors.

Chapter 11—How Does Suffering Relate to Our Eternal Occupation?

1. Pliny, "Letter to Trajan," *Internet Medieval Source Book: Pliny on the Christians*, accessed June 25, 2013, http://www.fordham.edu/halsall/source/pliny1.asp.

2. The second-century satirist Lucian writes of the Christians: "These misguided creatures start with the general conviction that they are immortal for all time, which explains the contempt of death and voluntary self-devotion which are so common among them." Lucian, *The Death of Peregrine*, Sacred-Texts.com, http://www.sacred-texts.com/cla/luc/wl4/wl420 .htm (accessed April 1, 2017).

3. Emphasis mine. We sometimes fail to comprehend the Roman prison's horror. Eyewitnesses tell us they were vile. Their toilets were buckets and they typically didn't have the smallest of windows (the sole ventilation being the result of the opening and then closing of the prison door) so they reeked of perspiration, vomit, feces, and urine. At night they were cold and unlit so that prisoners wouldn't see what bit them. Prisoners were filthy, their hair matted, their skin soiled; and their sweat rusted the iron chains that shackled them, sometimes fusing the chains to their ankles or wrists.

   For example, the 22-year-old Perpetua, who would later be put to death in Carthage (AD 202 or 203), wrote in her diary: "A few days later we were lodged in the prison; and I was terrified, as I had never before been in such a dark hole. What a difficult time it was! With the crowd the heat was stifling; then there was the extortion of the soldiers; and to crown all, I was tortured with worry for my baby there." Perpetua, "The Martyrdom of Saints Perpetua and Felicitas," *The Acts of the Christian Martyrs,* trans. Herbert Musurillo (Oxford: Oxford University Press, 1972), as found in "The Martyrdom of Saints Perpetua and Felicitas," *Frontline,* http://www.pbs.org/wgbh/pages/frontline/shows/religion/maps/primary/ perpetua.html (accessed November 22, 2005). See also Brian Rapske, *The Book of Acts in Its First-Century Setting*, ed. Bruce W. Winter (Grand Rapids: William B. Eerdmans, 1994), vol. 3, *The Book of Acts and Paul in Roman Custody*, 127.267 fn. 52: Perpetua, "The Martyr-dom of Saints Perpetua and Felicitas." Ibid.

4. NIV. "Endure," ὑπομένω, "means generally 'remain' or 'stay behind.' Among its derived meanings, that of 'endure' in trouble, affliction, or persecution is dominant in the NT and is seen here in the second line of the saying...The NT relates what is involved in enduring: Believers endure hatred by all for Christ's sake (Mt. 10:22 par. Mk. 13:13; cf. Mt. 24:13), they persevere in tribulation (Rom. 12:12), they endure great sufferings (Heb. 10:32) and temptation (Jas. 1:12), and they patiently endure suffering for doing good (1 Pe. 2:20)." George W. Knight, *The Pastoral Epistles: A Commentary on the Greek Text* (Grand Rapids: Eerdmans, 1992), 404. Those who disown or deny Christ don't endure. "The denial can also manifest itself in the moral realm. Some may 'profess to know God, but by their deeds deny him' (Tit. 1:16; cf. 1 Tim. 5:8)." Knight, *The Pastoral Epistles*, 406. "'Reign with him,' συμβασιλεύσομεν, only occurs twice in the NT (here and 1 Cor. 4:8 'Already you have all you want! Already you have become rich! You have become kings [βασιλεύω]—and that without us! How I wish that you really had become kings so that we might be kings with you [συμβασιλεύω]!'" Of this verse Knight comments, "Paul criticizes those who think and act as if they were already reigning with Christ. He wishes that it were so and then speaks of this present age as one in which 'when we are persecuted, we endure' (4:12)." Knight, *The Pastoral Epistles*, 405.

5. basileuō: "1. *be king, rule.*—a. of temporal princes b. of God and those closely united w. him—α. God β. Christ γ. God and Christ together δ. Saints, who have been called to rule w. God Ro 5:17b; Rv 5:10...20:4, 6; 22:5 (cf. Da 7:27). 2. *become king, obtain royal power.*" William F. Arndt and F. Wilbur Gingrich, *A Greek-English Lexicon of the New Testament and other Early Christian Literature* (Chicago: University of Chicago, 1969), 136.

6. nikaō: "1. intr. *Be victor, prevail, conquer*—a. in a battle or contest b. in a legal action 2. trans. *conquer, overcome, vanquish.*" Arndt and Gingrich, *A Greek-English Lexicon*, 541. There are some other words in the NT translated "overcome" but *nike* is most common.

7. Most translations translate *nike* as "overcome" in passages like 1 John 5:4: "everyone born of God *overcomes* the world." On the other hand, most translations use "conquer" in verses like Romans 8:37: "in all these things we are more than conquerors through him who loved us." I will use *overcome* or *conquer* interchangeably.

8. Endure means to "remain instead of fleeing...stand one's ground, hold out, endure in trouble affliction, persecution..." Arndt and Gingrich, *A Greek-English Lexicon*, 853.

9. Gordon Wenham comments: "Thus, like 'image,' *exercise dominion* reflects royal language. Man is created to rule." Gordon Wenham, *Word Biblical Commentary, Vol. 1: Genesis 1–15* (Nashville, TN: Nelson, 1987), 138.

10. Gen. 1:26-27. "The language of 1:26 reflects this idea of a royal figure representing God as his appointed ruler. This appears to be the understanding of Psalm 8, which focuses on human dominion, though without explicit mention of the 'image' or 'likeness.' This is further indicated by the term 'rule' (*rādâ*) in 1:26,28, which is used commonly of royal dominion. Human jurisdiction over animate life in the skies, waters, and land corresponds to the 'rule' (*māšal*) of the sun and moon over the inanimate sphere of creation. Our passage declares that all people, not just kings, have the special status of royalty in the eyes of God. It is strik-ing that God consigns jurisdiction to one of his creatures, since the major tenet of 1:1–2:3 is the sovereignty of God's creative word. It was this feature of creation that so astonished the

psalmist; for him the Infinite One crowned human infancy with the glory of his rule (8:5-8[6-9])." Kenneth A. Matthews, *The New American Commentary: Genesis 1–11:26* (Nashville, TN: Broadman & Holman, 1996), 169-170. Notice that it was the entire earth they were to subdue. Wenham explains the nature of the rule: "Man's divinely given commission to rule over all other living creatures is tempered, or better, brought into sharp relief, by that fact that such dominion does not allow him to kill these creatures or to use their flesh as food. Only much later (9:3, post-Flood) is domination extended to include consumption. Of the two verbs *rādâ*, 'exercise dominion,' and *kābaš*, 'subdue,' the latter connotes more force. Thus it refers to subjecting someone to slavery (2 Chr. 28:10; Neh. 5:5; Jer. 34:11, 16), to physical abuse and assault (Esth. 7:8), to treading (sins) under foot (Mic. 7:19 and Zech. 9:15, where it parallels 'devour'), and to militarily subjecting the population of a city (Num. 32:22, 29; Josh. 18:1). All these references suggest violence or a display of force. For reasons already indicated, it appears unlikely that we need to transfer the nuance of force and dictatorship into the use of *kābaš* in Gen. 1:28. Probably what is designated here is settlement and agriculture..." Wenham, *Genesis 1–15*, 139-140.

11. Dallas Willard, *The Divine Conspiracy* (San Francisco: HarperCollins, 1998), 21.

12. The serpent or snake is clearly identified with Satan: Revelation 12:9, "The great dragon was hurled down—that ancient serpent called the devil, or Satan, who leads the whole world astray. He was hurled to the earth, and his angels with him" (NIV). Also, Revelation 20:2: "He seized the dragon, that ancient serpent, who is the devil, or Satan, and bound him for a thousand years" (NIV). Matthews writes: "In accord with the traditional opinion, the snake is more than a literal snake; rather it is Satan's personal presence in the garden. We may interpret the role of the serpent in the same vein as Peter's resistance to Jesus' death, where the Lord responded to Peter: 'Get behind me, Satan! You are a stumbling block to me. You do not have in mind the things of God, but the things of men' (Matt 16:23). Jesus does not mean Peter is possessed with Satan as Judas was when 'Satan entered' him (Luke 22:3), nor was he threatened with possession (Luke 22:31). But Peter unwittingly was an advocate for Satan's cause." Matthews, *Genesis 1–11:26*, 234.

13. Albert Baylis: "It is a satanic *coup d'etat!* Satan not only incites them to sin in direct disobedience and rebellion against a divine command, but the sin also directly flouts the divine order. Humanity's charge to rule over the beasts is violated, and Adam capitulates his moral leadership." Albert H. Baylis, *From Creation to the Cross: Understanding the First Half of the Bible* (Grand Rapids: Zondervan, 1996), 46. Henri Blocher similarly comments, "The fact that the other party takes the form of an animal (the text underlines that the snake belonged to that category, Gn. 3:1) is not an insignificant detail. Reptiles were a part of the animal kingdom over which the man and the woman were to have dominion. If, as they sin, they obey the snake, there is evidence that orders established at creation are being twisted and smashed with violation of the divine covenant, either directly in the commission of the offense, or else in the repercussions..." Henri Blocher, *In the Beginning: The Opening Chapters of Genesis* (Downers Grove, IL: InterVarsity, 1984), 142.

14. Matthews comments on the lack of dominion: "Since 1:28 forms the background to the blessing (9:1), it is striking that the charge to 'subdue' and 'rule' (1:28b) is absent. This admits that the new circumstances of the sin-burdened world have altered this aspect of the Adamic blessing, which now will be difficult to accomplish in the hostile environs of the new world." Matthews further comments: "This appears remarkably different from the relationship that the first man and woman enjoyed in the garden with their animal residents (2:19-20). This would also be true of Noah's animal companions on board the ark, where evidently there

was a docile relationship. It is saying too much of the narrative to suppose that before the Noahic covenant there were no carnivorous animals. Rather, the Lord is formally announcing that this new enmity against humans cannot win out because the animal order is 'given in your hands' (v. 2). This expression describes the divine provision of Israel's victory over its enemies (e.g., Exod 23:31) and the handing over of a murderer to the blood-avenger (Deut 19:12). God has now put the life and death of the animal under the power of the human arbiter." Matthews, *Genesis 1–11:26*, 400-401.

15. NIV. Luke 4:5-7. Bock: "The meaning of the offer was clear: if Jesus would give Satan his heart and bow down before him, Satan would let Jesus rule." Darrell L. Bock, *Luke*, BECNT (Grand Rapids: Baker, 1994), 377.

16. Acts 26:18; John 8:34; Colossians 1:13; 2 Timothy 2:26; 1 John 3:10; John 8:44 NIV; 1 John 5:19; Ephesians 2:1-3.

17. Hebrews 2:14-15 NIV. "The devil did not possess control over death inherently but gained his power when he seduced humankind to rebel against God...The primary goal of the incarnation was the Son's participation in death, through which he nullified the devil's ability to enslave the children of God through fear of death." William L. Lane, *Word Biblical Commentary: Hebrews 1–8* (Nashville, TN: Thomas Nelson, 1991), 61. Beale: "Through his death Jesus nullified the devil's power to put others to death (Heb. 2:14) and took this power for himself (Rev. 1:18)." Beale, *Revelation*, 659.

18. Colossians 2:15 NIV.

19. A Roman legion comprised between 3000 to 6000 foot soldiers with cavalry.

20. John 18:36.

21. Of course, Jesus' disciples often misunderstood this. That's why in Matthew 16, when Jesus explained that He would have to suffer at the hands of the elders and be killed, Peter rebuked him: "This shall never happen to you" (verse 22). And then Jesus said something strange— He told Peter, "Get behind me, *Satan*! You are a hindrance to me. For you are not setting your mind on the things of God, but on the things of man." The trouble is that Peter was looking only from the human point of view and couldn't imagine Jesus, the Messiah of Israel, killed. But Satan knew that Jesus' submitting to suffering would defeat him. As Carson points out, at the temptation Satan had "already offered Jesus kingship without suffering." D.A. Carson, *The Expositor's Bible Commentary, Volume 8*, ed. Frank E. Gaebelein (Grand Rapids: Regency, 1984), 337.

22. This is the Greek word *nike* (from which Nike athletic shoes gets its name), and it means "to conquer" or "to overcome."

23. Revelation 5:2-8.

24. Beale: "The slain Lamb thus represents the image of a conqueror who was mortally wounded while defeating an enemy. Christ's death, the end-time sacrifice of the messianic Lamb, becomes interpreted as a sacrifice that not only redeems but also conquers." Beale, 351. "He was physically defeated but spiritually victorious. He willingly submitted to the unjust penalty of death, which was imposed on him ultimately by the devil. As an innocent victim he became a representative penal substitute for the sins of his people. While he was suffering the defeat of death, he was also overcoming by creating a kingdom of redeemed subjects over whom he would reign and over whom the devil would no longer have power...This does not mean that the Lamb's resurrection is not conceived of as a victory but only that there is an intention to highlight the death as a victory." Beale, 353.

25. Matthew 16:23.

26. Matthew 16:24.

27. Millard J. Erickson, *Christian Theology*, 2d ed. (Grand Rapids: Baker, 1998), 456.

28. Ephesians 6:12 NIV.

29. Ephesians 6:13 NIV.

30. 2 Corinthians 2:11; Ephesians 6:11 NIV.

31. 2 Corinthians 2:11.

32. 1 Corinthians 7:5.

33. Ephesians 4:27 NIV.

34. 1 Peter 5:8.

35. Romans 12:21.

36. Matthew 10:28 NIV.

37. Satan has always been the accuser: Job 1:6-11; 2:1-6; Zechariah 3:1-2; Revelation 12:10. But once Christ died for us, then the devil no longer had any basis for his accusation against the saints. Beale, *The Book of Revelation: A Commentary on the Greek Text*, NIGCT (Grand Rapids: Eerdmans, 1999), 659. Hebrews 2:14-15: The devil was the accuser and he held the power of death. Through Christ we have now overcome (conquered) those legal challenges so that neither "death" nor angels nor principalities can separate us from the kingdom of God. Paul was beheaded by Nero in AD 67.

38. "As sheep of slaughter...we overwhelmingly conquer." Beale, *Revelation*, 270.

39. Greek *hupernikao*—"to be more than conqueror—overwhelmingly conquer." Used only here in the NT. Beale translates it: "As sheep of slaughter...we overwhelmingly conquer." Beale, *Revelation*, 270.

40. Beale: "Through his death Jesus nullified the devil's power to put others to death (Heb. 2:14) and took this power for himself (Revelation 1:18). Therefore, the devil no longer had any basis for his accusations against the saints, since the penalty that they deserved and that he pleaded for had at least been exacted at Christ's death." Beale, *Revelation*, 659.

41. "Demons" is probably best translated "rulers," from the Greek *arche* [άρχή]—"beginning, origin." Moo comments: "Paul can use 'ruler' to denote a secular authority, but more often he uses it to denote authorities of the spirit world, sometimes those of an evil nature (Eph. 6:12; Col. 2:15) but also in a general way that makes it difficult to know whether evil, or evil and good, spirit 'rulers' generally are meant. If 'angels' refers to 'good' angels, it is natural to think that 'rulers' denotes spiritual powers, but the lexical evidence makes it impossible to be sure." Douglas Moo, *The Epistle to the Romans*, TNICNT (Grand Rapids: Eerdmans, 1996), 545.

42. Moo writes of "powers": "Since Paul uses the word to denote miracles [1 Cor. 12:10, 28-29; 2 Cor. 12:12], he may mean that nothing of such a nature—performed perhaps by Satan—can threaten our security as believers. But the occurrence of 'powers' with 'rulers' to denote spiritual beings suggests rather that some kind of spiritual forces are denoted here." Moo, *Romans*, 545-546.

43. In Romans 8:31 Paul asks, "If God is for us, who can be against us?" and in the verses that follow he seems to answer questions that are likely to arise. Namely, if God is for us, why do we suffer so? But Paul's point is that we conquer in the mistreatment. The suffering isn't strange or unusual: it is precisely the plan.

44. Philippians 1:29.

45. Beale: "Christ's conquering is ironically interpreted as accomplished through his death on the cross. Likewise, the description of suffering saints who overcome in Rom. 8:36-37 is strikingly similar to that of Rev. 5:5-6." Beale, *Revelation*, 270.

46. By endure suffering I mean that we learn to honor God without complaining in difficult situations that we cannot righteously change.

47. Alcoholism is an example of an unrighteous attempt to alleviate suffering.

48. Revelation 12:11.

49. Job 1:21.

50. Paul goes on in Ephesians 6 to tell us how we do conquer—he says, "Put on the whole armor of God" (verse 11). But, of course, Paul isn't talking about black belts, Kevlar vests, or handguns. No, our armor is to be honest, holy, witnesses for Christ who are full of faith, confident in our salvation, knowledgeable in the Word of God, regularly talking to the Father, and always alert.

51. Thomas à Kempis, *The Imitation of Christ*, trans. Aloysius Kroft, Harry F. Bolton (Milwaukee: Bruce Publishing, 1962), 59.

52. Perpetua, "The Martyrdom of Saints Perpetua and Felicitas," ibid.

53. I am not in the least suggesting that physical battle isn't sometimes necessary and even a part of the Christian's duty here. Of course it is.

54. C.S. Lewis, *Mere Christianity*, rev. ed. (New York: Macmillan, 1960), 173.

55. 1 John 5:4.

56. 1 John 4:4.

57. Revelation 22:5 (NIV).

58. Daniel 7:18, 27.

59. G.K. Beale, *A New Testament Biblical Theology: The Unfolding of the Old Testament in the New* (Grand Rapids: Baker, 2011), 2011.

60. Beale comments: "The 'overcoming' occurs before the believer inherits the promises...And this 'conquering' of sin (so 2:4-5, 14-16, 20-24) entails being conquered by the world, since, when believers refuse to compromise with the world, they are persecuted by the world... Hence, the church that perseveres in its witnessing faith wins a victory on earth even though it suffers earthly defeat." Beale, *Revelation*, 269. "It is not just how people die that proves them to be overcomers, but the whole of their Christian lives are to be characterized by 'overcoming,' which is a process completed at death." Beale, *Revelation*, 271.

61. Revelation 2:17; 3:22. We sit on Jesus' throne. And so Revelation 1:6 tells us that He "made us to be a kingdom and priests" (NIV). By our identification with Christ's death and resurrection, we inherit with Him. In his commentary on Revelation 1:6, Beale comments: "They not only have been made part of his kingdom and his subjects, but they have also been constituted kings together with him and share his priestly office by virtue of their identification with his death and resurrection." Beale continues, "Christ has made believers to serve as kings and priests in service to his Father, which is to be for his Father's eternal glory and dominion. The high point of vv 1-6, and of the whole chapter, is here: the achievement of God's glory through Christ's work and the service of his people as kings and priests." Beale, *Revelation*, 192, 194.

62. Also, as Jesus says in Luke 19:16-19, "The first came before him, saying, 'Lord, your mina has made ten minas more.' And he said to him, 'Well done, good servant! Because you have been faithful in a very little, you shall have authority over ten cities.' And the second came, saying, 'Lord, your mina has made five minas.' And he said to him, 'And you are to be over five cities.'" Bock comments regarding this verse: "Luke pictures additional responsibility in the future kingdom era. It is not limited to mere kingdom presence or additional church responsibility, but refers to full participation in the exercise of the kingdom's authority in the consummation (cf. 1 Cor. 6:2-3)." Darrell L Bock, *Luke*, vol. 2, BECNT (Grand Rapids: Baker, 1994), 1536.

63. Beale, *Revelation*, 1116. Revelation 22:5. G.K. Beale comments that it is probable that "the new creation will take some kind of material form and contain creatures to rule over. And even if there are no animals to rule over, it is probable that God's people will rule over holy angels, since angels were included in the creation over which Adam was to reign...Christ fulfills the role of the last Adam in order, partly, to rule over, in corporate solidarity with his people, the eternal new creation, which includes the holy angels (Heb. 2:5-16), who exist merely to be servants of the redeemed (Heb. 1:14; cf. Rev. 21:12). But exalted believers are different from the first Adam in that, whereas God only commissioned him to rule, now God *promises* that his people certainly will reign without end." Beale, *Revelation*, 1116-1117. However, Grant R. Osborne wrote regarding Revelation 22:5, "This sums up a major biblical theme on the future reign of the saints. Of course, this cannot be meant literally, for every saint will rule a kingdom that only saints inhabit (there is no hint in Scripture that we will reign over the celestial beings; rather, we are their 'fellow servants,' 19:10; 22:9). Thus, it probably means we will participate in the rule of Christ over the eternal kingdom." Grant R. Osborne, *Revelation* (Grand Rapids: Baker, 2002), 776. But Osborne is mistaken that we are not going to be reigning over other creatures, for several reasons. First, "no hint" is an interesting choice of words since the very word "reign" means to have authority over other creatures. That's the very denotation of reign or rule. We don't say we reign (unless we are kidding or crazy) over toasters or microwaves. Second, Adam's family was charged with ruling over the earth and the Bible tells us that Christians will share the reign of Christ. It would be strange if our authority was actually less than what Adam enjoyed. Third, Jesus says he will give those faithful here "cities" to rule (even if you take this as a metaphor, the question again still is, "metaphor for what?"). Fourth, I am not sure what Osborne means by "celestial beings" but the passages refer specifically to angels of whom 1 Cor. 6:3 says the saints will judge. But even if we don't reign over angels (the Scripture isn't explicit either way) that doesn't mean there won't be a host of other creatures over whom we will rule as was the case in Gen. 1:28. The Lord created everything from tigers to toucans on this planet and there is no reason to doubt creation's diversity in the life to come. Fifth, based on the preceding comments, it seems out of court to say that saints will only rule a kingdom that only saints will inhabit. Is there more than one kingdom? Are the saints getting their own little kingdoms somewhere? Of course not. And if this is the case, then there will probably be a myriad of creatures in the Kingdom." Osborne, *Revelation*, 776.

64. Revelation 21:5-7. Jesus says that the faithful manager who cares for his servants will be put in charge of *all* his master's possessions (Luke 12:32, Bock, 1180). Ephesians 2:6 says, "God raised us up with Christ and seated us with him in the heavenly realms in Christ Jesus" (NIV). Peter T. O'Brien writes, "Because they [believers] have been identified with Christ in his resurrection and exaltation, they, too, have a position of superiority and authority over evil powers. They no longer live under the authority and coercion of the 'ruler of the

kingdom of the air' (2:2)." Peter T. O'Brien, *The Letter to the Ephesians* (Grand Rapids: Eerdmans, 1999), 171.

65. See also Daniel 7:22: "Judgment was given for the saints of the most high." As for the 1 Corinthians passage, Gordon D. Fee writes: "Here he is speaking of the *final judgment* on 'the world' as a whole, the entire anti-God system of things that will come under God's judgment, in which God's people are in some way to be involved." Gordon D. Fee, *The First Epistle to the Corinthians,* NICNT (Grand Rapids: Eerdmans, 1987), 233. The angels who sinned await judgment.

66. Willard, *Divine Conspiracy*, 398.

67. Ibid., 397.

68. Christianity is either true or it's not. If Christianity isn't true, then we should all do something better with our time. But if Christianity is true, then we really have been forgiven of our sins, adopted into God's family, made inheritors of His kingdom, and chosen to reign with Christ for all eternity!

Epilogue: The Short Answer on Why God Allows Evil

1. Genesis 2:17 NIV.

2. Romans 5:8.

Appendix: Satan's Rebellion and God's Response

1. NIV.

2. John Milton, *The Christian Doctrine* in *John Milton Complete Poems and Major Prose*, ed. Merritt Y. Hughes (New York: Odyssey, 1957), 978.

3. C.S. Lewis, *Mere Christianity* (New York: HarperSanFrancisco, 2009), 49.

4. William A. Dembski, *The End of Christianity: Finding a Good God in an Evil World* (Nashville: B&H Academic, 2009), 27-28.

5. Although the early church fathers unanimously believed these verses *also* referred to Satan, many commentators say these passages refer only to earthly kings because Satan wouldn't have been the earthly author's intent. But this hermeneutic is being questioned (e.g., Vern S Poythress, "Dispensing with Merely Human Meaning: Gains and Losses from Focusing on the Human Author, Illustrated by Zephaniah 1:2-3" *JETS*, 27, No 3 [September 2014], 501-512), and some recent commentators are again applying these passages to Satan (e.g., Lamar Eugene Cooper, *Ezekiel*, NAC [Nashville, TN: Broadman & Holman, 1994]). After all, Satan is sometimes addressed through the creature he is influencing (Genesis 3:14-15; Matthew 16:23).

6. Revelation 12:4 (see also Daniel 8:10).

7. Anselm, *On the Fall of the Devil* in *Anselm of Canterbury: The Major Works* (UK: Oxford World's Classics, 1998), 202-203. Kindle Edition. Emphasis mine.

8. Ron Rhodes, *Angels Among Us: Separating Fact from Fiction* (Eugene, OR: Harvest House, 2008), 86.

9. Louis Berkhof, *Systematic Theology* (Grand Rapids: Eerdmans, 1993, reprint 1939), 145. Emphasis mine.

10. Rhodes, *Angels Among Us*, 71-72. Emphasis mine.

11. I don't know any theologians who argue that hell was created prior to Satan's rebellion.

12. C. Fred Dickason, *Angels, Elect and Evil* (Chicago: Moody, 1975), 136. I don't agree with much of Dickason's demonology, but I think he might have some input on this point.

13. NIV.

14. G.K. Beale, *The Book of Revelation: A Commentary on the Greek Text*, NIGTC (Grand Rapids: Eerdmans, 1999), 659. Grant R. Osborne: "The defeat of the dragon (12:7-9) is doubtless the same event as the victory of the Lamb (5:5-6), and both are to be located in the death and resurrection of Jesus Christ." Grant R. Osborne, *Revelation*, BECNT (Grand Rapids: Baker, 2002), 468.

15. Although I seriously disagree with some of his conclusions, Harold Chadwick's book *We Shall Judge Angels* provided some helpful insights for this appendix. Harold J. Chadwick, *We Shall Judge Angels: Understanding the Mysteries of Creation and Eternity* (South Plainfield, NJ: Bridge, 1994).